I0868661

Psychology Revivals

Adult–Child Conversation

Originally published in 1981, *Adult–Child Conversation* explores the dynamics of communication between adults and children and examines the structure, function, and implications of conversational exchanges in various contexts. It provides insights into the linguistic and psychological aspects of adult–child interactions, making it a valuable resource for researchers and practitioners in developmental psychology, linguistics, and education.

Adult–Child Conversation

Adult–Child Conversation

Edited by
Peter French and Margaret MacLure

Routledge
Taylor & Francis Group
LONDON AND NEW YORK

First published in 1981
by Croom Helm

This edition first published in 2026 by Routledge
4 Park Square, Milton Park, Abingdon, Oxon, OX14 4RN

and by Routledge
605 Third Avenue, New York, NY 10158

Routledge is an imprint of the Taylor & Francis Group, an informa business

© 1981 Peter French and Margaret MacLure

All rights reserved. No part of this book may be reprinted or reproduced or utilised in any form or by any electronic, mechanical, or other means, now known or hereafter invented, including photocopying and recording, or in any information storage or retrieval system, without permission in writing from the publishers.

Publisher's Note
The publisher has gone to great lengths to ensure the quality of this reprint but points out that some imperfections in the original copies may be apparent.

Disclaimer
The publisher has made every effort to trace copyright holders and welcomes correspondence from those they have been unable to contact.

For Product Safety Concerns and Information please contact our EU representative GPSR@taylorandfrancis.com. Taylor & Francis Verlag GmbH, Kaufingerstraße 24, 80331 München, Germany

A Library of Congress record exists under ISBN: 9780312005153

ISBN: 978-1-041-31726-5 (hbk)
ISBN: 978-1-003-78043-4 (ebk)
ISBN: 978-1-041-31731-9 (pbk)

Book DOI 10.4324/9781003780434

Adult-Child Conversation

Edited by
PETER FRENCH and MARGARET MACLURE

CROOM HELM LONDON

© 1981 Peter French and Margaret MacLure
Croom Helm Ltd, 2-10 St John's Road, London SW11

British Library Cataloguing in Publication Data

Adult-Child Interaction at Home and
at School *(Conference), University of Bristol, 1978*
Adult-child conversation.
1. Children – Language – Congresses
2. Children and adults – Congresses
I. Title II. French, Peter
III. MacLure, Margaret
401'.9 LB1139.L3

ISBN 0-7099-0069-4

Reproduced from copy supplied
printed and bound in Great Britain
by Billing and Sons Limited
Guildford, London, Oxford, Worcester

CONTENTS

LIST OF FIGURES

LIST OF TABLES

PREFACE

The majority of the papers collected together in this volume were delivered to an SSRC-supported conference on Adult–Child Interaction at Home and at School, held at the University of Bristol on 16–18 September 1978. However, in order more fully to represent the spectrum of approaches which are currently brought to bear on this topic, it was felt necessary to invite further contributions from researchers in the field. Specifically, the papers by Burton, Drew, Cuff and Hustler, Foster, and Wootton's chapter entitled 'Conversation Analysis' were solicited to fill the gaps which the editors felt the original collection left open.

We should like to express our thanks to Martyn Hammersley, Martin Montgomery, Mike Stubbs and Gordon Wells for their helpful comments and advice on the Introduction and on the organisation of the volume in general, as well as for their encouragement; to Maureen Shields and Bencie Woll who chaired the original conference; to David Satterley and Paul Whitely for editorial advice on particular chapters; and to Maureen Devoy, Debbie Lowe and Eileen Nash for their help with the preparation of the manuscript. Final responsibility for the volume rests, of course, with the editors.

PREFACE

INTRODUCTION

Collections of papers can usually be easily identified as falling within one particular discipline ('sociology', 'linguistics', etc.) or even some sub-branch of a parent discipline ('cognitive psychology', 'developmental psycholinguistics' and so on). While the rationale for collecting papers is often explicitly to define areas and highlight trends, to point to alignments and demarcations within the field, this is generally done against a background of shared assumptions and premises available to contributors and prospective readers alike.

In the case of this collection, there is no single theoretical-paradigmatic backcloth against which to locate the contributions. Talk between adults and children has become, of late, a focus of attention for a wide range of analysts of different academic persuasions, and the present volume reflects this spread, with contributions spanning linguistics, psychology, sociology and education, and various subdivisions and combinations within these categories.

The reasons for this convergence upon the study of adult-child talk are complex, and to some extent they reflect a contemporary reappraisal, within all the social sciences, of the part played by language and communication in the explanation of human behaviour. There seemed, therefore, to be a place for a forum where people working on adult-child interaction within different subject perspectives could come together to present their work and argue their positions. Individual disciplines are fairly well served with their own collections and anthologies but, to date, cross-disciplinary contact has been confined largely to private communication between workers and scattered journal articles. Where overviews of approaches have been offered, these have usually taken the form of a critical summary of other work from within one particular stance. It is hoped, therefore, that this collection will make available to a wider public in a single volume the range of perspectives which are being brought to bear on the examination of talk between adults and children, and some flavour of the rich body of work which this has stimulated.

It would be somewhat redundant to discuss here in detail the theoretical perspectives, affiliations and controversies informing the papers. It is expected that this will be one major outcome of the collection as a whole, and, with this in mind, many of the authors themselves reference their intellectual and historical context and enter into debate over competing approaches. In any case, it would probably be premature, in an area where new developments and theoretical advances are progressing rapidly, to attempt to set up tightly defined categorisations of the work being done. As will be evident on reading the included papers, the business of establishing foundations for further research, of formulating aims and objectives, is very much a live issue for analysts, and much current work is preceded or followed by a recommendation that its conclusions should be treated as tentative or preliminary.

We have, however, tried to organise the contributions by section around what appear to be particularly salient themes and issues in the study of adult-child interaction, and we shall confine ourselves to a brief discussion of each of these in turn.

Discourse Analysis

Until around the late 1960s, the attentions of most linguists had been directed towards the internal organisation of individual sentences. More recently, however, linguists have considered the possibilities of applying their theoretical principles to the systematic analysis of actually occurring conversation. Using principles derived from the work of the linguist Michael Halliday, the English Language Research Group at Birmingham University have attempted to characterise the structured aspect of classroom discussions by analysing them in terms of categories which have constrained and predictable ordering possibilities. The volume in which their analysis of classroom talk is presented, *Towards An Analysis of Discourse* (Sinclair and Coulthard, 1975), is in a sense the keystone around which the work included in Part I is built. As Burton's introductory chapter presents and clarifies the aims and principles of Discourse Analysis as compared with those of related disciplines, as well as the actual categories proposed for the analysis of teacher-pupil conversations, we shall not expound these here, but would recommend the reader unfamiliar with this mode of analysis to read Burton's paper before proceeding to the others in Part I.

Despite the fact that Discourse Analysis has enjoyed considerable success in representing classroom talk in terms of recurrent patterns of linguistic categories and their hierarchical organisation, it is precisely because it seeks to do this that Hammersley sees it as predicating a theory of classroom interaction which amounts to little more than simply following rules for speech production. For Hammersley, the reduction of what is essentially social action to linguistic categories excludes any reference to the concerns of the participants. Hence, possible conflicts of interest and consciously entered-into strategies for their negotiation are obscured.

This criticism itself, however, is in turn answered by Brazil, who suggests that it rests upon a misconception of the Discourse Analysts' enterprise. For Discourse Analysis to succeed as *linguistics*, Brazil argues, vocabularies of motive and intention are not essential components of the description.

The paper by Willes reports her attempts to chart the acquisition of classroom discourse competence by school beginners. Finding her initial choice of method – observer participation – inadequate to her purpose, in that it provided no means of discriminating the conversationally competent, yet silent, children from those who had not yet learned the 'rules', Willes outlines the development, implementation and results of an individual test of children's underlying competence at school discourse, defined by reference to the framework outlined by Burton.

The close integration of theoretical, methodological and educational concerns which Willes's paper represents is made explicit by Stubbs in the final chapter of the section. However, for Stubbs, the work also raises both theoretical and practical educational questions. For example, are Discourse Analysts' categories and their rules for combination as originally presented by Sinclair and Coulthard to be read as a model of underlying interactional competence (as Hammersley reads them), or is Discourse Analysis merely a system for describing symbolically the performance of the participants? Further, given that the rules are *at least* descriptive of performance and normative in character, should they be explicitly taught to school students?

Conversation Analysis

The papers in Part II are a collection of analyses by a 'school' of sociology which has its origins in Harold Garfinkel's ethnomethodology. Garfinkel's reformulation of the sociological enterprise constituted a radical departure from the traditional concerns of sociology in that it urged close examination of the methods by which routine, day-to-day activities are organised and managed by participants in interaction. Thus the papers in this part of the book are concerned with explicating taken-for-granted conversational activities – such as 'correcting', 'telling stories', the resolution of misunderstandings and other interactional matters.

Again, however, rather than expanding on theoretical issues here, we will merely draw the reader's attention to the paper by Wootton which introduces this section, and which provides a useful historical and theoretical exposition of ethnomethodology and the ethnomethodological focus upon conversation, known as Conversation(al) Analysis.

The chapter by Cuff and Hustler focuses on the production of stories by children in an infant school classroom. They suggest some specific ways in which the sequential patterning of pre- and post-story talk may be at variance with that in other more casual settings, and provide accounts of the ways in which participants may display story understanding and recognition of completion in story sequences or 'rounds'.

Wootton's analysis of the use of address terms in the speech of young children interacting with their parents suggests that the position of these items within utterances is related to the specific interactional work the address terms are doing. Further, he suggests that the placement of these items in certain positions may be a strategy children have available for overcoming the interactional problems they face as children.

Again, focusing on possible 'problems' in adult–child interaction, Langford examines previous literature on the resolution of misunderstandings. Arguing that prior statements on 'clarification request sequences' blanket what may be significant intricacies in their negotiation, he suggests various formal properties of the actual requests for clarification produced by parents which children might be attending to in deciding what sort of problem the parent has in understanding their utterance, and hence what steps to take towards a resolution.

Addressing Langford's paper, Hustler suggests that children may actually deploy their supposed incompetence at talk production to strategic ends. Like Wootton, Hustler considers that children may experience problems in engaging their parents in conversation, and one way of overcoming them might be to produce unclear or 'phonologically malformed' utterances which oblige the parent as recipient to request clarification – and thereby engage in talk.

Adult-Child Interaction and Developmental Analysis

The systematic study of the processes by which children come to be able to speak a language – their origins, development over time and variance across children – has been under way for at least twenty years. Yet it is only recently that developmental theory has looked to the interaction between child and adult, rather than to the language of the child alone, for potential explanations of the impetus behind development. The chapters in Part III are all concerned – some critically – with the attempt to formulate a theory of language development based on interactional principles.

In the introductory chapter, McTear presents a set of theoretical imperatives for an adequate developmental model of communicative competence, drawing on recent work in Discourse Analysis, Conversational Analysis, Linguistics and Pragmatics. Wells and Montgomery present the outlines of one particular developmental model and apply it to some excerpts of parent-child and teacher-pupil talk, going on to discuss similarities and differences in the dynamics of interaction in the two settings of home and school, as revealed by their analysis. Drew criticises this (Linguistic) approach from a Conversational Analysis perspective, arguing that the model fails to capture some important features of the interactional work accomplished by children and adults, and offering an alternative analysis of some of Wells's and Montgomery's data.

Foster, in the final chapter of Part III, carries out detailed and meticulous analysis of children's early interactions, and argues that, for a full understanding of the processes of development, all aspects of the communicative behaviour of both child and adult must be systematically described – including gaze, gesture, intonation, referents of utterances, etc., in addition to the verbal elements. She presents a method by which all the relevant parameters of the communicative situation can be captured.

Talk and Social Relations in the Classroom

Edwards criticises previous attempts by educationally oriented sociologists to infer social categories from isolated features of talk, and seeks to find a way of working with classroom conversations which will both reveal something of the social relationship between teachers and pupils and respect for the internal organisation of the talk itself. Focusing specifically on the patterns of turn-taking in formal classroom discussions, he considers, among other features, the teacher's control over turns at talk as evidence of an authority relationship based on the transmission of 'official' knowledge.

While we have drawn attention to what are potentially major issues and controversies to do with studying adult–child interaction from different perspectives, it is worth reiterating that the attempt to define areas and consolidate positions should be treated with caution. The business of describing, explaining and generally coming to grips with the processes of human interaction is still in its infancy, and as well as the 'paradigmatic' oppositions argued in the papers – e.g. linguistics *versus* sociology; discourse analysis *versus* conversational analysis; competence *versus* action and so on – it is possible to see trends and issues which cut across these larger boundaries. For instance, the search for internally organised conversational structure describable in rigorously defined ways is a primary concern of both discourse analysts and conversational analysts, while, on the other hand, on the question of the interactional or strategic significances attaching to conversational behaviours, conversational analysis as practised by some of the authors in Part II seems to share some of the concerns of what Hammersley called 'action' theory. Such issues cannot, therefore, easily be assigned labels such as 'a linguistic viewpoint' or 'a sociological concern'. We would not in any sense wish to talk away real and fundamental differences of approach as these are perceived by those concerned, but we would end on a note of caution against taking these as final statements or as the only issues open to debate.

It is not claimed, and was never expected, that some transcendental synthesis would be the outcome of this attempt to bring together different approaches. Labov (1978) talked about 'crossing the gulf between sociology and linguistics': it would be unwise to think that this or any other gulf has been crossed in these papers, and unrealistic to anticipate that the basic problems and puzzles confronting analysts of adult–child talk will be cleared up simply by airing them in concert.

The contributors would probably agree that, while the opportunity to discuss their work with others of different persuasions has been of use and interest in making visible the concerns and priorities which differentially motivate them, the result has not been, and could not be expected to be, any sort of marriage of minds over a common enterprise.

References

Labov, W. (1978). 'Crossing the Gulf between Sociology and Linguistics'. *American Sociologist*, 13, pp. 93–103

Sinclair, J.McH. and Coulthard, R.M. (1975). *Towards an Analysis of Discourse*. London: Oxford University Press

Part I

DISCOURSE ANALYSIS

1 THE SOCIO*LINGUISTIC* ANALYSIS OF SPOKEN DISCOURSE

Deirdre Burton

Objectives

In this chapter I hope to describe in useful detail the descriptive apparatus for spoken discourse developed at Birmingham University English Language Research by Sinclair, Ashby and Forsyth on an SSRC-funded project (1970–72), 'The English Used by Teachers and Pupils', which is written up in Sinclair et al. (1972) and in Sinclair and Coulthard (1975). This work is a substantial contribution to the rigorous linguistic analysis of discourse, quite different in orientation and construction from rather better-known work with a *socio*linguistic focus. Work in discourse analysis at Birmingham has been in progress for over a decade, but experience has shown that, for those outside the institution, or not in immediate contact with active members of the research unit, materials and methods are not at all easily accessible. This is because work is unpublished, published obscurely or, in the case of the main publication (Sinclair and Coulthard, 1975), written explicitly for at least two audiences. (See the opening to their Chapter 3 and the range of journals in which the book has been reviewed.) It is, therefore, difficult for those with specific research interests to use this important work in any practical way. It is my object in this chapter to explain, locate and comment on the basic aspects of this work. I hope to make explicit what I see as the most significant features of the descriptive system and to foreground problem areas. I hope, in so doing, to make it easier for those outside Birmingham to appreciate, and perhaps use and expand on, the characteristic features of this approach to the linguistic analysis of talk.

Background Assumptions

There are perhaps three main approaches to the analysis of conversation that are interesting and significant trends in humanities research in Britain and the USA. There are the *sociological* analyses of the ethnomethodologists and ethnographers (see, for example, Sacks, 1970 and

1972; Schegloff, 1968; Turner, 1974; Gumperz and Hymes, 1972), the *philosophically* oriented work on speech acts and conversational implicature (e.g. Austin, 1961 and 1962; Searle, 1969; Grice, 1957 and 1975; Kempson, 1977), and the *linguistically* focused work from Birmingham English Language Research. There are also, of course, many stray individuals whose particular concerns overlap in varied ways with the preoccupations of all these and, indeed, it would be perverse to see even these three models as distinct and hermetic: they too have overlapping aims, principles, references and results. Nevertheless, I think most analysts of conversation would agree that they represent three distinctive paradigms. Whilst all three are insightful, stimulating and rich in ideas, the difference in focuses is extremely important. The strong features of the Birmingham work, from the linguist's point of view, are well elaborated in Sinclair and Coulthard (1975). They are fully explicit about their allegiance to an established theoretical-linguistic framework – the early Hallidayan model – using terminology, apparatus and graphic representation that is contingent upon Halliday (1961), and proposing discourse as a linguistic level 'higher' than grammar, but which none the less displays a hierarchical rank scale analogous to those in the more-studied levels of grammar, phonology and graphology. They also make it clear that, in their search for organisation in discourse, they have borne in mind the sorts of organisation available for consideration at other levels of language – both in drawing parallels and in observing new features of patterning. They also reproduce a set of four criteria to be used in the construction of descriptive schema (see Sinclair, 1973) which puts them squarely within the general principles of linguistics, and distances them from the exciting, but less rigorous, notions and approach to data which characterise, say, the ethnomethodologists' work. They are in line here with an early pronouncement of J.R. Firth: 'We must avoid loose sociological linguistics without analytical rigour' (1935). The four crucial criteria to be borne in mind are as follows:

1. the descriptive system must be finite;
2. symbols used in the descriptive apparatus must be explicitly and precisely relatable to the data, so that coding is both clear and replicable;
3. the apparatus must account for all the data;
4. in order to make a structural statement of any standing whatsoever, there must be at least one impossible combination of symbols. (These points are elaborated and exemplified in Sinclair and

Coulthard, 1975, pp. 15–17.)

It is this sort of approach to the work – collecting a corpus of naturally occurring talk, and developing a descriptive apparatus that follows these sorts of criteria – that distinguishes the work of English Language Research from the other, undoubtedly rich and often brilliant, work produced by the scholars in the above-mentioned associated fields.

It would also probably be useful to locate where the Birmingham work stands in relation to both sociolinguistics and functionalism – both of which it lays claim to. The first of these is quite easy, in that we can make the usual distinction (see Fishman, 1972) between macro-sociolinguistics (language planning, correlational studies of substantial samples, work on class and sex differentials, large-scale cultural and political phenomena) and micro-sociolinguistics (the study of the minutiae of verbal interaction in a small data-based corpus). Undoubtedly, the macro and the micro have much to offer each other (see Burton and Stubbs, 1976, on this point) but certainly, in an area as new and relatively uncharted as the analysis of conversation, a small data collection, and a thorough, detailed and specific account of those data, is the only sensible way to proceed. There is an interesting comparison to be made here with several of the emergent fields within linguistics: children's acquisition of language, or pathological linguistics, for example, both of which require powerfully rich and detailed analyses of the case-study type if they ever hope to progress to work of greater generality – in either case the practical or the theoretical sense.

The precise relation of the English Language Research to functionalism is less easy to bring out. There is certainly a stated link with the anthropological-linguistic tradition of Malinowski-Firth-Halliday, where all instances of language are seen as instances of variations on the theme of 'I am communicating with you', and where 'things get done' through talk. But the Birmingham discourse work is placed, quite decidedly again, within a very microcosmic notion of functionality, so that, for example, the analyst needs to consider questions like 'What does this utterance do in terms of the discourse it contributes to? Does it request a verbal response? Does it mark a boundary in the flow of talk? Does it mark the fact that something interesting is coming later?' This, it seems to me, is a significantly different focus from other functionalist-based work, which considers functional relationships between the utterance and the wider situation which includes, of course, the rest of the discourse and participants to that discourse, but which usually looks outside the very minute relationships implied in Birmingham discourse analysis (see, for comparison, Jakobson, 1960; Soskin and John, 1963; Burke, 1945; Halliday, 1969; Hymes, 1972). Again, the larger-focused work and the smaller-focused work should have much to offer each other. For the time being, however, it is important to understand just what is being referred to in the Birmingham work when *functions* are mentioned. Perhaps a small example would help to make the point. The classroom description lists, amongst its *Acts*, an item labelled 'aside', where the teacher might mutter to himself something like 'now where did I put the chalk?' or 'brr, it's freezing in here'. In the description of the definitions and realisations of the 22 acts in Sinclair and Coulthard (1975), all the other acts are described – amongst other things – in terms of their function, but 'aside' is given no such description: implying that it has no function at all. Now, clearly, in some functionalist models it would have a very definite function – 'phatic', perhaps, or 'phatic/expressive' if one were considering Jakobson's model (Jakobson, 1960). Within the working of the *conversation*, however, it serves no prospective or retrospective function – that is, it neither sets up an expectation for a following utterance, nor fulfils one from a previous utterance. It is in this sense, then, that it has no function. It does not, in fact, contribute to the ongoing talk in any constructive way. Unless one has a very clear understanding of what is meant by 'function' in the Birmingham descriptive framework, much confusion can, and does, arise. Perhaps I have laboured the point rather, but the concept has substantial consequences for the rank scale, and particularly for any adaptations that researchers might want to make to it, and it is precisely because students and researchers have been confused by the issue (see, for example, McKnight, 1976, p. 25) that I have spent time and space here in an attempt to clarify the situation.

Both sociolinguistics and functionalism are foregrounded in the discussion of 'situation' and 'tactics' (Sinclair and Coulthard, 1975, pp. 28–34). These two labels indicate the ways in which individual utterances can be coded for 'what they do' in the real world and in the discourse. Turner (1971) very sensibly points out a particular problem for linguists working on real talk, which is that there is no simple, mechanical way in which the analyst can tell, simply from the words on his transcript, what speech act is being used and responded to. A classic example in Sinclair and Coulthard offers 'Is that your coat on the floor?', which is, of course, ostensibly an interrogative (in terms of syntax), or a question (in terms of sentence-action). In certain situations, though – for example, a father to a son in a cross tone of voice, when the son knows he is not supposed to leave his coat on the floor – the utterance constitutes a command, meaning 'pick it up and put it away!'. Sinclair and Coulthard state their position as follows:

> To handle this lack of fit between grammar and discourse we suggest two intermediate areas where distinctive choices can be postulated: situation and tactics . . . *Situation* here includes all relevant factors in the environment, social conventions and the shared experience of the participants . . . *tactics* handles the syntagmatic patterns of discourse: the way in which items precede, follow and are related to each other. It is place in the structure of discourse which finally determines which act a particular item is realising, though classifications can only be made of items already tagged with features from grammar and situation. (1975, pp. 28–9)

Clearly, 'situation' is and must be, a vague notion, where utterances may well be open to various types of interpretation from different individuals. This, in itself, is a fascinating area of study (see Garfinkel, 1967; Cicourel, 1973). It is, none the less, a reasonable, common-sense and workable state of affairs. Again, perhaps an example would help make clear the last part of the above quotation. Consider the difference between these two teacher utterances:

1. 'What about this one?' (pause)
2. 'What about this one? (no pause) This I think is a super one. Isobel, can you think what it means?'

Considering just the first four words: in the first (hypothetical) utterance they function as an *Elicitation* – a question eliciting a verbal response. In the second (genuine) utterance, the same four words are 'pushed down' to the position of *Starter* – a question, statement or command, the function of which is to draw attention to, or provide information about, an area, in order to make a correct *Response* to the *Initiation* as a whole more likely. In this case, the set of three (orthographic) sentences forms an Opening Move, the head of which is the Elicitation 'can you think what it means?' In terms of *tactics*, the first four words fill a possible pre-head position in the Move, the total possible structure of which is reproduced below:

Rank IV: Move (Opening)

Elements of Structure	*Structures*	*Classes of Act*
signal (s)	(s) (pre-h) h (post-h) (sel)	s:marker
pre-head (pre-h)	(sel) (pre-h) h	pre-h:starter
head (h)		h:choice of elicitation/directive/informative/check
post-head (post-h)		post-h:choice of prompt/clue
select (sel)		sel: ((cue) bid) nomination

Again, to avoid misunderstanding, I think it is probably advisable to say a little about the status of the descriptive system as published, particularly in relation to further work in discourse study. Sinclair and Coulthard indicate throughout that they hope that their work will be used and extended and modified in further conversational research: 'There will be a few . . . who will want to use the system in their own research work and for whom this chapter will have to act as a coding manual' (p. 19); '. . . we would stress the preliminary nature of this work, we are confident that sufficient progress has been made for more ambitious studies to be successfully undertaken' (p. 112). Again,

> We are hopeful that our efforts to provide a systematic account of samples of spoken language from a small number of classrooms will be of use to others with similar interests, and stimulate further empirical studies, both in educational and other contexts. (p. 112)

Implicit in these remarks, and more explicit elsewhere, is an acknowledgement of the limitations of their study: 'the most we can claim is to have begun to evolve one possible approach to the analysis of spoken texts, while working with a relatively small data sample taken from one situation type' (p. 112).

It is the 'one situation type' that is crucial to my point here. Elsewhere the authors again point out this problem with their analysis: 'The system . . . is now able to cope with most teacher/pupil interaction inside the classroom. What it cannot handle, and *of course was not designed to handle*, is pupil/pupil interaction in project work, discussion groups or the playground' (p. 6; my emphasis).

A particular problem I have encountered with recent researchers has been on this point, and in connection with the descriptive status of the discourse model as outlined in the book. The corpus itself was homogeneous, and a normative description inevitably emerged which, as the authors themselves stress, 'must be abandoned as soon as substantial sociolinguistic variables are allowed to vary' (p. 125). They are equally explicitly aware of the dangers of forcing new data into categories constructed for other data, but inevitably, of course, any later researcher wanting to test the strengths and weaknesses of the paradigm must begin by trying to force his data into those categories in order to see how near or how far the new material is, in terms of its organisation, and to see whether minor, or even major, amendments are feasible. The contingent danger is, of course, the difficulty in seeing what sort of new or modified structure might be required to handle the non-homogeneous data. Again, researchers have often mistaken the status of the classroom discourse model, and have reacted with surprise in finding that it fails to meet their needs precisely. It must be borne in mind that classroom discourse was originally singled out for study (see Sinclair and Coulthard, 1975, p. 6) because it was intuitively felt to be 'easier to handle', 'more highly structured than casual conversation' and, therefore, in some sense 'odd'. Since this is the case, it is similarly important for conversational analysts not to regard classroom discourse as central, and other situations as variations upon it. Again, as Sinclair and Coulthard point out (p. 123), a linguist who has intuitively selected a type of discourse as in some way unusual, then has the job of proving that there is any overlap between this type and others.

Classroom Discourse

As already stated above, the practical descriptive apparatus for handling classroom data is built on a rank scale model, with the usual hierarchical implications. The basic structure is as follows:

Lesson
V
Transaction
V
Exchange
V

Move
V
Act

where lessons are made up of Transactions, Transactions are made up of Exchanges, Exchanges are made up of Moves, and Moves are made up of Acts. The analogy with the grammar rank scale (Halliday, 1961) is helpful here, particularly at the lower end of the scale with a comparison between word-morpheme and Move-Act, since it is important to remember that, although the Act is the smallest unit, Move is the minimal free interactive unit and, although a Move may be realised by a single Act, Acts are essentially bound units, some of which cannot be used singly.

I find the informal presentation of the way this rank scale developed (Sinclair and Coulthard, 1975, p. 21) very helpful as a preliminary to understanding the rank scale in detail and depth, and will summarise this description briefly here.

1. The researchers began by considering two units only: the utterance (one speaker's contribution) and the exchange (two speakers' joint contribution to the talk – question and answer, for example).

2. They then noticed that a vast number of teacher utterances had a boundary in mid-utterance (c.f. Turner, 1971). A typical teacher utterance might have this form for instance:

> Paris, that's right.
> And Mary, what's the capital of Sweden?

They, therefore, decided to recognise a unit smaller than an utterance, which they labelled 'Move'. In the hypothetical example just given, the teacher uses two Moves – one which tells one pupil that he has just given her the right answer to a previous question, and one which asks another, specifically nominated pupil a similar question, requesting a different, but analogous, answer. It might be useful, at this stage, if I extend this hypothetical, but recognisably typical discourse, to produce two complete Exchanges – two Teacher-Eliciting exchanges – and lay them out using the graphic system given in Sinclair and Coulthard's book (see Fig. 1.1).

3. The researchers then decided that the typical Exchange structure for classroom discourse can be described as a three-part structure, comprising Initiation, Response and Feedback (IRF).

Figure 1.1: Two Teacher-Eliciting Exchanges, using Sinclair and Coulthard's System

Opening move	Act	Answering move	Act	Follow-up move	Act
John What's the capital of France?	n el	Paris	rep	Paris that's right	acc ev
And Mary What's the capital of Sweden?	n el	Stockholm	rep	Stockholm Good girl	acc ev

4. The next thing they noticed was a small set of words and phrases that recurred in teacher-talk, like 'right', 'well', 'OK', 'now', often produced with a sharply falling intonation and followed by a pause. These could be seen to be marking boundaries in the flow of talk, indicating the end of one stage, and the beginning of the next. This they labelled *Frame*.

5. This framing item was often followed in the data by a metastatement about the discourse. This they labelled *Focus*. Notice that Frame and Focus are both Moves, together with Opening, Answering and Follow-up moves. But whereas Opening, Answering, and Follow-up moves combine to form what are called *Teaching Exchanges*, Frame and Focus combine to form what are called *Boundary Exchanges*.

6. Frame and Focus provided the first positive evidence for a rank above the Exchange. This was labelled *Transaction*. As yet, there is no evidence for a structural description of Transaction. It is suggested that this may be a feature of different teachers' styles. Thus, for example, a particular teacher may mark the boundary of the Transaction, follow this with an Informing Exchange, follow that with, say, five Eliciting Exchanges, and follow that with a Directing Exchange; and when the

action that he has commanded the class to do has been completed, he may explicitly mark the end of the Transaction with another Boundary Exchange, in which the Metastatement in the Focusing move refers backwards to the job just completed.

7. They then realised that Moves had an internal structure of their own, and devised criteria for recognising 22 different *Acts*, some of which have already appeared in the example above: *Nomination* (n), *Elicitation* (el), *Reply* (rep), *Accept* (acc) and *Evaluate* (ev).

In the following pages I will set out the rank scale completely, more or less as it appears in Sinclair and Coulthard (1975), but with (a) a few minor modifications which, hopefully, make it easier to read and (b) corrections of misprints in the first edition of the book. I will also append comments, when appropriate, on some of the inherent problems contained in the scheme. In part, this reflects areas where the authors themselves are anticipating alterations to the model.

Rank One: Lesson

Elements of Structure	*Structures*	*Classes*
	an unordered series of transactions	

Notes

1. Clearly this is a very vague structural statement, and points up the difficulty inherent in any rank scale model *à propos* its highest unit. Notice, though, the implications for 'rule-bound creativity', for, whilst the lower ranks are very explicitly and tightly restricted, at the higher ranks there is clearly room for variation in 'discourse style' and 'teaching method' within an orderly and consensus discourse. (See Bernstein, 1971, on the notion of frames and freedom.)
2. For different speech situations, different common-sense terms are, of course, easily substituted: 'committee-meeting', 'interview', 'service-encounter'. For more abstract discussion, Hymes's notion of 'speech event' is an appropriate item to be borrowed (Hymes, 1972), wherever the interaction is co-terminous with that event.

Rank Two: Transaction

Elements of Structure		*Structures*	*Classes of Exchange*	
Preliminary	(P)	PM ($M^2 \ldots M^n$) (T)	P, T: Boundary	(II.1)
Medial	(M)		M:Teaching	(II.2)
Terminal	(T)			

Note

1. The optional terminal element is worth some consideration. Whilst it is quite a common option used in classroom discourse, where the teacher is often concerned to point out the structure of his/her talk as clearly as possible to his/her audience, it is not so obviously in use in other, less formal situations. It may often be the case that the closing of a particular Transaction can only be recognised after the event. That is, the hearer knows that the first Transaction has finished, because the second Transaction has explicitly started. Pearce (1977) and Tadros (forthcoming) have pointed out the same characteristic for the analysis of written discourse, and this may well be an important feature with regard to how participants understand all kinds of discourse. If it *is* the case that we assume we are still within one unit, or mode, or framework until the producer of the discourse we are reading or hearing explicitly indicates that we have moved to another, then this notion could well be used to explain various sorts of malfunctioning discourse – whether deliberate (like jokes, *avant-garde* writing) or accidental (foreigners' mistakes, socio-psychologically problematic situations).

Rank Three: Exchange (Boundary)

Elements of Structure	*Structures*	*Classes of Move*	
Frame (Fr)	Fr (Fo)	Fr: Framing	(III.1)
Focus (Fo)		Fo: Focusing	(III.2)

Note

1. The structure is represented thus in Sinclair and Coulthard (1975, p. 26): (Fr) (Fo). If it is intended to indicate that the Boundary Exchange can be made up of either a Frame or a Focus, or of both together, then linked brackets would make this clearer (Fr)(Fo), and would be more in line with current conventions. However, I understand that in the classroom data the Frame is obligatory and the Focus only optional (Sinclair, personal communication), so I have altered the structural statement as above.

Rank Three: Exchange (Teaching)

Elements of Structure		*Structures*	*Classes of Move*	
Initiation	(I)	I (R) (F)	I: Opening	(III.3)
Response	(R)		R: Answering	(III.4)
Feedback	(F)		F: Follow-up	(III.5)

Note

1. The basic rank scale is presented at primary delicacy only. Eleven sub-categories of this Exchange type are also isolated and presented in Sinclair and Coulthard (1975). Of these, six are Free Exchanges, and five are bound to preceding Free Exchanges:

Free		*Bound*	
Teacher-Inform	I (R)	Teacher-ReInitiation$_{(i)}$	IRI^{b}RF
Teacher-Direct	IR (F)	Teacher-ReInitiation$_{(ii)}$	IRF(I^{b})RF
Teacher-Elicit	IRF	Teacher-Listing	IRF(I^{b})RF(I^{b})RF etc.
Pupil-Elicit	IR	Teacher-Reinforce	IRI^{b}R
Pupil-Inform	IF	Teacher-Repeat	IRI^{b}RF
Teacher-Check	IR (F)		

Notice that in the discursive writing in the book, the authors claim that IRF is the most usual structure. This is, of course, the primary pattern only and, whilst it certainly does cover a large number of Exchanges in the data, a more delicate description is possible and desirable.

Rank Four: Move (Opening)

Elements of Structure		*Structures*	*Classes of Act*	
signal	(s)	(s) (pre-h) h (post-h) (sel)	s:marker	(IV.1)
pre-head	(pre-h)	(sel) (pre-h) h	pre-h:starter	(IV.2)
head	(h)		h:system operating at h; choice of elicitation directive informative check	(IV.3)
post-head	(post-h)		post-h:system operating at post-h; choice of prompt	
select	(sel)			

		clue (IV.4)
		sel: ((cue) bid) nomination (IV.5)

Note
1. I have corrected the rather misleading printing of the second column which appears in Sinclair and Coulthard thus:

(s) (pre-h) h (post-h)
(sel)
(sel) (pre-h) h (1975, p. 26)

Presumably the printer ran out of space, and the resulting presentation is somewhat confusing. My amendment is supposed to make the two alternative structures for an opening move.

Rank Four: Move (Answering)

Elements of Structure		*Structures*	*Classes of Act*
pre-head	(pre-h)	(pre-h) h (post-h)	pre-h: acknowledge (IV.6)
head	(h)		h: system operating at h; choice of
post-head	(post-h)		reply
			react (IV.7)
			acknowledge (IV.6)
			post-h: comment (IV.8)

Notes
1. There are several problems with the item Acknowledge which I will discuss below at Act rank. For the moment, notice that it is given here as occurring at two distinct places in the structure of this Move – pre-head or head. Taking account of the 'push-down' mechanism would simplify any coding problems with this item. That is, it would be coded as head if there were no following head realised by Reply or React.
2. The book misprints Acknowledge (as head) as IV.7 in the third column. I have corrected this to IV.6.

Rank Four: Move (Follow-up)

Elements of Structure		*Structures*	*Classes of Act*	
pre-head	(pre-h)	(pre-h) (h) (post-h)	pre-h:accept	(IV.9)
head	(h)		h:evaluate	(IV.10)
post-head	(post-h)		post-h:comment	(IV.8)

Rank Four: Move (Framing)

Elements of Structure		*Structures*	*Classes of Act*	
head	(h)	hq	h:marker	(IV.1)
qualifier	(q)		q:silent stress	(IV.11)

Note

1. The distinction between the head and qualifier is not immediately obvious since both of them are obligatory. The distinction resides in the fact that Markers can also occur in Opening Moves, but, if followed by the Silent Stress, the Move is recognised, and recognisable, as a Framing Move.

Rank Four: Move (Focusing)

Elements of Structure		*Structures*	*Classes of Act*	
signal	(s)	(s) (pre-h) h (post-h)	s:marker	(IV.1)
pre-head	(pre-h)		pre-h:starter	(IV.2)
head	(h)		h:system operating at h; choice of metastatement conclusion	(IV.12)
post-head	(post-h)		post-h:comment	(IV.8)

Note

1. Notice the similarity between this and the Opening Move: both begin with possible Marker and possible Starter, whilst the difference occurs in the choice of *head*. Whereas Opening Moves choose between Directive/Elicitation/Informative/Check, Focusing Moves choose between Metastatement and Conclusion. This has substantial implications for notions of the continuous classification of talk, in that hearers cannot tell, until the speaker produces the head of this utterance, whether they are supposed to be attending to a possible Opening Move or a possible Focusing Move.

Classes of Acts

Reference No.	*Label*	*Symbol*	*Realisation and Definition*
IV.1	marker	m	*Realised* by a closed class – well/ OK/now/good/right/alright. Falling intonation, and silent stress following when acting as the head of a framing move. *Function* to mark boundaries in the discourse. *Occurs* in Opening moves as signal Framing moves as head Focusing moves as signal
IV.2	starter	s	*Realised* by statement/question/ command. *Function* to provide information about, or direct attention to, an area in order to make a correct response to the initiation more likely. *Occurs* in Opening moves as pre-head Focusing moves as pre-head

Notes

1. Although there are no examples in the data, it would be quite feasible for this Act to be realised by a moodless item, e.g. 'easy one this'. Again, it is important to be quite clear about the relationship of the statements set out in the presentation of the system, and real discourse. The authors claim that they present only what occurs in the data. That these descriptive statements take on a categorical and definitive implication is unfortunate and misleading.

2. Notice the similarity between this item and Clues. They are indeed almost identical in terms of realisation, but they are labelled according to where they occur in the structure of the talk (see again Section 2; the discussion of Tactics). Thus, Starters occur in both Opening and Focusing Moves as pre-heads, but Clues occur in Opening Moves as post-head. This again points up the importance accorded to continuous

classification, and again has important implications when it comes to considering later researchers' suggestions for other Acts and Moves for different discourse types, some of which are extremely uneconomical.

Reference No.	*Label*	*Symbol*	*Realisation and Definition*
IV.3.1	elicitation	el	*Realised* by a question *Function* to request a linguistic response. *Occurs* in Opening moves as head (cf. IV.3.2/IV.3.3/IV.3.4)

Note

1. See below for remarks on an interesting overlap problem between Elicitations and Directives.

Reference No.	*Label*	*Symbol*	*Realisation and Definition*
IV.3.2	check	ch	*Realised* by a closed set of polar questions to do with being 'finished'/'ready', having 'problems'/'difficulties', being able to 'see'/'hear'. Real questions in the sense that the teacher doesn't already know the answer. *Function* to enable the teacher to ascertain whether there are any problems preventing the progress of the lesson. *Occurs* in Opening moves as head (c.f. IV.3.1/IV.3.3/IV.3.4)
IV.3.3	directive	d	*Realised* by a command. *Function* to request a non-linguistic response.

Notes

1. The original text states (as a misprint) that a Directive is realised by an imperative, thus confusing the distinction made on page 29 of the original, which presents the relationships between discourse categories, situational categories and grammatical categories. Since imperative is clearly a grammatical category, I have changed this to a discourse equivalent above.

2. There is an interesting problem of overlap between Directive and Elicitation when the teacher produces an utterance like: 'Tell me your name.' In one sense this is clearly an utterance that requests a verbal response (which is one criterion for classifying it as an Elicitation), in another sense it is clearly a command (which is one criterion for classifying it as a Directive). It is not an uncommon example. Either it is necessary to set up a new opening and answering pair (like Elicitation-Reply and Directive-React) to cope with this problem or, more economically, it is possible to see this *as* a *Directive*, to which the corresponding *React* happens to involve a verbal noise. It is this classification that seems more in line with a common-sense understanding of the discourse situation, in that, clearly, a Directive implies an instruction to perform something, and that performance might well include a verbal performance. Thus 'Sing the National Anthem backwards' would have the same classification.

It is interesting that Bauman (1976) uses the term 'solicitation' to cover both Elicitations and Directives.

Reference No.	*Label*	*Symbol*	*Realisation and Definition*
IV.3.4	informative	i	*Realised* by a statement. Differs from other uses of statement in that its sole *Function* is to provide information. The only necessary response is an acknowledgement of attention and understanding. *Occurs* in Opening moves as head (c.f. IV.3.1/IV.3.2/IV.3.3)

Notes

1. Notice the negative definition of this act.
2. In terms of classroom discourse this Act seems perfectly adequate,

but in other situations, particularly ones which are not set up as 'time for the transfer of information' but where, nevertheless, referential content is undoubtedly passed between the participants, a finer notion of this item is definitely called for.

Reference No.	*Label*	*Symbol*	*Realisation and Definition*
IV.4.1	prompt	p	*Realised* by closed class of items, e.g. 'go on'/'have a go'/'come on'/'quickly'. *Function* to reinforce a directive or elicitation by suggesting that the response is no longer requested but demanded. *Occurs* in Opening moves as post-head (c.f. IV.4.2)
IV.4.2	clue	cl	*Realised* by statement, command, question or moodless item. *Function* to provide additional information which helps the pupil answer the elicitation or comply with the directive. Thus subordinate to head. *Occurs* in Opening moves as post-head (c.f. IV.4.1)

Note

1. See the remarks on Starters above.

Reference No.	*Label*	*Symbol*	*Realisation and Definition*
IV.5.1	cue	cu	*Realised* by closed class of items (only three exponents in the data): 'hands up'/'don't call out', etc. *Function* to evoke an appropriate bid. *Occurs* in

			Opening moves as select (c.f. IV.5.2/IV.5.3)
IV.5.2	bid	b	*Realised* by closed class of verbal and non-verbal items 'Sir'/ 'Miss'/teacher's name/raised hand/finger clicks. *Function* to signal a desire to contribute to the discourse. *Occurs* in Opening moves as select (c.f. IV.5.1/IV.5.3)

Note

1. Notice that this description allows two speakers to contribute to a single Move which, if allowed to stand, has far-reaching consequences for the descriptive system. Sinclair and Coulthard are aware of the problem:

> . . . our rank of *move* is concerned centrally with each discrete contribution to a discussion made by one speaker. We resist recognising as a move a structure in which more than one speaker contributes, since that is more typical of the next rank up, *exchange*. (p. 123)
>
> It would be possible to suggest that teaching exchanges actually have a structure of five moves, with both bid and nomination as separate moves. The argument for this would be that a new move should begin every time there is a new speaker. We rejected this alternative, because it would have created as many difficulties as it would have solved. When a teacher nominated without waiting for a bid, we would have had to regard this as two moves, one consisting of a single word, and at times even embedded inside the other move. Such a solution would also have devalued the concept of move. We prefer to say that a move boundary signals a change in the speaker who is composing/creating the discourse, and that therefore a move boundary is a potential change in the direction of the discourse, whereas a child making a bid must choose from a very limited set of choices. Thus we regard the function of an opening move, with elicitation or directive as head, as not only requesting a reply or a reaction but as also deciding who should respond. An opening move ends after the responder has been selected (p. 46).

Reference No.	*Label*	*Symbol*	*Realisation and Definition*
IV.5.3	nomination	n	*Realised* by a closed class: names of all the pupils/'you' with contrastive stress/'anybody'/ 'yes'. *Function* to call on or give permission to a pupil to contribute to the discourse. *Occurs* in Opening moves as select (c.f. IV.5.1/IV.5.2)

Note

1. This is a very clear example of the way in which the analyst cannot move from a closed set of formal items (the children's names) to a functional categorisation. If, say, the class were an unruly one (and notice, in passing, that this descriptive analysis does not provide the tools necessary for describing unruly classes, since the data came from well-ordered classrooms), then the use of a child's name, spoken with, say, tone 4 (Halliday, 1970), could well be heard as a warning to stop behaving in ways that violated spoken and unspoken rules of classroom behaviour. (See Sinclair and Coulthard, 1975, pp. 30–32, for a full discussion of the overlapping interpretations of command/request and the dependence on situational knowledge for interpretive rules. See also Willes, 1975, for part of a case study of a child who clearly does *not* share situational knowledge.) As in Scale and Category grammar, used as a descriptive tool for the study of text, interpretation depends upon a combination of the examination of meaning, componence and structure (see Sinclair, 1972, p. 37).

Reference No.	*Label*	*Symbol*	*Realisation and Definition*
IV.6	acknowledge	ack	*Realised* by 'yes'/'OK'/'wow' and certain non-verbal gestures and expressions. *Function* simply to show that the initiation has been understood and, if the head was a directive, that the pupil intends to react. *Occurs* in

Answering move as pre-head
Answering move as head
(c.f. IV.7.1/IV.7.2)

Note

1. As in Informing above, it seems unsatisfactory not to distinguish between different types of Acknowledge like 'yes' and 'wow'. Again, this may not be particularly important in the classroom, where the range of choices open to the pupil is so very limited (although I can imagine sarcastic exploitation of 'wow' by unruly pupils that could totally demolish the planned lesson, and would thus need to be shown in the description of that discourse), but outside the classroom this is a rich and therefore problematic area. This matter of the rights and possibilities of answering speakers needs careful consideration.

Reference No.	*Label*	*Symbol*	*Realisation and Definition*
IV.7.1	reply	rep	*Realised* by statement, question, moodless item and non-verbal surrogates like nods. *Function* to provide a linguistic response appropriate to the elicitation. *Occurs* in Answering moves as head (c.f. IV.7.2/IV.6)
IV.7.2	react	rea	*Realised* by a non-linguistic action. *Function* to provide the appropriate non-linguistic response defined by the preceding directive. *Occurs* in Answering moves as head (c.f. IV.7.1/IV.6)
IV.8	comment	com	*Realised* by statement or tag question subordinate to the head. *Function* to exemplify, expand,

			justify, provide additional information. *Occurs* in Answering moves as post-head Follow-up moves as post-head Focusing moves as post-head

Note

1. The book again confuses grammatical and discourse categories. Tag question here means 'a declarative with an interrogative tag'. I have changed 'Realised by statement *and* tag question' to 'Realised by statement *or* tag question' to try to make this clearer.

Reference No.	*Label*	*Symbol*	*Realisation and Definition*
IV.9	accept	acc	*Realised* by a closed class of items 'yes'/'no'/'good'/'fine'/repetition of pupil's reply, all with neutral or low fall intonation. *Function* to indicate that teacher has heard/seen and that the reply or react was appropriate. *Occurs* in Follow-up moves as pre-head
IV.10	evaluate	e	*Realised* by statements or tag questions including words and phrases like 'good'/'team point'/'interesting'. *Function* to comment on quality of pupil reply, react or initiation. *Occurs* in Follow-up moves as head

Note

1. See my amendment above to Comment, with regard to tag questions. I have done the same here.

Reference No.	*Label*	*Symbol*	*Realisation and Definition*
IV.11	silent stress	ʌ	*Realised* by a pause, following a marker. *Function* to highlight the marker when it is serving as the head of a boundary exchange, indicating a transaction boundary. *Occurs* in Framing moves as qualifier

Note

1. It is not immediately obvious why this should be termed a 'qualifier' and not 'post-head', but see my comments on Boundary Exchanges above, where I point out that if, and only if, a Silent Stress follows a Marker, i.e. qualifies it, that Marker is heard as starting a Framing Move, rather than an Opening Move. The Silent Stress is thus only considered important as a bound qualifier to Markers.

Reference No.	*Label*	*Symbol*	*Realisation and Definition*
IV.12.1	meta-statements	ms	*Realised* by a statement which refers to future time. *Function* to help pupils to see the structure of the lesson and understand the purpose of the subsequent exchange. *Occurs* in Focusing moves as head

Note

1. Whilst the data have no examples of Metastatements referring to present time, this is by no means an impossible construct. For example, a teacher might well say 'What we're doing now is creating energy'.

Reference No.	*Label*	*Symbol*	*Realisation and Definition*
IV.13	loop	l	*Realised* by closed class of items 'pardon'/'what did you say'/'eh'/'did you say'/'do you mean'.

			Function to return the discourse to the stage it was at before the pupil spoke and from where it can proceed normally. *Occurs* Anywhere

Note

1. I am reminded of a method Garfinkel employed to 'create trouble', which was to get his students repeatedly to produce Loops to other participants' Informs (see Garfinkel, 1967). By no means did the discourse proceed normally! This means that, again, this item is open to disruptive exploitation.

Reference No.	*Label*	*Symbol*	*Realisation and Definition*
IV.14	aside	z	*Realised* by statement, question, command, moodless item. Seems to be the teacher talking to himself: 'It's freezing in here' for example. *Function* not given. *Occurs* Anywhere

Note

1. See my remarks on this item in Section 2 above. The fact that this item is not assigned a function means only that it does not contribute anything to the discourse and is not taken up in any way by other participants. I suspect that this item is far more a feature of formal talk situations than informal ones, where it could be an embarrassing item. It is also open to exploitation by perverse interactants.

Conclusion

In this chapter, I hope to have foregrounded and made clear the basic principles behind the work in Discourse Analysis from Birmingham English Language Research. I came to this type of analysis from a background interest in ethnomethodological work on the analysis of conversation, and have to confess to an initial scepticism about the descriptive adequacy of the Sinclair and Coulthard model. However, when I was forced to get to grips with the details of their work, in order to describe some problematic data, I was certainly impressed by the type of precise observations I could then make about the data – particularly in terms of comparing stretches of talk with one another. This is not, of course, to say that Sinclair and Coulthard (1975) is the last word on the subject. Interested analysts are recommended to see Coulthard and Montgomery (in press) and Burton (forthcoming). Nevertheless, the work reported in Sinclair and Coulthard (1975) represents a significant linguistic breakthrough for analysts of conversation, and deserves their attention.

References

Austin, J.L. (1961). *Philosophical Papers.* Edited by J.O. Urmson and G.L. Warnock. London: Oxford University Press

— (1962). *How to Do Things with Words.* London: Oxford University Press.

Barker, R.G. (ed.) (1963). *The Stream of Behaviour.* New York: Appleton

Bauman, R. (1976). 'The Development of Competence in the Use of Solicitational Routines: Children's Folklore and Informal Learning'. Mimeo, University of Texas Working Papers in Sociolinguistics, 34

Bernstein, B. (1971). 'On the Classification and Framing of Educational Knowledge'. In M.F.D. Young (ed.), *Knowledge and Control*

Burke, K. (1945). *A Grammar of Motives.* Englewood Cliffs, New Jersey: Prentice-Hall. (Republished by University of California Press, 1969)

Burton, D. (forthcoming). *Dialogue and Discourse.* London: Routledge

— and Stubbs, M.W. (1976). 'On Speaking Terms: Analysing Conversational Data'. *Midlands Association of Linguistic Studies*, II, 2, pp. 22–44

Cicourel, A.V. (1973). *Cognitive Sociology.* Harmondsworth: Penguin

Cole, P. and Morgan, J.L. (eds.) (1975). *Syntax and Semantics III: Speech Acts.* New York: Academic Press

Coulthard, R.M. and Montgomery, M.M. (eds.) (in press). *Studies in Discourse Analysis* (provisional title). London: Routledge

Douglas, J. (ed.) (1971). *Understanding Everyday Life.* London: Routledge

Firth, J.R. (1935). 'The Techniques of Semantics', in *Papers in Linguistics.* London: Oxford University Press

Fishman, J. (1972). 'The Relationship Between Micro- and Macro-Sociolinguistics in the Study of Who Speaks What Language to Whom and When'. Revised and reprinted in J.B. Pride and J. Homes (eds.), *Sociolinguistics*

Garfinkel, H. (1967). *Studies in Ethnomethodology.* New Jersey: Prentice-Hall

Grice, H.P. (1957). 'Meaning'. *Philosophical Review*, 66, pp. 377–88

— (1975). 'Logic and Conversation'. In P. Cole and J.L. Morgan (eds.) *Syntax and Semantics III: Speech Acts*

Gumperz, J.J. and Hymes, D. (eds.) (1972). *Directions in Sociolinguistics.* New York: Holt

Halliday, M.A.K. (1961). 'Categories of the Theory of Grammar'. *Word*, 17, pp. 241–92

— (1969). 'Relevant Models of Language'. *Educational Review*, 22, pp. 26–37

— (1970). *A Course in Spoken English: Intonation*. London: Oxford University Press
Hymes, D. (1972). 'Models of the Interaction of Language and Social Life'. In J.J. Gumperz and D. Hymes (eds.), *Directions in Sociolinguistics*
Jakobson, R. (1960). 'Concluding Statement: Linguistics and Poetics'. In T.A. Sebeok (ed.), *Style in Language*
Kempson, R. (1977). *Semantic Theory*. Cambridge: Cambridge University Press
McKnight, A. (1976). 'Large Group Conversation: Problems for Discourse Analysis'. Unpublished M.A. thesis, University of Lancaster
Pearce, R.D. (1977). 'A Stylistic Analysis of James Joyce's A Portrait of the Artist as a Young Man'. Unpublished Ph.D. thesis, University of Birmingham
Pride, J.B. and Holmes, J. (1972). *Sociolinguistics*. Harmondsworth: Penguin
Sacks, H. (1968-70). Lecture Notes. Mimeo, University of California, Los Angeles and Irvine
— (1972). 'On the Availability of Stories by Children'. In J.J. Gumperz and D. Hymes (eds.), *Directions in Sociolinguistics*
Schegloff, E. (1968). 'Sequencing in Conversational Openings'. *American Anthropologist*, 70, 6, pp. 1075-95
Searle, J.R. (1969). *Speech Acts: An Essay in the Philosophy of Language*. Cambridge: Cambridge University Press
Sebeok, T.A. (ed.) (1960). *Style in Language*. Cambridge, Mass.: MIT Press
Sinclair, J.McH. (1972). *A Course in Spoken English: Grammar*. London: Oxford University Press
— (1973). 'Linguistics in Colleges of Education'. *Dudley Educational Journal*, 1, 3
— , Coulthard, R.M., Forsyth, I.J. and Ashby, M. (1972). *The English Used by Teachers and Pupils*. (Report to the SSRC.) Mimeo, University of Birmingham
— and Coulthard, R.M. (1975). *Towards an Analysis of Discourse*. London: Oxford University Press
Soskin, W.P. and John, V. (1963). 'The Study of Spontaneous Talk'. In R.G. Barker (ed.), *The Stream of Behaviour*
Tadros, A. (forthcoming). 'The Structure of Economics Text'. Unpublished Ph.D. thesis, University of Birmingham
Turner, R. (1971). 'Words, Utterances and Activities'. In J. Douglas (ed.), *Understanding Everyday Life*
— (1974). 'Utterance Positioning as an Interactional Resource'. In R.J. Wilson (ed.), *Ethnomethodology, Labelling Theory and Deviant Behaviour*
Willes, M. (1975). 'Early Lessons Learned Too Well'. Paper presented to SSRC-supported Conference 'Collecting, Using and Reporting Talk for Research in Education'. University of Nottingham, September 1975
Wilson, R.J. (ed.) (1974). *Ethnomethodology, Labelling Theory and Deviant Behaviour*. London: Routledge
Young, M.F.D. (ed.) (1971). *Knowledge and Control*. London: Macmillan

2 PUTTING COMPETENCE INTO ACTION: SOME SOCIOLOGICAL NOTES ON A MODEL OF CLASSROOM INTERACTION

Martyn Hammersley

The study of classroom interaction has a quite surprisingly long history, and one of its distinctive features is a baffling array of approaches with different purposes, foci and terminologies. Despite this diversity, however, much of the most recent work in the field shares a fundamental idea which contrasts with the older 'classroom observation' tradition.[1] Crudely put, it is non-behaviourist: it has not sought to restrict itself to the description and explanation of 'observable behaviour'. Rather, the central aim has been to discover the assumptions, rules, strategies, etc. which underlie and produce classroom interaction. Nevertheless, within the boundaries of that common theme, there are still some major differences of approach and it is on one of these that I want to focus here.

Now, of course, the nature of the approach one adopts depends on one's purposes, and in the case of classroom interaction we are faced with several different disciplines as well as different schools of thought within those disciplines. My criticisms in this paper are not meant to suggest that there is only one set of proper purposes, or that classroom interaction is the 'territory' of one discipline. However, I do think that we should work towards the situation where the purposes, theories and findings of neighbouring disciplines are at least compatible and preferably complementary. It is certainly true that much sociology ignores linguistics, indeed much sociology ignores language, and that is a target for justifiable criticism. However, in this paper I want to point to some sociologically troubling aspects of some recent work in linguistics, sociolinguistics and the philosophy of language,[2] though I shall focus specifically on some recent work in the first discipline. I want to try to show that this work, while in many respects instructive, predicates a kind of sociological theory which is unsatisfactory in a number of different ways.[3]

I want to contrast what I shall call competence and action models of social interaction.[4] In the competence approach, particular instances or recurring patterns of human activity are treated as competent displays of culture membership, and the discovery of the rules or procedures by which that activity was, or could have been, produced is taken as the exclusive goal. I would count the following as examples of such an approach: 'the ethnography of speaking',[5] speech act analysis,[6] conversational analysis,[7] and discourse analysis.[8]

Action theory, on the other hand, while similarly anti-behaviourist, treats patterns of activity as the product of interaction between groups with different concerns and interests, who define situations in distinctive ways and develop strategies for furthering those interests, often by means of negotiation and bargaining with one another. In relation to any particular action, the action theorist asks what intentions and motives underlie it and how these relate to the actor's perspective or definition of the situation. Examples of an action approach can be found in interactionist ethnography,[9] transactional anthropology,[10] and social phenomenology.[11] Some work seems uneasily to span the divide between the competence and action approaches, that of Goffman being the most obvious example.[12]

At the risk of disclosing something of what is to come, I could say, baldly, that competence theories are concerned with explaining social order, action theories with detecting and accounting for patterns of social control.[13] However, for me this indicates the deficiencies of both, rather than the superiority of one over the other.

My argument is that, as an over-all framework, the action approach is the more promising. However, this framework is underdeveloped, in part, I think, because of a kind of empiricism whereby more emphasis has been placed on investigating the content of perspectives and strategies employed by particular groups of actors in particular settings than on developing the underlying theory. The result has been that the concepts which are central to the action model, 'perspective' and 'strategy', have an inadequate and usually implicit theoretical context which takes the form of a vague pluralism in which different groups simply have different interests and different views of, and strategies for dealing with, the world.

There are two implications of this implicit theory relevant here. The first is that definitions of the situation tend to be treated as though they are produced out of nothing. This ignores both the cultural resources which are used to produce them and the fact that perspectives often become institutionalised. The second relevant feature of this implicit theory is that it fails to recognise the problem of mutual understanding which arises if different groups have different perspectives. Unlike Mead, the founder of interactionism, latter-day interactionists have not tended to address the question of how communication and the co-ordination of action are possible.[14] Those working within competence approaches, on the other hand, have addressed both these problems and made some progress in dealing with them. I am not suggesting, therefore, that work done by those operating within a competence framework is simply mistaken and should be discarded, but rather that it must be recast into an action-based approach, a process which will transform the latter.

Having briefly sketched what I regard as the deficiencies of the action model, I want to turn now to the failings of the competence approach. To illustrate my arguments I shall focus on the work of Sinclair and Coulthard (1975), since this is the best-developed treatment of classroom interaction employing a competence approach.[15] However, I think my arguments apply equally to the other variants of competence theory.[16]

What I want to suggest is that the competence model amounts to a kind of cognitive functionalism sharing similar virtues and vices to normative functionalism.[17] The virtues are a disciplined search for systematic interrelation between the apparently unconnected, a concern with describing whole systems, and a willingness to seek explanations for the 'obvious'. Its vices are a reification of patterns of interaction as they exist at one socio-historical location into universal structures fulfilling universal functions;[18] an assumption of widespread consensus about rules and a neglect of the complex patterning of interests involved in social interaction; and an inability to explain change except as the result of the impact of external events. In this paper I shall try to show that these criticisms are also applicable to the competence model of classroom interaction.

Where normative functionalism, at least in its Parsonian form, is concerned with the norms and values that must be internalised by members of a society if that society is to function, those researchers working within the competence framework set out to specify the rules or procedures that underlie the competent performance of various kinds of social activity. In both cases the nature of the product – a properly functioning society and the performance of a particular activity – are treated as consensually defined and/or as analytically identifiable. Thus, in their introduction, Sinclair and Coulthard explain their choice of classroom interaction as a focus in terms of its characteristic structure:

> we decided it would be . . . productive to begin . . . with a more simple type of spoken discourse, one which has much more overt

> structure than 'desultory' conversation, where one participant has acknowledged responsibility for the direction of the discourse, for deciding who shall speak when, and for introducing and ending topics. (1975, p. 6)

Here we have the distribution of conversational rights as it typically occurs in the classroom proposed as a feature of a type of discourse. With this reformulation an element of necessity is added. Certain features of classroom interaction are 'fixed' as constitutive of that discourse type. Furthermore, these features seem to be thought of as in some sense functional:

> Verbal interaction inside the classroom differs markedly from desultory conversation in that its main purpose is to instruct and inform and this difference is reflected in the structure of the discourse. In conversation, topic changes are unpredictable and uncontrollable, for as Sacks has shown, a speaker can even talk 'on topic' without talking on the topic intended by the previous speaker. Inside the classroom it is one of the functions of the teacher to choose the topic, decide how it will be subdivided into smaller units and cope with digressions and misunderstandings. (Coulthard, 1977, p. 101)

One of the implications of the treatment of these features of classroom interaction as constitutive of a type of discourse is that any deviation from this pattern is conceived as resulting in meaninglessness:

> It is deviant to withhold feedback continually, and we have a tape of one lesson where a teacher, new to a class, and trying to suggest to them that there aren't always right answers, does withhold feedback and eventually reduces the children to silence – they cannot see the point of his questions. (Sinclair and Coulthard, 1975, p. 51)

As a result, there are no rational grounds for deviance, it is the product of whim:

> This category (teacher direct) covers all exchanges designed to get the pupil to do but not say something. Because of the nature of the classroom, the Response is a compulsory element of structure. This

> is not to suggest that children always do what they are told, but it does imply that the teacher has a right to expect the pupil to do so. Just as anyone can produce an ungrammatical sentence when he feels like it, so a pupil can break the rules of discourse. (Sinclair and Coulthard, 1975, p. 50)

Yet we have evidence that pupils often have different conceptions of how one should behave in the classroom from teachers, and this, in part, is because they have different patterns of interest.[19] And even if we did not have such evidence it would be cavalier to dismiss pupil deviance in this way. Now I don't want to deny that, in many senses, classroom interaction is a collaborative product, with teachers and pupils operating on the basis of similar working definitions of 'proper classroom behaviour'. I am not suggesting that the classroom is inevitably, or even typically, a setting in which there is an implacable conflict of interests between teachers and pupils: the relationship between the parties is much more subtle and complex; indeed, it is a mistake to assume that there are only two parties to classroom interaction and that these parties are stable.[20] However, conflicts do arise and these cannot be accounted for by the competence model except in terms of inappropriateness and irrationality.

But not only does this approach not provide us with any room for a satisfactory explanation of deviance, it also involves an implicit and quite inadequate account of conformity: participants conform because any other behaviour is 'inappropriate'. And yet, in many lessons, much teacher talk is expended in getting pupils to conform to the rules and even to respond to directives. Thus there arise what one might call disciplinary digressions, which can amount to anything from a look to a half-hour lecture. Furthermore, these often involve promises and threats of various kinds, which indicates that teachers recognise the possibility of rational alternative lines of pupil action even if rhetorically they often deny such a possibility.

In the same way, presenting the teacher's behaviour in terms of following the rules of discourse is unsatisfactory. We must investigate why these rules seem appropriate and, in part, the explanation is likely to be that such patterns seem to him to facilitate his goals; though sometimes they may not, as in the example quoted above of the teacher who seeks to avoid giving feedback.

As a result of its failure to deal with motivation, the competence approach is unable to account for the possibility of change in patterns of classroom interaction, or even for the processes of socio-historical development which have produced those patterns which currently exist. The rules of discourse are presented as static and somehow given. Furthermore, the status of the rules documented by Sinclair and Coulthard is unclear: is the evidence for their existence statistical regularity or is it that these are oriented-to features of interaction? If the former, the problem arises that statistical regularities are not always normative. If the latter, the authors certainly do not provide evidence that all the rules are oriented to, and even where they do provide such evidence they appeal to their own and their readers' knowledge of classrooms rather than establishing that these particular participants orient to them.

Now I think I can anticipate two kinds of response to these arguments. The first is that competence theorists do, of course, recognise the breaking of rules for strategic purposes. Thus, immediately prior to the extract from page 51 quoted earlier, Sinclair and Coulthard comment: 'So important is feedback that if it does not occur we feel confident in saying that the teacher has deliberately withheld it for some strategic purpose' (p. 51). The second response is that the competence model is being criticised for not doing something which it was never intended to do. According to this argument, its goal is the specification of the rules which define classroom actions and thereby make it possible for teachers and pupils to understand one another's actions. It is not intended to be a full account of what is actually done by teachers and pupils.

I want to reply to both these points simultaneously. It is perfectly possible for a competence theorist to recognise the strategic breaking of rules, so long as that strategy is not intended to modify, and does not result in modification of, those rules. Once this is admitted as a possibility, rules are no longer a sufficient basis for the explanation of action, nor can a useful distinction be drawn between rule-related and strategic considerations as bases for action. This is, I suspect, why Sinclair and Coulthard, after making the comment quoted above about the teacher's strategic withholding of feedback, then go on to say that, if this is done continually, the pupils are reduced to silence.

What I am arguing, then, is that the distinction between discourse rules, on the one hand, and the strategies employed by teachers (and presumably also pupils), on the other, is not viable. Sinclair and Coulthard do not provide us with any strong grounds for accepting a distinction between discourse and pedagogy. They base this distinction on the notion of 'linguistic patterning': thus 'a year's work' has no linguistic structure, whereas 'a lesson' does (1975, p. 20). But we are not told what 'linguistic patterning' is, or what the other forms of patterning are from which it is being distinguished. From what little is said about the pedagogic level it is quite unclear how the patterning there is similar to and different from that at the other levels. Indeed, the meaning of the term 'linguistic' is obscure. Sometimes it seems to mean speech, as when they talk about 'linguistic introductions' (p. 19) and linguistic and non-linguistic responses in distinguishing between elicitations and directives. Now this interpretation of 'linguistic' does not necessarily rule out linguistic order beyond the level of the lesson, though one would have to study the talk of the parties to lessons separately given their frequent dispersion before and after such occasions. And, indeed, it would allow us to deal with the important issue of topical coherence between lessons. However, it would rule out what the authors call 'reacts' since these are neither verbal nor 'non-verbal surrogates' for the verbal. Despite their inclusion of reacts, however, by the very nature of their data, and perhaps because of their disciplinary affiliations, the authors generally tend to restrict themselves to 'the linguistic' in this sense.[21]

This definition of 'linguistic' as 'the verbal' leads to a number of problems, one of which concerns the distinction between directives and elicitations. Elicitations are defined as requiring verbal responses, directives non-verbal responses. Here, it seems to me, the authors take what for them is an important consideration – the verbal/non-verbal contrast – to be a central feature of the orientations of participants. I think they are mistaken, and offer the following examples to suggest this:

(a) T: Now, who can tell me where Israel is? Go on then, Jackson.
(Pupil walks out to the front of the classroom and points to a place on the map drawn on the board.)

(b) T: Do you think that's clever?
P: No.
T: No what?
P: No sir.

While the teacher's utterance in (a) would presumably be classified by Sinclair and Coulthard as a directive, I suggest that it has more in common with elicitations. Conversely, 'No what?' seems best described as a directive even though it requires a verbal response. I suggest that the verbal/non-verbal distinction is not a satisfactory basis for distinguishing between directives and elicitations.[22]

There is, however, another way in which 'linguistic patterning' can be interpreted. It may be taken to mean the application of the notion of structure developed at the level of grammar to the analysis of social interaction. The goal here is the specification of rules of choice and chain. While linguistic patterning in grammatical terms is based on form, at the level of discourse it is to be based on function. Here again, though, we are faced with problems of interpretation: what kind of function is this and how are we to identify functions? The authors seem to identify function with teacher intention: 'Grammar is concerned with the *formal* properties of an item, discourse with the *functional* properties, with what the speaker is using the item for' (1975, pp. 27–8; original emphasis). Yet, clearly, only some kinds of teacher intention are to be included; much of what the teacher does in the classroom is left to the pedagogical level, but the basis for this allocation is not made explicit. So, for example, why is teacher direct-pupil react included while pupil deviance-teacher direct is excluded? In both cases the connection is complex because decision making, and not just rule following, is involved, though this is perhaps most obvious in the case of the latter connection.[23]

One final methodological point. Sinclair and Coulthard, quite rightly in my view, ground their functions in actor intentions, though there are times when they seem a little ambivalent about this, for example when they talk of 'discourse value'. However, the nature of the evidence at their disposal – transcripts – is an inadequate base for the identification of intentions, and the authors seem to place considerable tacit reliance on their knowledge of why teachers typically do what they do without testing it. An example occurs where they discuss 'starters':

> Starters are acts of which the function is to provide information about, or direct attention or thought towards, an area in order to make a correct response to the initiation more likely, even though this function is often only impromptu, when the teacher realizes that the intended elicitation was not adequate. What he has said can, however, serve as a starter to get the children thinking in the right area, and then the more explicit elicitation has more chance of success.
>
> 1. T *What about this one? This I think is a super one*. Isobel, can you think what it means?
>
> (Sinclair and Coulthard, 1975, pp. 34–5; original emphasis)

While this is quite a plausible interpretation, it is not the only one. I think one could equally argue that here we have an attempt to mobilise pupil participation *per se*, and there are, no doubt, other candidate descriptions. Which is correct has to be tested, but it may not be possible to do this relying on transcripts alone.

Conversational analysts, of course, would criticise the authors for attempting to ascribe intentions and motives in the first place (as would many sociological structuralists and functionalists). My point is a less severe one: simply that I believe the identification of intention and motive is more difficult than the authors seem to take it to be and that the use of other data sources, such as participant observation and interviewing, is necessary. All data sources are imperfect, but in different ways, and that means that, through their combination, we may be able to counter the major validity threats.[24]

In conclusion, let me repeat what I said at the start. I am not suggesting that the work of Sinclair and Coulthard be discarded as worthless. It is a very useful analysis, pointing to a number of important features of classroom interaction and indicating some of the requirements, hitherto ignored, which such analyses must meet. But it seems to me to restrict its focus to a sub-set of classroom interactional phenomena which is not a viable object of study. Furthermore, and for associated reasons, it conceptualises classroom interaction in terms of the following of constitutive rules, a conceptualisation which opens it up to the standard, and I think effective, criticisms which can be directed against normative functionalism. To escape such criticisms it is necessary to abandon the distinction between discourse and pedagogy and to treat classroom interaction as composed of interrelated actions which are the product not just of rule following, but also of decision making. What any particular action is, what its function is, should be assessed, in the first place, on the basis of some investigation of the patterns of intention and motivation which produced it, and this requires the use of a wider range of methods than just the analysis of transcripts of classroom talk.[25] This is not to deny that much classroom interaction is heavily institutionalised, and thus does amount to rule following. The point is, however, that these rules have become established through strategic thinking and actions and, at any point, may be suspended, modified or transformed as a result of strategic considerations. Only an action approach can take account of these features of classroom rules. However, as I remarked earlier, for it to become in any reasonable sense adequate, action theory requires considerable development, and this process of development must draw on the work already done within the competence framework.

Notes

1. For an outline and discussion of this tradition see Hamilton and Delamont (1974). For a more detailed account see Walker (1971).

2. They would not trouble all sociologists, of course, but only those committed to what, in this paper, I call action theory.

3. Incidentally, I recognise the perilous nature of this enterprise. It is very easy to misunderstand work in other disciplines – for example, because one is unaware of some crucial qualification which underlies all work in a discipline, or because one fails to allow for differences in purpose between disciplines. I trust my criticism will be taken in the tentative, constructive spirit in which they are intended.

4. These are convenience labels and may be misleading from the point of view of linguistics where the contrast to competence is performance. I am rather uncertain about the relationship between this distinction and the one I am proposing here. As I see it at the moment, the action approach would argue that the competence–performance distinction can only be made for particular points in the development of a sequence of social interaction, since performance is continually modifying competence in marginal respects, and sometimes in major ways.

5. Hymes (1977).

6. Austin (1962) and Searle (1965).

7. Sudnow (1972); Turner (1974); Schenkein (1978); also Part II of this volume. Conversational analysis is a difficult case. While in terms of ethnomethodological principles it escapes most of the problems I shall document here – though at enormous cost – in practice conversational analysts often seem to deviate from these principles in ways which leave their work open to these criticisms.

8. Sinclair and Coulthard (1975) and Coulthard (1977).

9. For examples concerned with classrooms, see Berlak *et al.* (1975), Woods (1977), A. Hargreaves (1979) and Hammersley (1974 and 1976).

10. There is no work in this tradition on classrooms, but see Kapferer (1976).

11. Berger and Luckmann (1967) and Schutz and Luckmann (1974). Hargreaves, Hester and Mellor (1975) represents an approach to classroom interaction which spans the interactionist and phenomenological approaches and also shows traces of a competence approach.

12. Gonos (1977) argues that Goffman's work has been misunderstood, that it is not interactionist but structuralist (i.e. not an action but a competence theory). However, this is rather unfair on Goffman's commentators since there seem to be elements of both approaches in his work (compare *The Presentation of Self* with *Frame Analysis*, for example), though I think it is probably correct to say that structuralism of a kind is dominant at least in his later work.

13. For the distinction between 'order' and 'control' theories see Dawe (1970).

14. This criticism is much less true of the phenomenologists but this approach has resulted in very little empirical work. For an expansion of these criticisms, see Hammersley (1978).

15. The only other work at a similar level of development is that of Mehan (1979).

16. With, as I remarked earlier, the partial exception of conversational analysis which, when it does avoid these problems, does so only at an exorbitant

cost: that of restricting the focus of research to 'possible methods' for producing accounts of social phenomena.

17. I am using 'functionalism' here in its sociological, not its psychological or linguistic, sense. That there should be such a similarity is not altogether surprising in the case of Sinclair and Coulthard's work, if one remembers the links between Malinowski, one of the founders of functionalist anthropology, and Firth; and, perhaps more significantly, between Durkheim and Saussure.

18. There are versions of functionalism which seek to avoid this problem, such as that of Merton (1957), but in my view their strategies for doing this undermine the functionalist scheme.

19. For example, D.H. Hargreaves (1967) and Lacey (1970).

20. Furlong (1976).

21. Incidentally, this tendency also appears in speech act analysis where what are in fact elements of social acts become designated as *speech* acts.

22. Having made this criticism, I suppose I ought to provide an alternative basis for distinguishing directives from elicitations. My current view is that directives demand compliance to a rule implied, or spelt out in, the utterance, where compliance is assumed to be within the capabilities of the target actor; and failure to comply, at least in the absence of a disclaimer (Hewitt and Stokes, 1975) or remedial action (Goffman, 1972; Lyman and Scott, 1970), will be read as unwillingness and/or deviance. An elicitation, on the other hand, requires the production of a sign (not necessarily verbal) which fills in a frame implied or present in the utterance (see Schutz, 1962, for the concept of sign as used here). Ability to provide this is not necessarily assumed and failure to provide an 'appropriate' answer is not necessarily treated as deviance, though ignorance can sometimes be treated as indicating incompetence or stupidity. There is a complicating factor, however: elicitations always presuppose a directive, and refusal to answer the questions will be treated as deviance.

23. It is, of course, possible to identify further patterns which seem to fit this notion of linguistic patterning: for example, one can distinguish between teacher questions designed solely to test attention or demonstrate the inattention of pupils, and those which are concerned with testing learning or knowledge. This is not in itself a criticism – this is the kind of distinction which can be picked up with increased delicacy. See Hammersley (1976).

24. This is the notion of triangulation which originated with Webb, Campbell, Schwartz and Sechrest (1966). For an account of the role of triangulation within ethnographic research, see Hammersley (1979).

25. I stress *in the first place* because I do believe it is possible to talk of unintended functions.

References

Austin, J.L. (1962). *How to do Things with Words*. London: Oxford University Press

Berger, P. and Luckman, T. (1967). *The Social Construction of Reality*. Harmondsworth: Penguin

Berlack, A. *et al.* (1975). 'Teaching and Learning in English Primary Schools'. *School Review*, 83, 2, pp. 215–43

Coulthard, M. (1977). *An Introduction to Discourse Analysis*. London: Longman

Dawe, A. (1970). 'The Two Sociologies'. *British Journal of Sociology*, 21, 2, pp. 207–18

Furlong, V. (1976). 'Interaction Sets in the Classroom: Towards a Study of Pupil Knowledge'. In M. Stubbs and S. Delamont (eds.), *Explorations in*

Classroom Observation. New York: Wiley
Goffman, E. (1971). *The Presentation of Self in Everyday Life*. Harmondsworth: Penguin
— (1972). *Relations in Public*. Harmondsworth: Penguin
— (1975). *Frame Analysis*. Harmondsworth: Penguin
Gonos, G. (1977). 'Situation versus Frame'. *American Sociological Review*, 42, 6, pp. 854–67
Hamilton, D. and Delamont, S. (1974). 'Classroom Research: A Cautionary Tale'. *Research in Education*, 11, pp. 1-15
Hammersley, M. (1974). 'The Organisation of Pupil Participation'. *Sociological Review*, 22, 3, pp. 355–68
— (1976). 'The Mobilization of Pupil Attention'. In M. Hammersley and P.E. Woods (eds.), *The Process of Schooling*. London: RKP and Open University
— (1978). 'What is a Strategy?'. Unpublished paper, Open University
— (1979). *Data Collection in Ethnographic Research*. Open University Course DE304, Research Methods in Education and Social Science. Bletchley: Open University Press
Hargreaves, A. (1979). 'Strategies, Decisions and Control: An Analysis of Interaction in a Middle School Classroom'. In J. Eggleston (ed.), *Teacher Decision-Making in the Classroom*. London: RKP
Hargreaves, D.H. (1967). *Social Relations in a Secondary School*. London: RKP
—, Hester, S. and Mellor, F. (1975). *Deviance in Classrooms*. London: RKP
Hewitt, J.P. and Stokes, R. (1975). 'Disclaimers'. *American Sociological Review*, 40, pp. 1-11
Hymes, D. (1977). *Foundations in Sociolinguistics*. London: Tavistock
Kapferer, B. (1976). *Transaction and Meaning*. Philadelphia: Institute for the Study of Human Issues
Lacey, C. (1970). *Hightown Grammar*. Manchester: Manchester University Press
Lyman, S.M. and Scott, M.B. (1970). *A Sociology of the Absurd*. New York: Appleton Century Crofts
Mehan, H. (1979). *Learning Lessons*. Harvard University Press
Merton, R.K. (1957). 'Manifest and Latent Functions'. In R.K. Merton (ed.), *Social Theory and Social Structure*. New York: Free Press
Schenkein, J. (1978). *Studies in the Organisation of Conversational Interaction*. New York: Academic Press
Schutz, A. (1962). 'Symbol, Reality and Society'. In *A. Schutz: Collected Papers*, vol. 1. The Hague: Nijhoff
— and Luckman, T. (1974). *The Structures of the Life-World*. London: Heinemann
Searle, J. (1965). 'What is a Speech Act'. In M. Black (ed.), *Philosophy in America*. London: Allen and Unwin
Sinclair, J.McH. and Coulthard, R.M. (1975). *Towards an Analysis of Discourse: The English Used by Teachers and Pupils*. London: Oxford University Press
Sudnow, D. (1972). *Studies in Social Interaction*. New York: Free Press
Turner, R. (1974). *Ethnomethodology*. Harmondsworth: Penguin
Walker, R. (1971). 'The Social Setting of the Classroom: A Review of Observational Studies and Research'. Unpublished M.Phil. thesis, University of London
Webb, E.J., Campbell, D.T., Schwartz, R. and Sechrest, L. (1966). *Unobtrusive Measures*. Chicago: Rand McNally
Woods, P.E. (1977). 'Teaching for Survival'. In P.E. Woods and M. Hammersley (eds.), *School Experience*. London: Croom Helm

3 DISCOURSE ANALYSIS AS LINGUISTICS: A RESPONSE TO HAMMERSLEY

David Brazil

It may be unfair to begin a response to Hammersley's interesting paper with a quibble. Quite early in his presentation, after having described what he sees as some of the shortcomings of an action model of social interaction, he goes on to propose that the work of those operating within a competence framework should be 'recast into an action-based approach, a process which will transform *the latter*' (p. 49 above; my emphasis). I hope I am not just being pernickety in finding this an odd piece of argumentation. I draw attention to it because it helps to focus something that I think is important. I am fully in sympathy with the wish to see how insights deriving from different descriptions can be made to complement and illuminate each other in the study of classroom language, but I should like to make it my first substantial plea that we should try to be very clear about what we are doing when we transpose the metaphors that facilitate progress in one field of academic endeavour into the metaphors that characterise another field. I should want, if I may put it bluntly, to have a clearer notion of who is buying what from whom than seems to be present in a proposal to transform one object by recasting another one.

My own contribution to the present cross-disciplinary enterprise is necessarily a one-sided one. Hammersley makes no pretence to amplify his notion of an action-based approach to the point at which it would be useful to criticise it. It is, indeed, unlikely that the job of criticism would fall within my competence if he did. I have to concentrate on his more detailed examination of the Sinclair and Coulthard model and see whether, by attempting some clarification on my own side of the disciplinary fence, I can make the process of calling across it rather more profitable.

Towards an Analysis of Discourse expounds a linguistic approach to supra-sentential structures as the latter occur in a small corpus of recorded classroom discourse. As a linguistic model, I see it as being vulnerable to two kinds of attack: it may be objected that it is bad linguistics; or it may be said that it fails to illuminate matters that interest observers of classroom language who have no particular interest in developing linguistic models. It is in relation to the latter desideratum that questions about how its conceptual framework and its categories match those of other disciplines might be held to be important. As a corpus-based study, it is potentially open to the specific objection that its categories are not generalisable beyond the corpus, but here the relevant perspective will be one which relates them not to pedagogically interesting events in the classroom but to a general theory of discourse analysis. The most useful form of response to Hammersley would seem to be to enlarge upon my own understanding of those features of the Sinclair and Coulthard approach that make it distinctive within linguistics. Having done this, and having admitted the limitations that its own inherent methodological commitment imposes, I should like to go on to ask whether it really obscures sociologically important considerations, as Hammersley thinks it does, or whether, as a first characterisation of the mechanisms of classroom interaction, it does not contribute to a theory in which such notions as 'strategy', 'conflict', 'decision making' and so on can be grounded.

I must reiterate that it is my own understanding that I am offering, notwithstanding the close contact I have had with the Birmingham discourse analysis research programme in recent years. I shall take the liberty, moreover, of going beyond the position expounded in *Towards an Analysis of Discourse*. As Burton (p. 21 above) has also suggested, some misunderstandings that have become evident to date may well arise from inexplicitness in the published exposition: such, I take it, has been the misfortune of most seminal works in most fields. It would not be much to our present purpose for me to say precisely how far I am trying faithfully to amplify or gloss that exposition, and how far I am modifying it in the light of subsequent thinking and research – even of my own, highly tentative speculations. I am conscious that a large proportion of what I have to say may appear tangential to the issues that Hammersley raises but I hope the attempt at clarification, which I think is a necessary preliminary to engagement with those issues, will be thought to be justified.

Hammersley's paper leaves me aware that, among the many issues to which we could be attending, two are central. These are the notion of competence and the relationship between what we can say of classroom interaction and interactive discourse as it occurs elsewhere. I shall begin with the first of these, partly because Hammersley chooses to use competence as an epithet to indicate the class of descriptions to which he sees that of Sinclair and Coulthard as belonging. Being thus presented as the basis of an either/or distinction, the use of the term clearly calls for careful scrutiny.

At least since 1957, with the publication of Chomsky's *Syntactic Structures*, competence has been equated by linguists largely with the ability to discriminate between well-formed and deviant sentences. The application of this criterion has never been unproblematical, and it is useful in the present context to consider why. All models of language recognise different modes of organisation within the continuum that relates sound to sense. Since the failure of Bloomfieldian structuralists to describe the sentence in terms of the patterned distribution of phonemes, it has come to be recognised that a quite different set of rules determines the combination of the latter from that which operates at the level of what, among linguists working in the Firthian tradition, is known as 'form'. If we begin at the level of phonology, we can see that 'deviance' there can be recognised fairly easily. The initial nasal / η /, for instance, excludes any sequence of phonemes from the set of well-formed English words, as does final / h /, and certain specifiable combinations of phonemes medially are similarly excluded. On whatever basis we may classify the segments that enter into the phonological structures of a given dialect of English, the membership of the classes does not vary. We may, perhaps, relate this to the fact that there are physical and physiological aspects to the classification and thus the distinction between allowable and proscribed sequences is not 'arbitrary' in the sense that it is at the formal level. Sorting into classes is not merely a matter of observing distributional privileges.

When we move to the formal level, the situation is not so simple. Admittedly, structure still enables us to reject certain sequences as ungrammatical. 'Cat the . . .' contravenes the rule that words of the word class 'determiner' always precede the head of the nominal group. However, in the pair of groups, 'the cuddly black cat' and 'the black cuddly cat', the structural frame contributes to meaning by producing a differential classification of 'cuddly': it resembles a large number of English adjectives in being able to indicate quality or classification, and it is the hearer/reader's knowledge of nominal group structure that enables him to interpret it in each of these two cases. The way the predictive power of structure can be exploited to allocate words to classes quite different from those to which they are normally thought to belong is a commonplace of literary commentary. A particularly vivid example is 'Thank me no thanking, nor proud me no prouds' (Romeo and Juliet, III, v) but the phenomenon is very common. The important point is that, although the semantics of such a sentence may present difficulties, there is no real problem in providing a grammatical analysis. To recall the comparison with phonology, we may note that such exploitation is possible because items like 'cuddly', 'thank' and 'proud', as they are used conversationally, do not have a necessarily stable relationship with anything that can be specified on an extra-linguistic basis. Exploitability would seem to be in inverse proportion to the stability of the relationship that is commonly held to apply for the word in question, a fact that can be related to the improbability of a closed-class item like 'the' being reclassified. In saying all this, we are, of course, declining to make the kind of abstraction away from observable language behaviour that transformational-generative grammarians make when they postulate a context-free speaker/hearer knowledge of the language, a knowledge which is held to include describable principles for 'semantic interpretation'. If we continue to use the term 'competence', we no longer place it in opposition to 'performance'.

The chief innovation of the Sinclair and Coulthard model is that a third mode of linguistic organisation is postulated, resulting in a three-level model in which the level of *function* is separated from the level of *form* by a discontinuity similar to that which separates the latter from the level of *phonology*.

The interrelationships between successive elements in interactive discourse, and upon the existence of which the coherence of such discourse depends, cannot be accounted for simply by reference to the grammar of the elements. For instance, grammar enables us to identify interrogative mood clauses, but there is no predictable relationship between clauses that have interrogative mood and elements of discourse structure that set up the kind of expectation of verbal response that elicitations do.[1]

The intermediate position given to the formal level accords with the observation already made that structure there sometimes separates the possible from the impossible, but sometimes provides the basis for interpreting whatever elements actually occur. Crossing the watershed between form and function, we find a situation that complements that at the phonological level in an interesting way. Here we are concerned with an object created by the combined efforts of more than one speaker. Under these circumstances it is difficult to see how anything can be ruled out as 'not discourse'. To set out with the expectation that such a ruling will be possible might, indeed, seem counter-intuitive. There does not seem to be any way in which one speaker can place absolute constraints upon another speaker in any sense comparable with the way his apprehension of grammatical rules might block the production of certain sequences within his own utterance. When mistakes occur, and are remarked upon, they are usually of the type:

A: So the meeting's on Friday.
B: Thanks.
A: No, I'm asking you.

Here, B wrongly classifies A's contribution, and rectification requires help of a metalinguistic nature from the latter. There is no way in which B can come to recognise the wrongness of his response by a process of self-monitoring in the way he might become aware of – and spontaneously correct – a grammatical mistake. A phenomenon that has attracted the interest of conversational analysts is the variety of 'remedial' procedures that exist for dealing with just such situations.[2] The most promising theoretical assumption seems to be that at the level of function a speaker can do anything he likes at any time, but that *what* he does will be classified as a contribution to the discourse in the light of whatever structural predictions the previous contribution (his own or another's) may have set up.

We may take an obvious and over-simplified example. An elicitation may get the response it predicts, or it may be followed by a totally irrelevant new initiation. Reflection upon the latter possibility forces us to focus upon two important factors. The first is that, because of the predictive power of the structural framework, the first speaker will be likely to treat anything as a non-response only after he has failed to discern a possible relevance. Utterance pairs like

A: So the meeting is on Friday?
B: Tom will be back in town.

where A hears B as meaning unambiguously either 'yes' or 'no' are common enough in most kinds of conversation. The absence of any deterministic relationship between form and function makes it possible for virtually any rejoinder to have coherence, given the shared background of understanding of the participants. In our example, B's classification of A's utterance as an elicitation could itself have been made only on the basis of assumptions arrived at intersubjectively. Recent work on discourse analysis has concentrated heavily on intonation, and it can be shown that the contribution of intonation to the communicative value of an utterance can be most usefully characterised by reference not to the grammatical structure of the utterance but to the here-and-now state of convergence between participants (see Brazil, 1975 and 1978). It is partly because a quality of relevance, accessible only to participants, and valid only at the time and place of utterance, can attach to any utterance regardless of its form, that no generalised judgements about well-formedness in discourse can be made.

The second point is that if a speaker's behaviour *is* heard as deviant, the deviance can be most satisfactorily characterised as deviance from a social norm. This is popularly recognised in the use of labels such as 'rude', 'evasive' and 'eccentric'. It is worth noting that, if speaker A fails to find any relationship between the two components of a pair like

A: Will you come for a drink?
B: My brother's just left for the States.

which would cause him to hear it as the predicted polar response, his precise label for B's behaviour will reflect his knowledge of B's manners, his drinking habits, or perhaps his state of mental health. As a linguistic event, it simply represents one of a set of options open to B at this point in the discourse. It is characterised not in terms of whatever judgements A may be induced to make of B but in terms of the prospective constraints that now apply to any rejoinder A might make.

Most of what I have said has direct relevance to the choice the Birmingham team made to begin the investigation of discourse structure by examining teacher-pupil talk in the institutionalised setting of the traditional 'lesson'. The fact that we cannot make intuitive judgements about what is and what is not well-formed discourse deprives the discourse analyst of that method of generalising his observations that has served linguists so well in their investigation of sentence grammar. A generative approach depends upon our being able to delimit the set of objects our rules can generate. The alternative is to describe a corpus and to extrapolate from one's findings with great caution and a willingness to revise one's categories. One advantage of classroom data as a starting-point, as compared, for instance, with desultory conversation, is that the kind of mutual understanding that gives operational coherence to the latter is less likely to create problems for the analyst. A response, for instance, is more likely to be publicly recognisable as a response.

The last assertion is in no sense a denial of Hammersley's contention that we may know less about what is going on between teacher and pupils than we think we do; but to deal with this objection we have, I think, to return to the distinction I made earlier between the discourse value of an utterance and its possible social significance.

A working sketch of the situation which a discourse analysis approach to classroom language invites us to contemplate is somewhat as follows. All discourse proceeds on the basis of rules which can be characterised in structural terms, the function of these rules being to classify speech events as they occur. Although the structures imply predictions – in a unit of discourse having structure XYZ the production of X predicts an occurrence of Y, and so on – the non-occurrence of Y is an exploitation of the system, not a breaking of a linguistic rule. Different situations, however, can be thought of as having different tolerances of exploitation. Clearly, for instance, the act of ignoring a question by making an irrelevant observation would be unacceptable in certain situations but might be perfectly acceptable in others. The characterisation of a 'situation' and its postulated 'discourse type' raises problems similar to the task of identifying situationally conditioned 'styles' or 'registers'. These latter can be defined by reference to their tendency to exploit some sub-set of the total lexical and grammatical resources of the language rather than others. In a similar way, we may expect that our postulated discourse type will have its total set of speaker-options described in a general discourse theory, but will be distinguished on the basis of its preference for exploiting some of them and avoiding others. I say 'expect' because we are, of course, still a long way from being able to formulate the general theory. Very importantly, though, we must be clear that 'discourse competence', as we have described it, *does not in itself constitute* 'the rules or procedures that underlie the competent performance of various kinds of social activity'. Hammersley suggests it does. In so far as one's view of classroom behaviour is a normative one, the norm is socially defined. To specify the linguistic options that are available to participants is to identify, in a neutral, non-normative way, the means whereby they do or do not conform to the socially accepted pattern.

Some discussion of the three-part exchange might help to clarify the last point. In the data that Sinclair and Coulthard examine, there is a marked preference for exchanges which begin with an elicitation for the structure: initiation-response-feedback. So marked is the preference, in fact, that they feel able to say that, when teachers with-hold feedback persistently, the pupils cease to respond. This pattern of behaviour can be interestingly compared with exchanges in other discourse types. A three-part exchange also occurs frequently in doctor–patient interaction:

I. How often do you get these pains?
R. About twice a day doctor.
F. Yes.

But the exchange differs from the classroom type in at least two important respects. A teacher's 'yes' in a similar case would normally signify 'Yes, you are right' or 'Yes, I agree'. Without going into details, we may note that the two kinds of evaluation would be distinguished intonationally. Different again would be the intonation of the doctor's 'yes'. Here, neither of the evaluating versions would be very sensible: if the doctor were in the situation the teacher is usually in of being in a position to evaluate the answer, he would scarcely have asked the question. The low-pitched 'yes' we should expect can mean little more than 'That's that part of the business satisfactorily concluded'. The other difference is that, if the doctor does not supply feedback in this way, it has no effect upon the patient's willingness to respond to a subsequent elicitation; for him, the expectation that his information will be approved or rejected is no part of the game, as it is for the pupil. Going now outside the range of discourse types on which we can claim much work has been done, we can say with some confidence that the low-pitched 'yes' we have associated with the doctor is often an indication that the speaker, whoever he is, intends to initiate the next exchange; and to generalise still further, frequent recourse to this way of pre-empting the distribution of turns seems to be the prerogative of the 'superior' party in a non-symmetrical interaction. I do not think, for instance, that a pupil would often produce a doctor-like 'yes' after the teacher had given him a piece of information he had requested, even if he had a whole list of further questions to put. In symmetrical conversations, the device is available for exploitation as a means of staking a claim to the next initiation.

Of the two points I wish to make, the first is that the statement about the prevalence of three-part exchanges in teacher–pupil talk is an observation about how, in given circumstances, the total set of available options tends to be drawn upon. The other is that the selection can be related, speculatively but with a fair measure of cogency, to non-linguistic factors in the situation. It is, however, these non-linguistic factors that define the event. To describe the linguistic concomitants of such matters as role relationship, location of knowledge, purpose of interaction and so on, is in no way to reify a particular configuration of all these variables. It is rather to show the linguistic options in their proper relationship to other available linguistic options and so to expose some of the mechanism whereby such a configuration may be maintained or altered. When a given situation tolerates a number of different role relationships, as many educationists would maintain the classroom does, the analysis can show how the differences are manifested in so far as they involve different selections in discourse systems. This last qualification is essential in order to keep in mind the limits of what can be accounted for in the kind of description we are discussing, a point I shall return to later.

Meanwhile, when it is commented that 'It is deviant to withhold feedback continually' (Sinclair and Coulthard, 1975, p. 51), we must be clear that 'deviant' means failing to play the game according to the rule which, in this case, the pupils assume to be inherent in the activity. The behaviour of the latter, as Sinclair and Coulthard report it, suggests that this novel exploitation of the linguistic options goes beyond what their experience of classrooms has led them to believe is the limit of tolerance. When Hammersley says that such a departure from the expected pattern 'is conceived as resulting in meaninglessness' (p. 50 above), he seems to me to be making – disapprovingly – a very proper assessment of a situation that results from a unilateral change of the rules of the game. But to see such a change as a result of mere whim is surely to overlook the conscious and deliberate intention a teacher may have to instigate a quite different relationship, in which he would want to be seen as relinquishing the role of evaluator.

We might perhaps consider this apparently unsuccessful attempt to innovate as potentially a contribution to the process of socio-historical development of which, like Hammersley, I should certainly wish to take cognizance. The point I have already made still applies. No one, presumably, would deny that what is deviant today may be normal classroom behaviour at some future date. But this simple example shows how the change might take the form of a different selection from the same set of options. (We may, of course, at some time have to consider a diachronic dimension in discourse studies, but the possibility need hardly concern us now.) Presumably, too, a pattern which is so closely related to a regularly recurrent state of affairs – very crudely: teacher knows something / teacher wants to know whether pupil knows it / pupil wants to know whether his suggestion is right – will be fairly resistant to change.

What has just been said about changes of practice historically viewed applies equally to co-existent discourse types in different classrooms, in schools catering for children of different ages, and in lessons or parts of lessons occurring at different times in the school day. In each case, however, it is possible that the categories that have proved adequate for Sinclair and Coulthard's corpus will require modification. In theory, two kinds of modification are possible: either the options that are specified might be supplemented by more delicate ones in accordance with the principles of the Hallidayan model that is used, or an attempt might be made to replace the specifically classroom categories with categories belonging to a general theory of discourse. Some progress has been made in the latter direction at the rank of the Exchange and its constituents (see Coulthard and Brazil, 1979). For those engaged in the application of the description to data of their own it ought to come as no surprise that one or other kind of modification may be necessary, particularly if those data have been produced in a different set of circumstances. Indeed, noting the extent to which it is necessary, and the kinds of misfit that occur, it might be seen as an important contribution towards characterising their own data.

The abstraction of corpus-specific categories was unavoidable in a first descriptive exercise where there was no existing theoretical base to build upon. It has, however, had the unfortunate effect of suggesting a closer relationship between the structurally defined speaker-options, on the one hand, and the motives and intentions of a speaker, on the other hand, than can, in fact, be specified. The point about the rank scale and its associated categories is that the units 'act', 'move', 'exchange' and 'transaction', and the classes into which they enter, are all defined with reference to each other. The argument for using this particular model cannot be rehearsed here, but by way of explication we may cite, for comparison, the grammatical unit 'clause', the definition of which depends upon its potentiality for entering into the structure of a unit above it, the 'sentence', and its own constituency stated in terms of the unit next below it, the 'group'. Such abstract, mutually-defined units are not easy to find without recourse to contextual meaning. The grammarian has the advantage of widely recognised aids to conceptualisation of the kind that have formed the staple of traditional school grammars: it is salutary to contemplate the problems of appreciating a relationship such as that holding between, for instance, subject and predicate, without the help of ultimately over-specific notions like 'actor' and 'action'. To begin the task of identifying the abstract categories of discourse, it is obviously an advantage to work on a corpus where there is a fairly transparent correlation between those categories and what we can say, in some reasonably principled way, the speaker is doing at the time. The ascription of intention and motive to teacher or pupil is to be seen, however, as a tentative and heuristic device.

One reason why this must be so is that intentions and motives are not, as far as we know, susceptible to the kind of either/or classification that would make it possible to match them with linguistic choices. More importantly, there is no way of discovering precise motives from the data. Obviously, a teacher's initiation may be intended simply to discover whether a particular pupil remembers something from a previous lesson, or he may wish to check that the pupil is listening, or to encourage him to participate by asking a question to which he thinks he knows the answer; he may even have the malicious intent of getting one over on him by exposing his ignorance. We could hardly expect these, or the multiplicity of other motives he may have, to be distinguishable in a publicly available record of the lesson, even, I suspect, if the latter included all the paralinguistic and visual accompaniments of the verbal material. A distinction has to be made between describing the repertoire of options and the strategic purposes that selections from that repertoire may be exploited to serve. The linguistic description stops short of the latter. This does not mean, however, that it is irrelevant to the study of the classroom as a place where shifting interests and the possibility of conflict are important factors. If some other techniques – such as asking participants what they thought their intentions were in saying certain things – are thought to have value in exploring these matters, then the value of an analysis which identifies the options in a principled way would seem to be obvious. A first approach to the study of strategy might reasonably be thought to be the identification of those points at which strategically important decisions are taken. It will, I think, be clear from what I have said that at the abstract level of function there is no opposition between 'rule following' and 'decision making': the one implies the other.

It must, of course, be conceded that the general answer to the question 'What is a function?' admits of no simple answer; but neither can we easily assign a status transparent to common sense to linguistic organisation at the formal level. What, for instance, is meant, in traditional terminology, by 'a part of speech'? I should like to conclude, however, by insisting on the precedence of structural criteria over the attribution of intention, and to do so by glancing briefly at the trouble Hammersley (pp. 53–4 above) has with elicitations and directives.

One of the examples he chooses to demonstrate the problem is:

T: Now, who can tell me where Israel is? Go on then, Jackson. ((Pupil walks out to the front of the classroom and points to a place on the map drawn on the board.))

Hammersley's complaint is that to distinguish between elicitations and directives on the basis of their requiring verbal and non-verbal responses leads us wrongly to regard the teacher's utterance as a directive. There is, admittedly, a difficulty in applying a simple verbal/non-verbal distinction in that it takes no account of the difference between the non-verbal activity that has interactive significance solely by virtue of being an action, on the one hand, and the non-verbal surrogate for verbalisation, on the other. It is a characteristic of the first that there is no verbal alternative: the directive 'Close the door, will you' is satisfied only by the addressee doing something non-verbal. By contrast, an elicitation always leaves open the possibility of a verbal response, even if another way of responding seems to be indicated: Jackson could, had he so wished, have stayed in his place and said something like 'In the bottom right-hand corner of the map, about six inches to the north-west of where it says "Scale" '. The teacher might then, had he been disposed to be flexible, have evaluated the response just as one would expect him to do if evidence of knowledge had been provided non-verbally. If we introduce the question of whether or not Jackson is carrying out the teacher's wishes, we are confronted with the inherent ambiguity of any analysis which invokes intentionality. Did the teacher intend to find out whether Jackson knew where Israel was, or did he intend him to make an excursion to the front of the classroom; or did he intend both?

It is the assumption underlying the structural approach to such a case that any follow-up provided by the teacher will be classifiable by reference to the status of the initiation. For instance, any formulation which is interpretable as 'Yes, you are right', being an evaluation of information offered, would seem to be an option only in an exchange which began with an elicitation. It is hardly necessary, nor in fact is it possible in the present state of our knowledge of general discourse theory, to demonstrate in detail that there is a different range of possibilities for the speaker at the third place in exchanges of the two types. A pair of unfavourable rejoinders will serve to illustrate the kind of difference we might expect:

No, it isn't there. That's Egypt. (after an elicitation)
No, I wanted you to show me, not tell me. (after a directive)

What is interesting about Hammersley's transcript is that the feedback is omitted. If (as we are free to suppose) he has *not* done what the teacher wanted him to do, we have no evidence in the text to indicate wherein he has offended; whether by signalling wrong information or by going out to the map when the teacher really wanted him to stay put and give a verbal answer. One's experience of classrooms would probably lead one to conclude that the former is more probable, but this is really beside the point. ('Go on' is ambiguous.) An important function of a linguistic description is to identify the sources of ambiguity in a text. If we had the teacher's feedback in this case, it is highly likely that the ambiguity would be resolved, but it is not difficult to imagine a similar exchange in which the teacher decides on the nature of the feedback in the light of the pupil's response: a correct answer incorrectly indicated might be treated as failing to comply with a directive ('Write it down, don't call out'); an incorrect answer to the same question might be negatively evaluated as a response to an elicitation. The possibility helps to underline the fact that the initiating move is classified on the basis of its operation as a constituent of the unit next above it, namely the exchange, and not on the basis of anything that can be said about it in isolation, whether with reference to grammatical description or to any surmised intention. It also exemplifies the operation of what we might call 'the dynamic element' in classroom discourse. Hammersley conceptualises this element in terms of 'rules . . . (which) may be suspended, modified or transformed' (p. 55 above). An alternative is to characterise discourse in terms of a rule system which, precisely because it is *not* subject to modification, can be exploited for tactical ends. Recognition of the ambiguity built into the system is a necessary step towards understanding the process.

Notes

1. See also Burton's chapter in this volume, on the nature of the 'fit' between grammar and discourse, as it is conceptualised in the Sinclair and Coulthard framework.

2. The papers by Drew and Langford in this volume make reference to such 'remedial' procedures.

References

Brazil, D.C. (1975). *Discourse Intonation*. Discourse Analysis Monographs no. 1, English Language Research, University of Birmingham

— (1978). *Discourse Intonation II*. Discourse Analysis Monographs no. 2, English Language Research, University of Birmingham

Chomsky, N. (1957). *Syntactic Structures*. The Hague: Mouton

Coulthard, R.M. and Brazil, D.C. (1979). *Exchange Structure*. Discourse Analysis Monographs no. 5, English Language Research, University of Birmingham

Sinclair, J.McH. and Coulthard, R.M. (1975). *Towards an Analysis of Discourse*. London: Oxford University Press

4 LEARNING TO TAKE PART IN CLASSROOM INTERACTION

Mary Willes

Introduction

For some time now, I have been attempting to observe as closely as I can the processes by which children learn how to interact with their teachers. In this paper I hope to indicate something of the ways in which the problems that arose at each stage determined changes of method and approach in the text. I want to suggest reasons for thinking that learning to participate in classroom discourse constitutes a very considerable part of the learning most children do in the initial months of exposure to schooling – learning not generally acknowledged in those terms by those professionally concerned with young children's education or with the preparation of their teachers. I want to suggest that there are wide differences in the rate at which such learning is accomplished and (more unexpectedly and more tentatively) that there are differences in the learning strategies children employ. I shall try to indicate some of the false starts and unanswered questions that have troubled the course of this work.

The General Direction of the Study

The subject of my inquiry is the way in which children, new to school, learn to participate as pupils in the discourse of the classroom. It assumes that participation requires them to interpret what teachers say, to respond suitably, and to make a contribution of their own of a sort, and at a time, that teachers recognise as appropriate. I began work supposing that the regularities of classroom discourse have to be learned by those entering the educational system, and that in societies like our own, where early schooling represents the first step taken unaccompanied from the family into a wider society, learning to participate in the discourse of the classroom must represent for the individual a significant step in the development of sociolinguistic competence, a representation (and a fairly readily observable one) of the process of becoming a member of a speech community. Since the rules, when set out, appear to be quite complicated, I expect that the business of learning them must take place over an extended period of time, and I thought it likely that learners would make mistakes indicative of stages in the process. I expected to find evidence of different rates of learning, and I expected, too, to find teachers explaining to pupils, carefully and repetitively, what was required of them. Only gradually, I surmised, would the talk in the reception class come to resemble the discourse in the primary and secondary school and be analysable in the same terms. Initially, I undertook periods of observation and recording in two reception classrooms. Even with hindsight, these assumptions seem to me not unreasonable, nor do I think they were unproductive. However, in at least one fundamental particular, the expectations with which I began were contradicted. It seemed not to be the case the children learned to be pupils by a process of steady accretion. What was happening was certainly not that. Learning to respond as teachers expect pupils to do appeared to be more rapid and easy, altogether less dependent on explicit instruction, than I had anticipated. Of course, mistakes in comprehension between speaker and hearer, and the fact that some of the speakers were so young, made it a little easier than usual to relate mistakes to each discoursant's necessary ignorance of the shape and the limits of the knowledge available to the other.

It was not the case that all the children participated in anything like equal degree. Of course, in a sense, nothing could be more obvious. At every level of institutionalised education, teachers take it for granted this will be so and make efforts, necessarily intermittent, to identify and encourage those of their pupils who are reluctant to offer answers. It is, however, difficult not to ignore them a great deal of the time, although they are by no means an unimportant minority. For the observer, the difficulty is different from the teacher's, but it is still serious. Taped and transcribed texts of classroom discourse overlook altogether the non-participating pupils, and represent the discourse as if the class were a single entity making a collective response in a reciproca relation to the teacher. For some purposes, this may be immaterial, but not for mine, since it is certain that, by whatever means, each child has severally to learn what is expected of him in the role of pupil and what he must in his turn expect. It was clear that the evidence of spontaneously occurring talk needed to be supplemented by other evidence, having its own limitations, but avoiding these. In the most recent stages of the study, I have returned to the evidence of classroom talk, with different expectations and reformulated questions.

Framework for the Study: the Birmingham Work on Classroom Discourse

Nobody whose concern with classroom talk is immediate and practical, who (as Britton, 1970, puts it) wants to 'listen with more understanding to children and adolescents, and who has for any reason a concern for what becomes of them' (p. 7), need complain of any sparseness in the literature related to these concerns. What has been lacking until recently has been a model of the developed classroom discourse which newcomers to school have to learn, which can offer a clear and replicable classification of all the data, and which establishes what are the units of discourse and how they are related to each other. In the absence of such a linguistically motivated model, it is entirely possible that there should be detailed, interesting and sensitively interpreted observation of what goes on in classrooms. Coherent explanation remains out of reach. The work of Sinclair, Coulthard and their associates, available since 1975 in the form of a published monograph, and anticipated by less formal publications, provides such a model, and in fact anticipates the present study:

> a study of teacher-pupil interactions in the reception classes of junior schools and nursery schools could shed more light on what the rules for discourse are, as well as how they are established and learned. How does the five year old who speaks when he wants to become the ten year old who waits to be nominated? (Sinclair and Coulthard, 1975, p. 113)

It is to the work of the English Language Research Unit at Birmingham University that this study is immediately and heavily indebted, and remains so through the changes of method and emphasis which I shall describe. It is to just these questions that it is addressed. Some part of my intention was to put to practical exploratory use the analytic tools that had been developed at Birmingham.

Some Limitations of Direct Observation

From the inception of the study, it was my intention to take into account the sort of talk children produce when they play at schools, on the grounds that some significant part of their perception of what is usual, expected and proper, in terms of the actualities of the classroom, must find expression in such activity. When I talked about this possibility to teachers, they repeatedly confirmed my supposition that pupils play the role of the teacher as an authoritarian stereotype, extremely different from the teacher's image of herself, and having a great deal in common with the representation of teachers in some sorts of children's fiction. My difficulty was to catch them at it, and I am inclined to attribute the difficulty to the accidental circumstance that the time at my disposal was narrowly limited. A naturalist misses much if he can spend only limited time in his hide. The children I observed engaged in every other sort of make believe. They played at buses, at mothers and fathers, at hospitals, shifting from one set of imagined circumstances to another with dream-like rapidity and inconsequence. They seemed to have no need or wish to represent to themselves the situation of the classroom. Could they be persuaded to do so?

With this question in mind, I introduced a commercially available toy school. The classroom, its furnishings, the teacher and the individual members of the (multi-racial) class are on a miniature scale, but the blackboard and chalks, magnet board, letters and figures are a size a child can handle easily and are designed to invite the users to play the parts of teacher and taught. Groups of children were invited to play with it. What I observed when they did so was not quite what I had hoped. In each group, one individual firmly asserted the right to 'be teacher'. There was no argument and no question of taking turns. Having asserted her claim, she did all the talking, without interruption from the others, and played the teacher, not as one who dispenses information or asks questions, but as one who divides up the day. Coming in and going out, register and milk money and 'staying to dinner' followed each other without intermission and, once exhausted, began again. The unlucky 'pupils' quickly grew fidgety in response to a monologue they did not interrupt. If it is the case, as this experience suggests, that for some newcomers to school, at least, it is the new organisational routines of school that have vitality and importance, and it is her control of *these* that constitutes the authority of the teacher, then that is a matter of some interest in itself. However, the children whose perceptions were made accessible by this device were the very children who, in the real classroom, had much to say. It was clear that this sort of play could afford no indication of the problem with which I was at this stage preoccupied, that of discovering how the quieter children, the less assertive, the less confident, perceived the roles of pupil and teacher. I needed to devise some other means by which it would be possible to uncover the perceptions of a representative sample of children, including those whose quickness is responsible for the impression I had received of rapid and easy learning by a class of newcomers, and those who are slower, who rely heavily on imitation, or who rarely respond without prompting.

A Method for Checking what Children Know about Classroom Interaction

If a child is to respond in a way that is acceptable in his teacher's terms, he needs to understand what is said in this limited sense, that he can predict what is going to happen next. He can rely on his teacher to take initiatives. I wanted to find a device that would enable me to offer children, singly and separately, opportunities to show me whether they could do this, and that would in addition give me control over the kind and the number of their responses, so that I could make comparisons between children and between the same child at different stages of his school experience.

The material I came up with is very simple. It consists of an illustrated story book put together so as to look as much like those commonly in use in classrooms as my limited resources would allow. In two respects the book differs from the stories from which, at very frequent intervals, teachers read aloud to groups of children. It is a story about children and their teachers in school. (It was always possible to point to the supply of fiction displayed in each classroom and to say truthfully that not one of the stories available had so ordinary and familiar a setting.) Secondly, the story is incomplete. Only the illustrations and part of the story is there: all the important parts, the parts that tell you what happened, and what the people actually said and did, are still to be written. The observer invites the pupil to help to finish the story properly and, if the idea is welcome, writes his name boldly on the cover. Within the story (which, of course, is read aloud), there are at each point opportunities for the observer to say: 'What do you think happened then? What shall we make the teacher say? What do you think that little girl did?' In this context it is natural enough for the observer to act as the person who writes into the book a story that becomes each child's own. The completed story is his to keep, but not before the observer has transferred each child's contribution onto previously prepared sheets.

My hope was that I would, as a result, get an indication of the extent to which individual children were able to predict that initiating moves, of more than one kind, are made by teachers, that responding moves are made by pupils, and that these are followed by feedback moves, again made by teachers. I hoped to find evidence of understanding that situations must be taken into account in interpreting utterances. I hoped that my sample (necessarily limited in size but in principle extendable) would be, none the less, representative and would include a range, from the confident to the timid, and from the naturally talkative to the taciturn, and that I might get from the completed stories some indication of what those children can do who rarely participate in classroom talk without some degree of persuasion from their teacher, if then.

First trials, in a small pilot study, were reasonably reassuring. The materials seemed, in broad terms, to discriminate. Four-year-olds found the task quite taxing; children approaching six managed confidently; seven- to eight-year-olds found it very easy and were inclined to be disdainful. The materials seemed to be usable, after minimal briefing, by other people. The procedure seemed to be not at all upsetting, even to the youngest children. I set about the selection of a sample of children entering full-time compulsory schooling in September 1977, who I would study at intervals during their first year of schooling, and a smaller sample who had already passed through the first two years of infant school and would enter the junior school on the same date.

Interpreting the Evidence of the Completed Stories

What was not apparent to the children is that the story is organised in three sections, and that this organisation is 'concealed' in the sense that it does not coincide with divisions in the narrative. In the first part (the 'Preliminaries'), that part of the story which the pupil is asked to supply is largely independent of his understanding of the role of pupil. What he knows about interacting with adults in other everyday settings is enough. Only one question in that section relates to what goes on in school. I needed to identify unwilling participants and, if necessary, to bring the whole matter to a speedy and friendly conclusion. I wanted some way of differentiating between predicting what follows what in the classroom and outside it. The second part (the 'Exchanges') is a sequence of exchanges in a pre-reading session. It is a long series: each page offers several parts to be supplied, and I deliberately took the risk of boring the children, since it seemed to me that the ability to predict what is going to happen next in discourse of this sort is critical to the process of participating as a learner, and I wanted to give the children sufficiently varied and repeated opportunity of demonstrating that this was within their scope. Part three ('Situational') requires for its completion an understanding of the situational rules that apply to classroom discourse and of what is entailed in the process of bidding. (This last is exceptional in that teachers are very well aware of the need to instruct children in it, and repeat the lesson well beyond the earliest years of schooling.) I did not include anything that would check children's ability to interpret the occurrence of boundary exchanges. I set myself the limited objective of discovering something of the way in which they learned enough to be able to operate successfully in the responding role, the role that is for them accustomed and obligatory.

Of the sample of newcomers to school, only one, Louise, was as silent and (apparently) as uncomprehending as her teacher told me she had been since she arrived. She turned away from me, raising her hand as if to protect her averted gaze. From Nigel I had, on the first occasion, replies only to the initial cues. After that, his volatile attention was elsewhere, and I was as unable to recall it as his teachers had been. One boy sighed heavily and complained of boredom. Otherwise the children seemed at ease with what was required, understood my explanations and were quite ready to have a go, and very pleased to have a tangible reward in conclusion. There were, in a sense, no 'right' answers and no scores. In using and interpreting the material, I took no response at all as a signal from the child that the question was too hard. He just couldn't say what would happen next. When this happened I let a little time elapse, but I did not urge or prompt, I made little of it and I turned to the next page. By 'well-formed' replies is meant 'readily analysable in terms of the Birmingham model of classroom discourse'. It is, of course, entirely possible for a reply to be incomplete or factually quite wrong, and still to be unmistakably well-formed. The generalisations that have emerged so far from studying the replies are displayed in the tables at the end of the chapter and brief comment is enough. (It should be emphasised that the tables are presented purely as a simple way of displaying the apparent trends which have emerged from this preliminary study: further work and analysis would be required to provide statistical support for these.) It is necessary to remember that the four-year-old children are the new entrants; the five-year-olds are the same children after a lapse of seven months; the seven-year-olds are a different, and smaller, group of children.

There is a steady increase in the number of well-formed answers and a corresponding decrease in the number of nil replies (Tables 4.1 and 4.2). The first seven months of schooling produce almost as marked an increase in the number of well-formed replies as does the subsequent longer period. The difference is not evenly distributed: it is less in the preliminary exchanges and more marked in those that relate specifically to the classroom. The first table displays the individual production of well-formed responses on each of two occasions. With one exception, the children produced more well-formed answers on the second occasion. This table illustrates the variation within the group, both in the number of well-formed answers they were able to produce and in the contrast between the number on the first and on the second occasion. In general, it is true that the low scorers remained low and that the high scorers retained their leadership. The seven-year-olds produced fewer nil and more well-formed responses than did the four- and five-year-olds (Tables 4.3 and 4.4). Those children who produced many nil responses on the first occasion show a sharp drop on the second, feeling, no doubt, more confident after seven months of schooling and a task of which (even though they denied it) they probably retained some memory. The examination of nil and well-formed responses to each cue indicates that the task was not evenly difficult (Tables 4.5 and 4.6): the third of the preliminary exchanges regularly caused trouble and probably should be eliminated. The tables indicate clearly the increase in the ability to predict well-formed exchanges and to apply situational rules that comes with seven months' schooling.

So far, the inferences from the study confirm observation: children do not start formal schooling in simple ignorance of what to expect. In so far as their response to this task genuinely reflects knowledge that is available for their use in the classroom, they differ considerably from the outset and, though learning is rapid, these differences persist. A group, in which there are some children who are well able to participate and who appear to the teacher satisfactorily responsive, may include a number of individuals, even a majority, who are not, and whose understanding of what is going on may be very hazy indeed, or who, alternatively, may have quite different reasons for their reluctance to make overt responses.

It is not, of course, the case that the responses I had from the children were all either nil replies or well-formed responses. The most interesting were neither. The answers that were difficult to classify persisted on the second occasion though their numbers dropped as the numbers of well-formed replies increased. Some children supplied a single stock answer to almost every question. What had been learned by the children who handled the situation I presented in this way? Others produced answers that derived directly from the preceding one, and these again were sometimes (though rarely) interpretable as well formed. Some answers struck the adult hearer as, in different degrees, implausible. Some of these implausible answers coincided with the observation frequently made by teachers that children represent teachers as much more severe than they are. Predictions of a negative response on the part of a teacher were often expressed in terms of 'hitting' and 'belting'. The most straightforward explanation seems to me to be that young children are very much aware that the world belongs to adults. Power and authority reside in them. Children may not often experience the exercise of power in simple, undisguised terms, but these are the terms in which they find it natural to represent it. Some responses struck the observing adult as strange, and I can only illustrate, from one pupil's answers, the quality of this strangeness. It was as if the speaker were intermittently immersed in private fantasy:

Investigator: If you were as near to Miss Smith as the children in the picture you would see that this card says 'dog'. What do you think Miss Smith is saying to them?
Heather: He's dead and somebody buries him underground.
Investigator: What do you think Miss Smith said then?
Heather: Is it a tortoise, and does it walk?

By the standards of the classroom, Heather's replies were, on the first occasion, conspicuously inappropriate. She was, I must emphasise, not alone in doing this: she simply did it more consistently, and at greater length, than a number of the others. It is certainly the case, as has been pointed out (and notably by Hasan, 1971), that children's language use is not just, in Chomsky's (1965) sense, innovative: it is also, in general, suitable to the context in which it occurs. Communicative competence includes the ability to say what is appropriate. Heather seemed, at four, not to recognise that there was a topic of conversation, agreed between us, which either of us could change, but only after indicating our intention to the other. Most of the children seemed to have reached a point where they could manage better than Heather, but several of them could only do so with mistakes and lapses. Their control of appropriateness, and Heather's most notably, was insecure relative to that of the older children. Seven months later, the qualitative change was most marked. Heather made no mention of death or of tortoises (the subjects that had recurred in her earlier replies). Not only were her answers entirely appropriate, they were more substantial and detailed in terms of classroom reference than those of the majority of five-year-olds.

Observation of the Least Successful Children

By 'least successful' is meant those children who, unlike the others, seemed to make little headway in the initial months of schooling, judged by their failure to produce conspicuously more well-formed responses on the second occasion than on the first. I was able to see four of these, to talk to their teachers, and to see whether I could at all usefully intervene and attempt to teach them what I expected and what they could expect. In this last I failed pretty completely, which does not mean that the attempt was necessarily misguided, though it may have been.

The children I saw for the third time were four in number. With the exception of Robert, the youngest child in the sample, they had been identified by teachers, independently of my inquiry, as giving cause for concern. Information had been offered to me before I sought it. Mark was one of twins, and regarded as backward – less backward, however, than his brother. Both children had defective eyesight. Nigel was the youngest of a large family. Little was expected by his teachers of him; he was regarded as certainly in need of special schooling. Louise was to quite an exceptional degree shy and retiring at the start – so much so that I decided to see her for a third time even though she provided a number of well-formed answers on the second occasion. Her Head Teacher was very positive about the reasons for Louise's early reluctance; she was certain, she assured me, that Louise was regarded as someone of little ability and no consequence in contrast with her lively elder brother. The comments made spontaneously by teachers did seem to support the view that the children least able to predict what would happen in a story about the classroom were having difficulty in satisfactory participation in actual classroom interaction. My hope was that, with these children, I might be able to use the toy school and the possibilities of imaginative role taking it offered, in a different, and perhaps a more positive and purposeful, way than I had done earlier with other groups. If they would accept me as a playmate, we might exchange the roles of teacher and taught. I could say, 'now, *I'll* be teacher first: this is what *I* do, and this is what *you* do'; and then 'now it's *your* turn. *You're* the teacher, you ask the questions: you tell *me* what to do.' I would be, as I had until then avoided being, overtly and intentionally didactic.

The responses I got were neither expected nor uniform. Neither Nigel, nor Robert, nor Mark, was willing to play with the materials in the way that to other children, and to adults, seemed natural. The playground apparatus and the school bell, the items that could be manipulated noisily, caught their attention to the exclusion of the teacher, the pupils, the desks and the classroom materials. When I drew their attention to these and invited make-believe play, they disregarded these suggestions as if they had no meaning for them at all. Louise responded quite differently. In one particular she defeated my expectations. I assumed that the toy would have novelty for the children, but Louise claimed (and I believed her) to have a very similar toy at home. Her play with it, which was wholly unlike that of the others, may, therefore, have been well rehearsed. She was quite unwilling to accept me as a playmate and turned a deaf ear to the offer of a shared make-believe game. Her teacher had warned me that on this occasion I should meet a changed, and much happier, little girl. Louise had blossomed. She had learned to read and had received the accolade of a hymn book of her own, which in her school rewards the attainment of a reading age of seven. Without delay, she unpacked the contents of the box, set out the pupils in rows of desks, with the teacher facing them, and assumed the teacher role. As teacher, she produced a series of directing moves: 'You've got to write your names out proper', she announced. Minutes later, she informed me 'the teacher's got to go to a meeting', and removed the teacher from the sight of the class. '*This* little girl is going to be the teacher.' However, this delegation of duty was not a success. 'They've been very naughty', Louise cheerfully announced. 'All of them have been very naughty. These children are doing very naughty.' And she added, 'The teacher's talking to thin air!' Her 'school day' was punctuated by 'playtime' and 'hometime', and at the end of it she carefully and quickly packed up all the toys and asked if she could return to the classroom. Louise sustained her make believe by telling herself a story, and she used the toy pieces to support and illustrate her narrative. She gave me clear evidence that she saw teachers as those who organise and control (and not as those who serve as resources of information or as those who check whether information has been assimilated). She perceived teachers as having duties that sometimes remove them from the classroom. 'Being a teacher' was, for her, at the end of her eight months of schooling, a role that can be assumed temporarily by someone whose usual role is that of pupil: it had, for her, obligations attaching to it that can be successfully or unsuccessfully discharged. Good children comply; naughty children don't. Good teachers get compliance; the pupil delegated the role of teacher gets disobedience. Neither offers information nor asks questions. From the usual adult standpoint, neither *teaches* at all. It is a view of the classroom in some ways sophisticated, in other ways not just simplistic but actually opposed to the assumptions teachers share with those responsible for the organisation, design and equipment of classrooms.

Problems Outstanding

This is work in progress, and I have still to examine some of the material that I have. In particular, I want to continue to examine the contrast between the children's response to the story-telling activity on the first and on the second occasion that I undertook it. The task of teaching those children who seemed to be learning more slowly than most what to expect, and assisting them to understand that what goes on is essentially orderly and predictable, proved to be much trickier than I had supposed. Like their teachers, I met at once the intractable difficulty of securing the volatile attention of these children.

I want to look more closely than I have yet done at what I have tentatively identified as contrasting learning strategies of children on the way to the production of well-formed classroom discourse. It does look as if these are not equally useful. I suspect that those strategies that sometimes produce answers interpretable as well formed, and sometimes not, must get responses from teachers that are, from the viewpoint of the pupil, quite arbitrary, and that this arbitrariness requires learning. I suspect also that the interested attention of teachers is attracted by utterances that strike the adult as fanciful or odd, and that this is a kind of response that favours rigid learning in children like Heather. I suspect that, for some groups of children (and since I work in the Midlands the children of Caribbean origin come immediately to mind), there are particular difficulties involved in learning to predict, from moment to moment, what is going to be said or done next. I think I am learning (and I hope to put into practice the lesson) the need for flexibility, for caution and for particularly close attention to those children who say or do what I least expect.

Table 4.1: Number of Well-formed Responses to Cues by Each Child in the Younger Group on Entry to School (Occasion 1) and Seven Months Later (Occasion 2)

Child[b]	No. of Well-formed Responses: Occasion 1[a]	No. of Well-formed Responses: Occasion 2
1	0	3
2	4	11
3	8	19
4	7	17
5	10	20
6	1	5
7	10	21
8	11	18
9	4	15
10	11	16
11	8	21
12	13	18
13	14	22
14	5	14
15	6	13
16	13	18
17	14	23
18	11	19
19	9	16
20	8	19
21	3	4
22	3	13
23	11	11
24	2	13
25	3	9
26	10	13
27	4	10
28	7	14
29	0	11
30	4	9
31	10	20
32	11	22
33	10	12
34	13	15
35	17	19
36	7	5
37	11	16
38	0	2

a. Total number of cues presented = 25.

b. Children arranged in ascending order of age within the group. Children it was not possible to see on Occasion 2 are not included (4 children).

Table 4.2: Number of Nil Responses to Cues by Each Child in the Younger Group on Entry to School (Occasion 1) and Seven Months Later (Occasion 2)

Child[b]	No. of Nil Responses: Occasion 1[a]	No. of Nil Responses: Occasion 2
1	23	1
2	1	0
3	6	3
4	0	0
5	10	3
6	12	7
7	1	0
8	1	0
9	0	0
10	0	0
11	1	1
12	0	1
13	0	0
14	14	2
15	3	0
16	1	2
17	0	0
18	2	0
19	4	2
20	0	0
21	21	3
22	14	0
23	0	0
24	12	1
25	3	1
26	2	1
27	4	1
28	6	1
29	25	7
30	9	1
31	3	0
32	1	0
33	0	2
34	1	0
35	0	0
36	0	1
37	1	2
38	22	0

a. Total number of cues presented = 25.

b. Children arranged in ascending order of age within the group. Children it was not possible to see on Occasion2 are not included (4 children).

Table 4.3: Number of Well-formed Responses to Cues by Each Child in the Older Group (Seven-year-olds)

Child[b]	No. of Well-formed Responses[a]
1	21
2	15
3	16
4	18
5	21
6	19
7	24
8	14

a. Total number of cues presented = 25.
b. Children arranged in ascending order of age.

Table 4.4: Number of Nil Responses to Cues by Each Child in the Older Group (Seven-year-olds)

Child[b]	No. of Nil Responses[a]
1	0
2	5
3	2
4	1
5	1
6	1
7	1
8	2

a. Total number of cues presented = 25.
b. Children arranged in ascending order of age.

Table 4.5: Breakdown of Number of Well-formed Responses to Individual Cues by Younger Group on Entry to School (Occasion 1) and Seven Months Later (Occasion 2)

Cues	No. of Well-formed Responses: Occasion 1[a]	No. of Well-formed Responses: Occasion 2
'Preliminary'		
1	27	27
2	17	28
3	13	17
4	30	32
5	30	32
'Exchange'		
1	4	20
2	2	17
3	2	13
4	1	10
5	2	16
6	3	8
7	5	14
8	14	28
9	15	24
'Situational'		
1	14	22
2	17	31
3	12	12
4	5	22
5	25	28
6	14	25
7	10	16
8	17	16
9	24	26
10	23	28
11	13	32

a. Out of a possible total of 38 (i.e. number of children in younger group visited on both occasions).

Table 4.6: Breakdown of Number of Nil Responses to Individual Cues by Younger Group on Entry to School (Occasion 1) and Seven Months Later (Occasion 2)

Cues	No. of Nil Responses: Occasion 1[a]	No. of Nil Responses: Occasion 2
'Preliminary'		
1	2	0
2	5	1
3	15	9
4	3	0
5	4	0
'Exchange'		
1	8	2
2	9	0
3	8	0
4	13	4
5	6	0
6	10	1
7	11	0
8	6	0
9	7	0
'Situational'		
1	8	4
2	13	4
3	8	0
4	15	2
5	9	2
6	10	4
7	10	2
8	10	4
9	10	2
10	7	2
11	7	0

a. Out of a possible total of 38 (i.e. number of children in younger group visited on both occasions).

References

Britton, J. (1970). *Language and Learning*. Harmondsworth: Penguin

Chomsky, N. (1965). *Aspects of the Theory of Syntax*. Cambridge, Mass.: MIT Press

Hasan, R. (1971). 'Syntax and Semantics'. In J. Morton (ed.), *Biological and Social Factors in Psycholinguistics*. London: Logos Press

Sinclair, J.McH. and Coulthard, R.M. (1975). *Towards an Analysis of Discourse*. London: Oxford University Press

5 THEORY AND PRACTICE: A RESPONSE TO WILLES

Michael Stubbs

Perhaps one of the functions of a discussant is to be rather more pedestrian and literal-minded than the paper being discussed. I propose, in any case, to take this approach to Willes's paper, because it seems that what she has done is to move very skilfully from descriptive theory to both methodology and practical educational concerns, and back again, throughout the paper. It may, therefore, be worth while attempting a rather more pedestrian and explicit commentary on what she has in fact done. It is rare to find a paper which successfully manages this kind of integration, and a discussant is perhaps in a better position to make the feat explicit than is the original author. Also, although the paper is clearly indebted, as Willes acknowledges, to research by Sinclair and Coulthard (1975), this research is adapted in an imaginative way, and some of the links are fairly well hidden: it may, therefore, be worth while making some of these links more explicit. Finally, it is rare to find a paper which is so disarmingly straightforward about problems and dead-ends in research, and this is also worth a comment.

Willes has succeeded in integrating points at three different levels of interest. First, there is discussion of interest to sociolinguistic theory, about the acquisition of communicative competence and about the nature of that competence; second, there are several methodological points about problems encountered during the research and about possible devices for generating crucial data required to answer particular questions; and third, there is discussion of problems of immediate practical concern to teachers. The paper demonstrates, in fact, that it *is* possible to relate these different concerns, although this is so seldom achieved. The findings, about the different rates at which children learn the rules of classroom discourse, are of equal interest to researchers and to teachers.

As Willes says, she has put to 'practical exploratory use' the model of classroom discourse proposed by Sinclair and Coulthard (1975). The work is superficially rather different from Sinclair and Coulthard's: it is clearly an innovative and imaginative development of some of their ideas, rather than a mechanical application of them. But the work is still based firmly on the approach to discourse which they propose, not only in its use of various descriptive categories (*Initiation, Response* and *Feedback*), but also in its whole notion of discourse being highly predictable from one utterance to the next. A central idea in Sinclair and Coulthard is that utterances can be classified according to what follows: 'the meaning of an utterance is its predictive assessment of what follows' (p. 120). This concept of discourse underlies the very neat set of experimental materials in the form of the incomplete illustrated story book which Willes has developed: a kind of cloze procedure for discourse sequences.

However, Willes also seems to have inherited various problems from Sinclair and Coulthard. She regards their work in the following ways: (a) as a model of developed classroom discourse; (b) as a way of coding actual verbal behaviour; (c) as a way of coding responses elicited in an experiment; and (d) as a model of a norm from which other kinds of classroom discourse may be seen as deviating. This final concept of a norm is, at least, proposed in a previous paper by Willes (1978). She distinguishes clearly between competence and performance: silent children may know things for which they give no evidence. But she nevertheless does not discuss the problem of whether the same descriptive system can be applied equally to actually occurring verbal behaviour and to perceptions as represented by responses to an experiment, and in addition be regarded as a norm. As I say, this problem is inherited from the original work. Sinclair and Coulthard present their work as a system for describing naturally occurring classroom discourse, although they do not justify this at any length. It could also be regarded as something more abstract: an ideal-typical model of underlying discourse competence. A detailed discussion of the children's responses to the incomplete story book would be fascinating in its own right, and might answer some of these queries about the relationship between children's verbal behaviour in real and in simulated discourse.

On methodology, Willes is usefully candid about the way in which researchers' expectations and preconceptions can be contradicted in the field. It is useful to have a reminder that everyone's research is usually a muddled and untidy affair, although few of us admit this, and manage to draw clear lessons from it. She then makes a very simple (but possibly unfashionable) point about the limitations of spontaneous talk as data. Silent pupils will not be recorded on the tape-recorder, and naturalistic data may therefore have to be supplemented by experimental methods which will generate the rich data required to answer specific questions. This is a theoretical/methodological point: you cannot infer competence from production, and theoretical sampling (c.f. Glaser and Strauss, 1968) may be required to supplement naturally occurring data. But she turns it also into a practical point for teachers: that a teacher may assume that the whole class has the same discourse competence as the vocal minority.

When I first read Willes's paper, I found her findings rather contradictory. On the one hand, some children seem to remain at a loss about the rules of classroom discourse. On the other hand, learning classroom discourse seems 'more rapid and easy' than one might expect: children learn their early lessons 'too well', as she has put it in another paper (Willes, 1978). The point appears to be that some children do learn the rules of classroom discourse very quickly, these children are highly visible, and the teacher may assume that the whole class has their competence; but other individual children may have more difficulties. The question then arises as to whether it is a good idea to set out to teach classroom discourse directly, when a problem often encountered later by teachers is how to get pupils to break away from merely making short responses to teachers' initiations.

Next, the findings. First, I was left wondering about the explanations of some of the findings. The data on children's perceptions of school are interesting, if depressing! It is perhaps not very surprising, however, that children's role playing is confined to teachers' organising talk. This is, after all, less creative, more repetitive and more predictable than teaching talk. It is therefore easier to imitate. To imitate teaching talk you have to know something! The children might know much more about classroom talk than is revealed in their performance. It is not clear, in other words, whether this finding is simply an artefact of an inadequate research strategy, although I am not sure, on reflection, how this might be demonstrated. Other perceptions may be elicited by other research devices, but perhaps the perceptions which are most easily observed have some special validity purely by virtue of this fact? This may be partly what is meant by 'stereotype'.

More important are the reasons for the different rates of children's learning about classroom discourse. One possibility lies in different amounts of continuity between the discourse at home and at school. I have certainly recorded mothers and children using discourse which is easily analysable by the procedure set out in Sinclair and Coulthard (1975), and presumably such discourse differs in frequency in different homes (Stubbs, 1976, p. 98). This is a major research area which is now open to investigation.

So I feel now that I have been left with highly productive questions at different levels of interest. What does work of this type tell us about the nature of children's communicative competence? Could we investigate the reasons for the findings about differences in competence? Is it 'misguided' to attempt to teach children about classroom discourse? These are all at present unanswered questions, but Willes has proposed interesting ways of investigating them.

The prevailing theoretical orientation of Willes's paper is clearly linguistic, but not narrowly so. She combines linguistic insights with genuine participant observation and ethnographic work, making her paper comparable to work reported in Cazden *et al.* (eds.) (1972): especially, for example, the well-known studies of American Indian classrooms by Philips and by Dumont.

In addition, she selects particular theoretical insights which can illuminate educational practice. Note that the selection is not of superficial facts, but of concepts (as I emphasised at the beginning of this article) of a more powerful and general kind: the concept of discourse as a system, the concept of predictive or prospective structure, the concept of cloze procedures and so on. There is a great deal in contemporary linguistics that is of value to educationalists. But there is also a great deal of linguistic work that is of no immediate relevance. Modern linguistics is, however, so vast that only someone with a full-time professional interest in language could hope to find a way through this amount of work and select out those findings and concepts which are likely to be relevant to teachers. It is, therefore, to be hoped that more linguists will develop an interest in presenting their discipline in an accessible way to educationalists, as Willes does in this paper.

References

Cazden, C., John, V. and Hymes, D. (eds.) (1972). *Functions of Language in the Classroom*. New York: Teachers College Press

Dumont, R.V. (1972). 'Learning English and How to be Silent: Studies in Sioux and Cherokee Classrooms'. In Cazden *et al.* (eds.), *Functions of Language in the Classroom*

Glaser, B.G. and Strauss, A.L. (1968). *The Discovery of Grounded Theory: Strategies for Qualitative Research*. New York: Weidenfeld and Nicolson

Philips, S. (1972). 'Participant Structures and Communicative Competence: Warm Springs Children in Community and Classroom'. In Cazden *et al.* (eds.), *Functions of Language in the Classroom*

Sinclair, J.McH. and Coulthard, R.M. (1975). *Towards an Analysis of Discourse*. London: Oxford University Press

Stubbs, M. (1976). *Language, Schools and Classrooms*. London: Methuen
Willes, M. (1978). 'Early Lessons Learned Too Well'. In C. Adelman (ed.), *Uttering Muttering: Reporting and Using Talk for Social and Educational Research*. Mimeo. Bulmershe College of Higher Education, Reading

Part II

CONVERSATION ANALYSIS

6 CONVERSATION ANALYSIS

A.J. Wootton

From within child language studies a number of warrants have emerged for the study of children's interaction with those around them. Such analysis can, for example, disclose features of children's speech production which seem associated with particular types of recipient and situation. Furthermore, through analysis of the adult 'input' to children in interaction writers have attempted to illuminate the developmental trajectories to be found in language acquisition: parent and child speech are scanned to assess the extent of their linguistic isomorphism; the systematic features of 'baby talk' by adults are described and evaluated for their linguistic nutritiousness; the implicit ways through which parents make available to children, in discourse, semantic and syntactic knowledge are examined. The explicit concern in studies of this kind is to use interaction analysis either as a way of extending our knowledge of the linguistic competence at children's disposal, or as a potential basis for arriving at explanations of developmental profiles. The systematic analysis of social interaction has, of course, also been the concern of other disciplines, such as sociology, as well as other sub-branches of psychology, notably social psychology. Yet much of this work also has not been concerned with the organisation of interaction as such, but with such issues as the way in which the interaction facilitates the development of skills or the abilities of participants (analogously to much work on adult-child interaction), the way that it leads to particular decision outcomes, its use as a basis for making inferences about the concepts of one or more participants and so on. Studies of teacher-pupil interaction, for example, seem overwhelmingly concerned with the consequence of particular interaction patterns in terms of their conduciveness to various forms of learning by pupils. If, for convenience, we can accept Bates's distinction between pragmatics and sociolinguistics:

> pragmatics is the study of rules for using language in context – rules that can, at least in principle, be part of the linguistic competence of a single speaker. Sociolinguistics, on the other hand, is the study of differences between social groups in the use of a given language or set of languages. (1976, pp. 541–2)

then we can say that such work on interaction has given us much sociolinguistic information but little pragmatic information,[1] much information about variabilities in speech and behaviour patterns, less about the ways through which the orderliness of co-ordinated conduct is achieved. Some branches of social psychology and sociology are now engaged in treating the organisation of interaction as a phenomenon in its own right.[2] Within sociology, such a concern was probably initiated by Simmel (1950), though it was radically reshaped and extended by Goffman (e.g. 1959, 1972). Most recently, a body of knowledge sharing these concerns has emerged from the work of conversation analysts (CA) working within the ethnomethodological tradition of sociology, and it is their work that is to be introduced here.

By virtue of working within the ethnomethodological tradition, CA work has distinctive qualities which must appear puzzling to those first reading it. It is, for example, single-mindedly anti-theoretical, non-experimental and inductive, and it does not sit easily in that vein of language study which traditionally has been left free for sociologists to work, namely sociolinguistics. To understand something of why it has this character, it is necessary to mention briefly how it emerged from within the discipline of sociology.[3] It emerged specifically from ethnomethodological observations about procedures of analysis within sociology, and the crux of these observations centred around categorisation practices. In describing aspects of the social world, sociologists and anthropologists have assigned aspects of interaction processes to various types of analytic category. Sometimes such categories have represented attempts to discriminate types of interaction *per se*, as when, say, different types of exchange relation or teacher-pupil interaction are distinguished, but similar issues arise when, for example, social scientists have sought to recover the categories in terms of which people structure their experience from interactional evidence. Ethnomethodologists have claimed that the assignment of specific instances to such categories is problematic in a variety of ways. In general, they argue that no exhaustive account can be given, in terms of the features of the categories, as to how instances of such categories are recognised, that such practices, as ends in themselves, always leave open the question of what methods are used to render instances into instances of X or Y. The categories (e.g. the vocabulary) that both laymen and social scientists use, it is argued, are 'specifically vague' (Garfinkel, 1967) in their application, 'vague' in that the warrant for their use is reliant on knowledge which is either indefinite or inexplicit, 'specific' because, in spite of such vagueness, people usually do operate with a sense that what they see and hear is of a specific, definite kind. The problem for most ethnomethodologists is to give an account of how activity can take on for people this definite character, to disclose the methods through which people repair the irremedial indexicality of the sign systems around them.

In the context of interaction, it is clear that such methods need to be public because, if interaction is to be the co-ordinated enterprise that it often is, then participants must have mutual access to design principles which allow for the orderly production and recognition of conduct.[4] Such design principles are crucial because the relevance of things like known information about co-participants and guesses as to their intentions are contingent on the recognisable state of the interaction at some *specific* time, and their relevance is formulated through the shape of the interaction as it proceeds. Interaction analysis must be at least partly concerned with the ways through which co-ordination is achieved, where co-ordination can be partly a matter of satisfying the technical requirements posed by engaging in any particular form of discourse, notably the specifics of the turn allocation system, but where, more importantly, co-ordination is also a matter of doing some activity in concert with co-participants, the activity which is the 'point of' the interaction – making a request, telling a joke, conveying bad news, etc. The possibility CA investigates is that people's understanding of what goes on around them is based on a close monitoring of design specifics, notably the positioning of items in relation to prior items within sequences and the specific format of items (the format specifics being describable at any of the conventional levels of linguistic description, such as syntax, lexis, prosody, as well as taking account of accompanying non-verbal behaviour, if available to the investigator).

It is the organisation of co-ordinated *actions* which CA seeks to examine, the way that people accomplish their various implicit or explicit interactional business. Talk is of interest only in so far as it is partly through the organisation of talk that people accomplish this business. Schegloff and Sacks, for example, say in their discussion of the closings of conversation:

> it should be clearly understood that the 'closing problem' we are discussing is proposed as a problem for conversationalists; we are not interested in it as a problem for analysts except in so far, and in the ways, it is a problem for participants. (1974, p. 234)[5]

They then go on to pose as an issue how participants collaboratively can bring a conversation to a close, focusing especially on the placement and properties of general types of what they call 'pre-closings': that is, types of turn which allow recipient to initiate further unmentioned matters, but which also offer the opportunity for recipient, at that point, to choose not to continue the conversation, thus warranting the initiation of what they call the 'terminal exchange' (i.e. 'goodbyes'). The problems around which the analysis revolves are interactional ones, just as the problems concerning the articles in this section are essentially interactional: Cuff and Hustler are partly concerned with the ways through which teachers and children build their remarks to display the situated character of stories not just as stories, but as invited stories which are part of an ongoing round of such stories; Langford is concerned with the work recognisably achieved through the use of different forms of clarification requests by parents; Wootton is concerned to specify, through conversation analysis, the kinds of interactional work accomplished through the use of address terms in different utterance positions.

Great care is taken in this work in the characterisation of actions achieved through the design specifics of turns. Just as the problems which interest those working in CA are interactional problems which are oriented to as such by participants, so also turn designs are only considered equivalent where there is some evidence that they are treated as such by participants: where, for example, there is sequential evidence suggesting an equivalence of treatment by recipient in next turn. Thus Drew (this volume) points out that a CA approach to corrections would want to discriminate between a variety of correction turn types which seem to have different sequential correlates and that such discriminations do not appear to be made within meaningful potential models. Similar points can be made about speech act analyses of discourse. Labov and Fanshel (1977), for example, lay out a variety of ways in which requests can be rejected but, although they notice that outright rejections (i.e. 'no') are rarely used, there is no attempt to examine the differential treatment of rejection types, nor the systematic ordering of such rejection turns across utterances by the same speaker, in order to assess differential implications for the development of the dialogue. Any conversation analysis must surely come to grips with the specific way in which the introduction of some turn channels the course of the dialogue, and to do that one must get involved in finding evidence as to the bases on which participants treat different utterance forms (e.g. of corrections, or of rejections) as having a different character. If this is not a prerequisite for certain linguistic analyses it is clearly a prerequisite for any form of analysis attempting to show how people accomplish various interactional work in co-ordinated ways and, as a result, there is some work in CA on the nature of cross-turn constraints existing in dialogue, the ways in which certain sets of actions are contingent on the occurrence of priors.[6]

In approaching interaction, then, it is the problems confronting participants which are of interest in CA, and the systematic procedures and designs through which such problems are displayed and resolved. There is no prior analytic 'theory' of interaction being applied and there is no assumption that interaction is always perfectly co-ordinated, that participants are everywhere able to decode talk. In contrast with previous work on interaction, issues of misunderstanding, lack of coherence, error and suchlike have been given a great deal of attention within CA.[7] This is partly because the occurrence of repair procedures, procedures designed to remedy such problems, themselves locate phenomena that *for participants* are in need of repair, and in doing this provide important clues to relevant normative structures in dialogue. Bur the organisation of repair procedures in their own right has proved to be of great interest in that their internal organisation exhibits orderly properties. In the case of corrections, for example, Schegloff, Sacks and Jefferson (1977) have shown that sequences in which corrections occur generally seem to be organised so to allow the error maker to self-correct. Recipients do not interrupt turns at points where they can hear errors; in fact, they often delay their turn and/or employ turn designs which avoid correction and create a subsequent opportunity for error maker to self-correct. The articles by Drew and Langford in this volume both explore these themes. More generally, the organisation of repair in conversation constitutes an enormous area of inquiry and, in different ways, it is the main theme of the articles by Langford and Wootton in this part of the book. Even so, detailed analysis of the distinctive interactional properties of different types of repair turn within correction and clarification sequences has barely begun, and this promises to be a rich area of inquiry, especially within children's interaction sequences, given their frequency of clarificatory and remedial comment.[8]

Most work in CA has examined interaction among adults rather than that involving children, and a picture is emerging in which particular types of speech sequence seem to be organised in ways which attend the non-equivalence of actions which take place within those sequences. Pomerantz (1975 and 1978,b), for example, has shown within agreement/disagreement sequences that, whereas agreements are characteristically non-delayed in relation to the prior turn, include agreement tokens (e.g. 'yes') and are matched to the turn being agreed with, disagreements come in a much wider variety of turn designs. Many are delayed in time after the initial turn, and the disagreement turn itself is often prefaced by weak disjunction markers such as 'well' rather than 'no', although a variety of other preface types are outlined by Pomerantz, such as turn initial agreement components (e.g. 'yes I agree though . . .'). Viewed as a type of sequence, agreement/disagreement sequences seem to be organised by participants so as to minimise the occurrence of disagreement, and for this reason Pomerantz has argued that, through turn and sequence design, participants exhibit a preference for agreement in such sequences. Other studies, in similar ways, have suggested that correcting is displayed as non-equivalent, and dispreferred, to self-correcting (Schegloff, Sacks and Jefferson, 1977); that rejecting a child request is displayed by adults as non-equivalent and dispreferred, to granting (Wootton, forthcoming).[9] The different types of turn design within these sequences show systematic internal relationships with each other; for example, within request sequences, parents systematically move to more negative and outright rejection forms if they have not initially used such forms and if the child continues with the request. Furthermore, in these request sequences, there is some evidence of children's monitoring rejection turn designs in that they appear differentially to respond to different types of design. This suggests to me that such preference organisations may constitute some of the major axes which allow for the principled production and interpretation of verbal conduct, and in some sense competence in adults consists in the mastery of these delicate design features through which the character of actions is conveyed. Although, in the case of requests, it may be that children are capable of monitoring such designs, their productive mastery of them is more questionable. To my knowledge, no studies have explicitly examined whether children, as recipients of requests, employ even the same range of turn types as their parents but, from the examples given by Garvey (1975) of four-year-olds, it seems unlikely to be the case. It remains, of course, as a possibility that young children could convey such differential actions in alternative ways but, until they at least employ the range of adult turn type, internally ordered and used in similar ways to adults, there seems little ground for claiming that children's management of requests at age four bears much resemblance to that of adults. And precisely similar points could be made regarding the other preference organisations that workers in CA have identified. At present, the precise status of such forms of preference organisation is difficult to pinpoint, but there is no doubt as to the orderliness of the phenomena through which they are exhibited and they may form an important basis for specifying in more detail those features of communicative competence which children do not exhibit at, say, age four.

Although CA may shed light on ways in which the handling of interaction through dialogue may be managed differently by adults and children, the main thrust of ethnomethodological writing on children, to date, has been more concerned to enlarge our conception of children's communicative competence. Cicourel and his collaborators have shown,[10] for example, that children's inappropriate answers to standardised test problems are often based on forms of reasoning which, in their own right, appear both systematic and comprehensible in adult terms. Furthermore, similar characteristics have been accorded to children's responses deemed inappropriate/incorrect in teacher-pupil dialogue. In these ways, it is argued, displays of 'deficiency' by children can be analytically transformed into displays of competence, occasions on which all children employ shared interpretive procedures, shared in the sense of being mutually comprehensible and based on 'rational' forms of reasoning. The upshot of this work seems to me to be a recommendation for the systematic examination of the interpretive procedures used by children. Cicourel has outlined some examples of such procedures, as employed by adults, but the relationship between the procedures specified by him and a systematic conversation analysis based on ethnomethodological premises is quite unclear. One of his interpretive procedures, for example, concerns the retrospective-prospective sense of occurrence. He writes: 'Routine conversation depends upon speakers and hearers waiting for later utterances to decide what was intended before' (1973, p. 54). In what sense conversation 'depends upon' the possibility of such a phenomenon occurring is quite unclear; such a phenomenon can occur and, where it does occur in such a way as to be recognisable to participants as occurring, it becomes an interactional phenomenon; I take it that part of the art of being a teacher consists in having ways of detecting when it is that a child now understands something, when it is that an activity like clarification can cease. In fact, a similar issue often arises for the child in the clarification sequences explored by Langford in this part of the book, in that the child has to decide just when it is that further clarification is not required by the parent, when it is that the parent 'now' understands. In these cases, presumably there are systematic and recognisable bases for making such inferences; in fact, it is the systematics of such a process that analyses like those of Langford are concerned to disclose. But because such a phenomenon can take place does not imply that conversation depends on the possibility of subsequent talk elaborating what has gone before. Clearly, conversation can take place in which opaque items or intentions are never clarified, yet the occurrence of subsequent conversation is not prejudiced by virtue of this. Again one can devise circumstances/tasks, as has Garfinkel (1967), in which one makes it possible for subjects to revise their earlier notions of the meaning of some talk in the light of later turns, but, while that may tell one interesting things about the variety of meaning attribution consistent with any given surface form, it cannot stand as some kind of model of what always occurs in conversation. It is possible for revisions of meaning to occur; the conversation analyst needs to concern himself with whether he can trace orderly features of those interactions in which such revisions do occur (where such revisions become overt interactional phenomena), the procedures through which they are exhibited as such and the systematics of their treatment. In the last analysis, Cicourel's concerns do not focus around the collaborative management of interactional issues and for this reason his work has been most useful as a critique of prevailing modes of description within semantics and child language study, rather than as laying the basis for cumulative work on the organisation of interaction.

To summarise, CA is not primarily concerned with using interaction as a basis for making claims as to the development of attributes among participants;[11] it is concerned with tracing systematics in the management of interactional matters. In doing this, it examines in detail the format and positioning of turns within sequences with the aim, stated in most ambitious terms, of disclosing general forms of organisation which are not speaker or situation specific. To this extent it falls within the domain of pragmatics rather than sociolinguistics. Because it lays great stress on the identification of issues and actions which are of significance to participants, and because it has no theories about interaction that it is concerned to test, the procedure of analysis is primarily inductive.[12] Some within CA are able to make interesting headway from the analysis of single fragments of data – many of Sacks's important unpublished lecture notes are in this mould – and, in the last analysis, any general claims do have to be grounded in specific data fragments; but finalised analyses are usually making claims which to the analyst seem consistent with the general corpus of conversation at his disposal, a corpus which is roughly equivalent to the corpus of acceptable sentences with which grammarians work.

The aims of the analyses in this part of the book differ in terms of their generality. Cuff and Hustler are partially concerned with the way in which 'the fact that' a particular set of activities in the classroom centring on story time are being engaged in is accomplished. That is not guaranteed by our general common-sense knowledge that such activities occur in such settings; rather: 'Activities, agenda, responsibility have all to be achieved in the then-and-there of that particular occasion; the occasion has to be brought off in, by and through the talk in a localised (utterance-by-utterance) manner' (p. 135). So their analysis leads them to look at the variety of ways through which the character and organisation of the occasion was documented in talk: in doing so they refer to phenomena such as invitations, closings, stories, all of which can and have been subjected to detailed analyses in their own right. The remaining papers are more narrowly concerned with the organisation of specific actions: Langford with the sequential properties of different types of clarification request; Wootton with the kinds of remedial work achieved through the use of address terms by children. This, and other CA work relating to child interaction,[13] must represent only a modest beginning, modest in that the range of such work within CA is limited, and even here there is clearly unevenness in the extent to which the articles represent finalised conclusions on the issues that they discuss. Nevertheless, I have tried to indicate that mainstream work within CA may be of more than marginal interest to those working on child language and, given the increasing concern with systematic, pragmatic and interactional analysis within child language study, this body of work, and the rationale for its adoption, may merit some attention from those interested in such matters. It is this work which has emerged as one of the more significant and cumulative attempts to analyse interaction from within the sociological and anthropological traditions, traditions which have, after all, been concerned with tackling such matters for some time.

Notes

1. A similar point is made, in fact, by Bates (1976) in her discussion of these issues.

2. As this is intended as an introduction to conversation analysis, I shall not attempt to describe and interrelate the important work concerned with the organisation of interaction which has been taking place within certain branches of social psychology. For fairly recent overviews of that work see Argyle (1975) and Kendon (1977).

3. The remainder of this paragraph really only hints at the programmatic basis of ethnomethodological work. For fuller and more adequate discussions the reader is referred to Garfinkel (1967), Sacks (1963), Garfinkel and Sacks (1970), Coulter (1971, 1973), Drew (1977, Chs. 2 and 3), Wootton (1975) and Heritage (1978a and 1978b).

4. In the most general sense 'recipient design' is, therefore, both a necessary and investigable type of systematicity within any community of speakers and hearers.

5. In order to clarify the nature of the 'problems' which CA typically investigates, it is worth while continuing the quotation from Schegloff and Sacks. They go on, in parenthesis, to say:

> By 'problem' we do not intend puzzle, in the sense that participants need to ponder the matter of how to close a conversation. We mean that closings are to be seen as achievements, as solutions to certain problems of conversational organisation. While, for many people, closing a conversation may be a practical problem in the sense that they find it difficult to get out of a conversation they are in, that problem is different from the problem of closing that we are concerned with. The problem we are concerned with sets up the possibilities of a practical problem but does not require that such practical problems occur. Our discussion should then be able to furnish bases for the existence of practical problems of closing conversations. (1974, p. 234)

6. Some of the more important discussions are to be found in Schegloff and Sacks (1974), Jefferson (1972a), Schegloff (1972) and Sacks, Schegloff and Jefferson (1974).

7. Jefferson's work (1972b, 1974) has been especially concerned with these themes, but see also Schegloff (1977).

8. This area is also one which is being increasingly addressed from within other approaches to interaction; some of this work, such as that of Garvey and Corsaro, is referred to in the chapters by Langford and Hustler in this volume.

9. Later work, such as that of Heritage (1978b), explores the preference for agreement, while other work done by Pomerantz (1978a and 1978b) and Sacks and Schegloff (1979) is concerned with the operation of multiple preferences.

10. See, for example, Cicourel *et al.* (1974), Mehan (1973), Mackay (1974) and Cicourel (1973).

11. That is not to say, of course, that its findings have no bearing on claims made about the attributes of participants. For those interested in such things as perspective taking by children, my article in this section may be of interest in that it demonstrates how children's re-solicit items post non-response to an initial remark contain different types of proposed analysis as to how their prior turn came to get no response from the parent.

12. Unfortunately, there is no satisfactory exegesis of the methodology (ies) employed in CA, and to characterise it as a form of induction is to risk trivialisation. From my points earlier concerning the description of turns it must be clear that both evidence, and a variety of evidence, is routinely used by CA to warrant characterisations. It has generally proved possible from the highly detailed analysis of ongoing talk to find sources of evidence which bear on specific claims being made. For the inventive use of self-correction data, for example, see Sacks and Schegloff (forthcoming).

13. See, especially, Speier (1971, 1973) and McHoul (1978).

References

Argyle, M. (1975). *Bodily Communication.* London: Methuen

Bates, E. (1976). 'Pragmatics and Sociolinguistics in Child Language'. In D.A. Morehead and A.E. Morehead (eds.), *Normal and Deficient Child Language*

Cicourel, A.V. (1973). *Cognitive Sociology*. Harmondsworth: Penguin

— Jennings, K.H., Jennings, S.H.M., Leiter, K.C.W., MacKay, R., Mehan, H. and Roth, D.R. (1974). *Language Use and School Performance*. New York: Academic Press

Coulter, J. (1971). 'Decontextualised Meanings: Current Approaches to Verstehende Investigations'. *Sociological Review*, 19, pp. 301–23

— (1973). 'Language and the Conceptualization of Meaning'. *Sociology*, 7, pp. 173–89

Douglas, J. (ed.) (1971). *Understanding Everyday Life*. London: Routledge

Dreitzel, H.P. (ed.) (1973). *Childhood and Socialization*. Recent Sociology no. 5. London: Macmillan

Dressler, W. (ed.) (1977). *Current Trends in Text Linguistics*. Berlin; New York: de Gruyter

Drew, P. (1977). 'Some Moral and Inferential Aspects of Descriptions of Violent Events in Northern Ireland', Unpublished Ph.D. thesis, University of Lancaster

Garfinkel, H. (1967). *Studies in Ethnomethodology*. Englewood Cliffs, New Jersey: Prentice-Hall

— and Sacks, H. (1970). 'On Formal Structures of Practical Actions'. In J.C. McKinney and E. Tiryakian (eds.), *Theoretical Sociology*

Garvey, C. (1975). 'Requests and Responses in Children's Speech'. *Journal of Child Language*, 2, pp. 41–63

Goffman, E. (1959). *The Presentation of Self in Everyday Life*. New York: Doubleday

— (1972). *Interaction Ritual*. Harmondsworth: Penguin

Heritage, J.C. (1978a). 'Aspects of the Flexibilities of Natural Language Use: A Reply to Phillips'. *Sociology*, 12, pp. 79–105

— (1978b). 'Negotiating Conversational Realities: Aspects of Confirmations and Disconfirmations to Formulations'. Paper presented to Third Annual International Institute in Ethnomethodology and Conversation Analysis, University of Boston

Jefferson, G. (1972a). 'Side Sequences'. In D. Sudnow (ed.), *Studies in Social Interaction*

— (1972b). 'Sequential Analysis of Two Types of Conversational Disruption'. Unpublished Ph.D. thesis, University of California, Irvine

— (1974). 'Error Correction as an Interactional Resource'. *Language in Society*, 2, pp. 181–99

Kendon, A. (1977). *Studies in the Behaviour of Social Interaction*. Indiana: Indiana University Press

Labov, W. and Fanshel, D. (1977). *Therapeutic Discourse*. New York: Academic Press

McHoul, A. (1978). 'The Organisation of Turns at Formal Talk in the Classroom'. *Language in Society*, 7, pp. 183–213

Mackay, R.W. (1974). 'Conceptions of Children and Models of Socialization'. In R. Turner (ed.), *Ethnomethodology*

McKinney, J.C. and Tiryakian, E. (eds.) (1970). *Theoretical Sociology*. New York: Appleton

Mehan, H. (1973). 'Assessing Children's School Performance'. In H.P. Dreitzel (ed.), *Childhood and Socialization*

Morehead, D.A. and Morehead, A.E. (eds.) (1970). *Normal and Deficient Child Language*. Baltimore: University Park Press

Pomerantz, A. (1975). 'Second Assessments: A Study of Some Features of Agreements/Disagreements'. Unpublished Ph.D. thesis, University of California, Irvine

— (1978a). 'Compliment Responses: Notes on the Operation of Multiple Constraints'. In J. Schenkein (ed.), *Studies in the Organisation of Conversational Interaction*

— (1978b). 'Agreeing and Disagreeing with Assessments'. Unpublished MS, University of California, Los Angeles

Psathas, G. (ed.) (1979). *Everyday Language: Studies in Ethnomethodology*. New York: Irvington Press

Sacks, H. (1963). 'Sociological Description'. *Berkeley Journal of Sociology*, 8, pp. 1-19

—, Schegloff, E. and Jefferson, G. (1974). 'A Simplest Systematics for the Organization of Turn-Taking for Conversation'. *Language*, 50, pp. 696–735

— and Schegloff, E. (1979). 'Two Preferences in the Organization of Reference to Persons in Conversation and their Interaction'. In G. Psathas (ed.), *Studies in Ethnomethodology*

Schegloff, E. (1972). 'Notes on a Conversational Practice: Formulating Place'. In D. Sudnow (ed.), *Studies in Social Interaction*

— (1977). 'On Some Questions and Ambiguities in Conversation'. In W. Dressler (ed.), *Current Trends in Text Linguistics*

— and Sacks, H. (1974). 'Opening up Closings'. In R. Turner (ed.), *Ethnomethodology*

—, Sacks, H. and Jefferson, G. (1977). 'The Preference for Self-Correction in the Organization of Repair in Conversation'. *Language*, 53, pp. 361–82

Schenkein, J. (ed.) (1978). *Studies in the Organisation of Conversational Interaction*. New York: Academic Press

Simmel, G. (1950). *The Sociology of Georg Simmel*. New York: Free Press

Speier, M. (1971). 'The Everyday World of the Child'. In J. Douglas (ed.), *Understanding Everyday Life*

— (1973). *How to Observe Face-to-Face Communication*. Pacific Palisades, California: Goodyear

Sudnow, D. (ed.) (1972). *Studies in Social Interaction*. New York: Free Press

Turner, R. (ed.) (1974). *Ethnomethodology*. Harmondsworth: Penguin

Wootton, A.J. (1975). *Dilemmas of Discourse*. London: Allen and Unwin

— (forthcoming). 'The Management of Grantings and Rejections by Parents in Request Sequences'. *Semiotica*, forthcoming

7 STORIES AND STORY TIME IN AN INFANT CLASSROOM

E.C. Cuff and D. Hustler

Introduction

In this paper, we outline some features of a particular sociological approach which has the social organisation of talk as a central concern. We attempt some illustrative analyses which might serve to document the potential relevance of this approach for an understanding of talk in classrooms, especially, perhaps, talk in infant classrooms. As such, the paper does not claim to produce 'findings' with regard to the infant classroom, nor does it express strong interest in warranting the analyses which are developed. In the course of the paper we do, however, take up and discuss several important methodological issues as and where they become pressingly relevant to the argument. Finally, we briefly touch on some of the implications of the approach for such matters as 'competence at talk-production'.

For some time, we have been tape-recording and transcribing talk in school classrooms in order to provide materials for the analysis of social interaction from a sociological standpoint. For this chapter, the material for analysis is the following transcript, which derives from a collection of recordings of 'story time' in infant classrooms. (Transcription conventions are set out on pp. 140-1.)

ST 2

1. C: (   )
2. T: That's a nasty cut isn't it
   Did you fall over
3. C_1: Don't know
4. C_2: (nasty cut)
5. C: I think m –   my mummy and daddy says
   (   ) fall over   or anything
6. C: (/ /   )
7. C: (/ /   )
8. T: Anyway – it's time for your story now / / (   )

9. C: ( )
10. T: Look this way – – Look this way that's right the story I'm going to tell you today is about – rather ( ) Christmas (about a donkey) do you know anyone that rode on a donkey at Christmas. Yes (/ /)
11. C: Mary and Joseph
12. T: Yes well Mary rode on a donkey didn't she / /
13. C: Yes
14. T: ( ) Very tired on her legs
15. C: Bethlehem
16. T: Yes
17. C: ( ) n my brother and me and my cousin made an ( ) and I made an angel
18. T: Did they
19. C: Uhm it took 5 weeks to get back
20. T: Did it take 5 weeks
21. C: and wh ( ) going to make a donkey when I get home
22. T: You made them at home
23. C: Yes
24. T: Well this story isn't about a donkey a long time ago it's a story about – – – a donkey that's – – – – around today a little donkey and it lived in a field – – – – a little black donkey in a little green field – – – at the time of the story snow was falling – – the little donkey in the field were all covered with snowflakes – – – – he wasn't cold though because he ran round the field – but he was lonely – – – – whenever he stopped he threw back his head he said EE-AW EE-AW – there was no other little donkey to say ee-aw back so he was a lonely donkey – – – two little girls came past the field and they stopped and they looked over the gate – and they stroked him and patted him ....

....

((the telling of the story continues for seven minutes with occasional utterances from the children which can be heard as displaying their monitoring of the story as it develops))

77. T: .... and so both the little donkeys and the little girls had a very – – happy – – Christmas ((whispered)) – and so the little donkey wasn't lonely any more.

78. C: (   )

79. T: Have you ever felt lonely have you ever felt lonely

80. CC: Mmmmmmhh ((several children make similar type utterances))

81. C: Yeh yeh

82. T: When did you feel lonely Colin

(1.0)

83. Colin: Uhm – – – – we went out one day and – me dad said uhh we're going to (bridge   ) you want to come with me now

84. C: Hahh

85. Colin: and I stayed in the tent

86. T: You stayed in the tent on your own – and then you felt lonely

87. C: (   )   ((very softly))

88. T: Yes (Sarah) when did you feel lonely

89. Sarah: (   )   ((very softly))

90. T: and you felt lonely on your own

91. Sarah: (Yes)

92. T: What about you Wendy

93. Wendy: Well uh – I got lost / / (one day)

94. C: KATHY

95. T: Yes

96. Wendy: and uh – – and – – I can't remember (the rest)

97. T: You got lost did w– were you going shopping

98. Wendy: Uhm – yes I (was with) Mummy (   ) a– a– no I wasn't going shopping with (   ) and uh she uhm she was in the shop and I went down and no she wasn't in the shop

99. C: hahhhh

100. Wendy: and I went and looked in the shop and she wasn't there (   ) and she (caught) up (   )

101. C: hahhhhh

102. T: and did you think for a moment you'd been left on your own

103. Wendy: Y (hhh) es

104. T: and you felt lonely – – Yes Melanie
105. Melanie: Wh – when my mummy – when we were going to the shopping and then my – my mummy – – – – – when (/ /)
106. C: hehhh ice cream
107. Melanie: and then she (forgot) it to bring home and then when my mummy come for us
she said you you ( )
Eleanor – – Eleanor / / and we will go and get that ice cream
/ / ((someone enters the room and speaks in the background))

((further child talking right through this stretch of talk))

108. ? = Hehh
109. T: Oh I see – – what about you Richard have you never been lost or felt lonely – – – – never what about you Paul
(1.0)
110. C:) hehhh
111. Paul:) I have uh – – I have once when I was in the house fast asleep – – – and uh I woke early in the morning looking round for them. ( )
in the house I jumped up up in the air and uhh I thought that was Mummy and Daddy in bed (somebody else)
112. C: HA HA
113. T:) Hehhh
114. C:) Hehhh
115. Paul: and so : : o – – i the – uh me Aunty and me aunty said to me cos me mummy went to uh – – me mummy went to hospickle to get the baby –
((one child laughing hard throughout))
116. T: Was that when you had a new baby
117. C: Yes
118. Paul: and m – then me dad was poorly he had to go to hospital (as well) because he couldn't e:at <u>well</u>

and then – / /
119. C: / / ( )
120. ? / / ( ) Aunty ( )
121. Paul: do you know what happened when I came downstairs
– – – well hehh something really funny – – came
downstairs – I turned round me head and then I
turned round – and me aunty ((laughs and talks))
me aunty stuffed me head in the ice cre:::am
((rising crescendo of laughter by Paul through last
part of his utterance))
122. T: / / uhhh
123. Paul: hehhh and then I went outside to play and came back
in – an went to bed and no-one was in the 'ouse =
((one child is laughing throughout the utterance))
124. T: = and-that's-when-you-felt-lonely what about you
Kevin
125. Kevin: (Well) One day when I when I was at Huyton ((one
child is laughing through his utterance)) I went out
and I had my flippers and my snorkle and my goggles
in my bag and there was a river so so I get them (on)
/ / then I went in the river
((school bell rings))
(0.5)
126. T: You did
127. Kevin: (N) – I was lonely
128. T: Were you – well does anybody know – – of
anybody that lives on their own perhaps.
129. CC: ( )
130. T: Yes Colin
131. Colin: Me Grandma did –
him and grandma, me mum and grandad did –
132. C: (quiet)
and grandad did
133. T: often old people – live on their own and at Christmas
time – it's a nice time for families to be together isn't
it – – we all like to see our relations and aunties and
uncles and all like to be together at Christmas time –
and sometimes old people that live on their own
perhaps th – they haven't got any children – and
they haven't got anybody to visit at Christmas – and
they feel very very lonely – just like the little donkey

– and they'd often wish for a visit – from somebody – what do you think you could do if you knew somebody that was lonely / / uh yes Melanie.

134. Melanie: Um um my (n-nan ( ) Um is lonely and we go to ( ) in ( ) every Saturday and sometimes um I ask them if I can stay and one day I stayed for a whole week / / and and a weekend.
135. C: / / (ooh)
136. T: Well that's nice isn't it ( ) I live next door to a very old man he's eighty-six – and he lives on his own – and sometimes his – children come to visit him and his – grand-children and even his great grandchildren – but he's rather lonely – so do you know what my little boy does – – whenever we're doing any baking or making anything nice to eat
137. C: He gives him he he g- g- ( ) wh / / a cake
138. T: / / think
139. T: Yes we go round n my little boy goes to visit Mr B x x – Mr B x x likes to see him – doesn't go round too much in case he feels tired – usually after three thirty – because old people often like to rest as well – – he goes and takes him a cake or something to eat.
140. Paul: uh
141. T: Yes Paul
142. Paul: Old people old people can get co:old by their doors sometimes when the doors ( ) open but once I – when someone was lonely and never had a house I I let them come in my house and stay and when they were very hungry – – / /
143. ? ( )
144. Paul: that time when she came in the house I gave her loads of Chris– we had a nice time and at Christmas time do you know what I gave him
145. T: What
146. C: A dolly and a (/ /)
147. Paul: Wh / / I gave him/ /
148. C: ( )
149. Paul: Uh – – – – and me mum and the family/ /
150. ? hehh
151. Paul: uh uh

and me dad built me dad built a nice nice nice
wh– – – – / / /what is it)
152. C: shed
153. Paul: bungalow and he built built him one there and he he sticked in the sides of the door in case these tiny bits opening
154. T: Yes ( )
155. C: Uhm one day when we were uh when uh we just been in the bookshop we went to find a toilet and on the way we saw a man lying on the floor
156. T: Oh (/ /)
157. C: and th– uh outside the – shop and an ambulance came to take him and we put a a jacket over him – ( ) him / / to hospital
158. CC: uhhhhh
159. T: Perhaps he he was very ill wasn't he
160. C; Just lying on the floor in / / the cold
161. C:) Yes
)
162. C:) Mmmmm
163. T: Yes Colin
164. Colin: My mum will be lonely in the shop now
165. T: She'll be lonely in the shop
166. Colin: Yes uhm cos sh– no help uhm ( ) me friend grandma's friend comes in this afternoon so she'll be lonely this morning with uh she ca– ( ) (a lot of fuss) ( )
167. T: Well the thing about a shop is that you can <u>never</u> really be <u>too</u> lonely in a shop because – people often come in to buy things don't they and so – if your mummy's working in a shop she can have a chat with customers when they come in – but I think it's a nice thing to remember <u>old</u> people at Christmas time
((child coughs))
168. T: And perhaps – you can ask your mummy or your daddy – if you can go round and visit them if you know they're on their own and if they're lonely it's a good idea to ask somebody first
169. C_1: I got uh somebody at Trafford (Edge) called Aunty Betty / /
170. T: Yes

171. C_1: She's on her own and I – go and wh – visit her sometimes and st:ay
172. T: Do you oh that's nice
173. C_1: And she gives me some cake
174. C: ( )
175. T: Does she
176. C: Uhhhhh
177. C: (Well she)
178. C_1: And Timmy ( )
179. T: And Timmy as well yes
180. Paul: Well we been to the shops but w– we were going to go home get on the bus and we just saw someone ly:ing in the pavement ( ) know I know what will happen he's drunk
181. T: I see
182. Paul: Well and then my dad came across the road to see what it was he thought it was a – Guy Fawk or something
183. C: hehh
184. Paul: Like that and and he looked worried and so we took him on the bus – we took him on the bus lying on the chairs and people st– people tried to sit him standing but we tried to get them we we said you can't because he's – poorly so when we went home yu know what happened!
185. T: What ( )
186. Paul: My mum was looking for the cake when someone was sit sitting down on it ((another child laughs))
187. T: I see
188. Paul: And you know what happened – we said you're sitting down on it and d'you know when she g– when she came up she turned out and she couldn't help it she just fell away down in the sticking in the cake on the head

((several children laugh))

189. Paul: And and th (hhh) en she had to have a wash and you know the man woke up he he roared because he didn't know where he was – – and we we we //
190. ? ( )

191. Paul: asked him where his home was – and we – and we were trying to help him cos he couldn't go out all the time and buy – food because cos you get too much wind really for old people

192. T: Well what about Marianne do you know anybody that's alone

193. Marianne: (   )

194. T: (   ) a lady

195. C: ((softly – whispers))

196. T: No no it's alright just leave that there that's it ((something bangs on table))

197. C: Owww

198. T: Yes – Wendy

((several children laugh))

199. Wendy: I got whm – wh my mum goes every Sunday to see whm a man called wh – –

((several children laugh))

200. Wendy: Uncle Harry and he – his wh wife just whm died before – – but he's still got a pussy cat

((several children laugh extendedly))

201. T: Well that's nearly the end of our story time about the little donkey – the lonely little donkey – and perhaps you might think about people you know that are lonely – and hm and help them out sometime – will you do

202. C:) Yes
)

203. C:) Yes
)

204. C:) Yes

205. C: You know

206. T: Yes Paul

207. Paul: Some people some people might get dressed up at – and they might be big bad men (   ) and try to take you away =

208. C: = Yes
209. Paul: So so you'll have to ask your mummy first / / really
210. T: Yes yes I did say it was a good idea even if it was a neighbour – even if the man next door to where I live often my little boy Daniel likes to go round and see him – sometimes he wants to go round when I think that Mr B x x would like a rest and it's a good idea if – even if it's a neighbour and especially if it's someone you don't know to ask your mummy or your daddy – first of all (isn't / / it)
211. C: (   )

((child coughs))

((tape-recorder is switched off))

As may be widely known, it is a common practice in infant schools to conclude the school day with a story read or told by the teacher, followed usually by some teacher-pupil talk about the story or related matters. Occasionally, the story is preceded by some story-related activity which may be characterisable as an introduction to the story. In these respects, our materials are 'typical'. Their particular interest for us is in the nature of the post-story talk. It appears that the teacher is attempting to continue story time by encouraging the children themselves to produce stories, in that they are asked to tell about themselves and what they have been doing with respect to certain matters of concern to the teacher (loneliness and helping the lonely).

For the purposes of analysis, it is helpful to characterise the talk in transcription ST 2 as having a number of stages. Later on, in Section V, we shall show in our discussion of the 'classroom agenda' that it is more than an analysts' device in that the parties to the talk may themselves use such notions as a resource for helping both to constitute and to bring off the classroom agenda. The stages that we shall refer to are:

Stage 1: Story introduction.
Stage 2: The teacher tells a story about a lonely donkey.
Stage 3: The teacher makes opportunities for children's stories by asking 'Have you ever felt lonely . . .' (utterance 79) immediately on completing the story about the lonely donkey. Thereafter, seven children can be heard to respond

to the teacher's request.

Stage 4: The teacher then asks 'does anybody know – – of anybody that lives on their own' (utterance 128); asks 'what do you think you could do if you knew somebody that was lonely' (utterance 133, part); and then goes on to tell a story about what she and her son, Daniel, do in fact do (utterances 136 and 139). One pupil, Paul, then appears to volunteer a story, which is the first of a number produced by the children in this stage.

We recognise that this particular characterisation of the materials can give rise to a number of further observations and a variety of further issues. To begin with, some aspects of the children's stories might appear to document our knowledge that they are 'only six-year-olds'. At times, the stories in the third stage seem to have little or no relevance to 'having felt lonely' and, on almost every occasion during this stage, the teacher has to produce utterances which seem to generate relevance for the preceding child's contribution. We could, in other words, consider the relative incompetence of young children in producing 'well-formed' and 'appropriate' stories. Secondly, we could argue that the materials represent an instance of 'poor teaching', of misguided assumptions about the abilities of six-year-old children. We could, in short, point to teacher incompetence as an issue for argument and analysis. Thirdly, we could use the materials to argue a case for the sort of basic interpretive procedures the children 'must' be using to generate the utterances that they produce and this would involve contrasting this basis of competence with the previous argument about competence in story telling (Mackay, 1974). A further possible issue we should mention is to look at the structure of the talk to see what it reveals in terms of 'power differentials' between teacher and pupils. Classroom talk has received considerable attention from researchers who find such talk as fundamentally displaying authority relationships. Sequencing analysis and an analysis of how identities are formulated (Payne, 1976, provides some interesting classroom examples) can readily be brought to bear to show how social structure is, in this respect, simultaneously expressed, constituted and maintained through the talk (Edwards, in this volume, makes a useful survey and a particular contribution to this approach).

Our initial characterisation of the materials might seem to make any one of these approaches viable as a starting-point and we would not wish to deny their viability. In fact, several of these issues will eventually be touched on.

Our particular starting-point, however, is the observation that story telling appears to be taking place, and our interest in drawing attention to those crudely observable features of the transcription characterised as Stages 1-4 is as follows: they appear, *prima facie*, to display an organisation of talk on which there has been interesting and illuminating sociological research. This research has been produced mainly by the late Harvey Sacks and concerns the ways by which 'stories' are interactionally produced in settings of 'natural conversation'.

I

In the broadest terms, Sacks was concerned to explicate the methods and practices members of society have for collaboratively and interactionally achieving any particular occasion or setting – e.g. a conversation about X, a debate about Y, a radio programme on Z. He pursued this study of members' 'sense assembly procedures' mainly by examining transcriptions of talk in 'natural' settings (i.e. settings which are not a product of contrivance, experimentation, etc., but are, rather, routine and everyday activities of members of society). From his very large output of analyses and findings about the organisation of talk (Sacks, 1964-72), our particular interest here is some of what he had to say about 'stories'.

For Sacks, 'stories' in natural conversation are not located by using a definition as a search procedure, but rather they are analytically describable in terms of their functions in talk. Thus, in multi-party talk, a speaker may wish to talk extendedly about something he has done, heard, knows, etc. In order to do so, he requires to secure both the co-operation and the attention of the other parties to the talk so that he can hold the conversational floor without interruption or subversion of his intentions until he has finished what he has to say. In fact, this question of completion points and speaker change is vital not only for stories, but also for much wider considerations of turn allocation in the organisation of talk (Sacks, 1974). Here, we can focus only on those stretches of talk which both member and analyst alike can recognise as 'stories' (or, at least, 'candidate stories') and Sacks (1970) suggested that they have an interactional structure, which we schematise as follows:

(a) Story Preface (Request) e.g. A Something terrible

			happened on the way here.
(b)	Acceptance	e.g.	B Oh dear, what?
(c)	Story	e.g.	A ((A tells what happened))
(d)	Hearing/Second Story	e.g.	B Oh, that's terrible. ((and B may go on to tell a 'similar' story))

To clarify, the story preface (a) seeks permission to talk about something that happened, i.e. a story, over what may well be an extensive piece of talk. It also indicates what sort of a story it will be and what an appropriate completion point might look like – e.g. when hearers can find something terrible has happened. It therefore also indicates what an appropriate hearing will look like. If the request embodied in the story preface is accepted (and not declined, diverted, put off with, for example, 'Never mind, have you heard the latest Test score?'), then A can embark on his story. Although others may properly speak in the course of the story (e.g. to produce 'continuers' like 'hmmm', 'yes', 'I see', etc., or 'clarifiers' like 'he did what', 'pardon', etc.), such interventions need not come off as 'interruptions' or 'subversions' to the extent that hearers honour the story acceptance (b) and the conversational floor is returned to the story teller to continue his story. Finally, hearers are interactionally required to monitor the story in order to take up the talk when its completion is reached, i.e. to discover an appropriate completion and speaker transition point and, as we have noted, the materials of the story preface can provide a useful resource for this purpose. In addition, there are conventional syntactic and prosodic devices which can provide clues about the imminence of an ending. A typical example can be found in the way the story about the lonely donkey is completed in our materials (see line 77), although it should be noted that we have not attempted to produce a transcription which fully represents the relevant intonational contours.

Taking up the talk at an appropriate place and repeating the materials of the story preface might do more than indicate that hearers have been monitoring the story sufficiently only to recognise a possible completion point. A way of doing the interactional work of displaying rather than asserting that close attention has been paid is for hearers to continue the talk by producing further stories which build off the one they have just heard. Sacks called these further stories 'second stories' and adduced several reasons for their strong interactional relationships. 'First stories' can be found to provide basic resources for the production of 'second stories'. Not only do they appear to occasion and organise the memories of hearers for the production of 'second stories' which are then-and-there appropriate, they also provide structural models for them. For example, the relation of tellers to events and activities in 'second stories' tends to resemble that initially presented in the 'first story'. Consequently, a party to the talk can strongly display his close attention to and understanding of the 'first story' through his construction of a 'second story'. Moreover, a 'first story' often generates a 'round' of stories in multi-party conversation, and the stories in the round or clump which has been touched off by the 'first story' have in common these topical and structural similarities.

At this point, we would like briefly to draw attention to two problematic issues which have been raised in the exposition of Sacks's work and which we will take up later in some detail. The first is the interactional accomplishment of a story completion, since unit-types such as a sentential construction cannot on their own provide a basis for recognition of a possible completion point and a potential for speaker change. The second is that the recognition of a story completion by the hearer, where it is displayed by taking up the floor at an appropriate point, does display monitoring of the story, but does not strongly demonstrate close attention and understanding on the part of hearers.

II

As we have suggested, the materials for transcription ST 2 appear, *prima facie*, to reflect some of these analytical features of stories, particularly with reference to the possibility that there are two rounds of stories (i.e. Stages 3 and 4) and with reference to the topical coherence (loneliness and helping, respectively) and structural similarity (the relationship of each teller to these activities) within each round of stories. More than a cursory inspection, however, reveals major differences from, as well as similarities to, Sacks's analysis of the generation and functioning of stories in natural conversation. In fact, these differences could appear so striking as to deny the relevance or usefulness of this analysis to these materials.

One obvious basis for differences can be seen to be generated by the orientation of the parties to the setting which they are constituting in, by and through their talk. This setting, which might be classed as story-time-in-an-infants-classroom, is one in which we will suggest that some or all of the parties are aware of and orient to the fact that there is an 'agenda' to be got through (i.e. a story to be told and all that that entails for these parties on such occasions), a specified time in which to do the agenda (i.e. the time before going home), and the knowledge that there is someone assigned to steer and control this agenda (i.e. the teacher).

Later on, we shall take further this matter of the occasioned nature, the 'settingedness', of the talk (Garfinkel, 1967). We shall also explore the significance of the fact that the parties to the talk comprise one adult and a number of young six- to seven-year-old children, with some reference to the question of 'competence' at talk production. For the present, however, we wish to refer to the occasioned nature of the talk, to draw out some of its grossly observable features: overwhelmingly, the talk is so partitioned that alternate slots are occupied by teacher and pupil, respectively. Furthermore, next-speaker is usually, although not invariably, selected by the teacher. There are no examples in the transcription of publicly available, i.e. 'classroom', talk being conducted between the children. Presumably, talk of the pattern C-C-C, rather than T-C-T, would effectively subvert the classroom agenda and reconstitute the occasion as something other than what the parties consider it is or should be. Features such as these have been noted by several researchers and have received considerable attention (e.g. McHoul, 1978, and Edwards, in this volume).

This particular organisation of multi-party talk (T-C-T, etc.) clearly produces difficulties for analysing story production by attempting a straightforward application of Sacks's analysis. For example, the teacher's long story about the lonely donkey does not produce from the pupils any volunteering of 'second stories'. Nor does the teacher appear to expect her story to have this effect, for she goes on immediately to ask (in utterance 79), 'Have you ever felt lonely have you ever felt lonely', and, then, after a chorus of apparently affirmative responses, the talk continues with what appears to be a different organisation for the production of stories, i.e.

(a)	Story Invitation	82.	T:	When did you feel lonely Colin.
(b)	Story/Acceptance	83.	C:	Uhm – – – – we went out one day . . .
		85.		. . . and I stayed in the tent.
(c)	Story Closing/ Hearing	86.	T:	You stayed in the tent on your own – and then you felt lonely.

(d) Story Invitation 88. T: Yes (Sarah) when did you feel lonely.

This pattern appears to persist through a round of stories in which the children respond to the invitation to tell about when they felt lonely.

We can contrast this pattern with the one we adduced earlier from Sacks's work:

Pattern (i)

Speaker

A (a) Story Preface/Request
B (b) Acceptance
A (c) Story
B (d) Hearing/Second Story

Pattern (ii)

Speaker

A (a) Story Invitation/Request
B (b) Story/Acceptance
A (c) Story Closing/Hearing
B (d) Story Invitation (to C)

Here we note that pattern (ii) is itself preceded by an exchange which establishes a pool of children who have identified themselves as 'having felt lonely' and presumably, therefore, as potential story tellers regarding that experience.

Pattern (ii) seems to exemplify a class of stories found in natural conversation, which can be termed 'invited stories' (Cuff and Francis, 1978). This research analyses the talk of persons invited to tell the story of their marriage breakdown. Their 'invited stories' differ from 'volunteered' stories not only in terms of turn-organisation and functions as indicated by patterns (i) and (ii), but also in terms of some important interactional features. First, the teller (or, rather, invited or candidate teller) may not be as ready, willing or able to produce a story at the request of the inviter in the same manner and with the same ease as someone who has remembered a story and who deems it to be appropriate at that place in the talk. Second, the teller of an invited story is required adequately to fulfil the terms of the inviter's request. There may be difficulties in knowing exactly what these terms are and how they might be achieved and when 'enough' has been said/produced. Thus the teller might offer only a candidate closing, and the onus of finding it to be adequate might be oriented to, as properly being the responsibility of the inviter. Thus a proffered closing might have only candidate status in so far as the inviter can seek to extend the story by asking for more detail, clarification, etc. Although such interactional work can and does occur in 'volunteered' stories, it can be more fraught with interactional perils or troubles, in that such probings might more readily come off as impugning, subverting, undercutting both the teller's story and his character. As we have indicated, such interactional troubles can be avoided by demonstrating both understanding and agreement or sympathy by means of an appropriate second story. This member's method might not be available for an inviter who is seeking to generate a round of invited stories.

III

Again, it will be readily apparent that this analysis of features of invited stories might still not provide sufficient analytic machinery to provide for the stories in our materials. Whereas the inviter of the stories about marriage breakdown knew beforehand that her interlocutors did, in fact, have those stories to tell, in our materials the teacher cannot be confident that her pupils have available a story about feeling lonely. As we have noted, however, her question, 'have you ever felt lonely have you ever felt lonely', serves to produce a number of affirmative responses from the pupils which can be used to indicate the availability of a pool of candidate and 'voluntary' story tellers about this experience. Secondly, the brevity of most of the children's responses to the invitation might indicate that they resemble something like 'answering a question' rather than 'telling a story'. Of course, such a characterisation cannot be ruled out as 'incorrect'; but it involves a different analytical purchase on the materials, and one to which our hearing does not lead us. This hearing must rest, in part, on what the child produced, but we note that a 'story' does not simply consist of what the child produced. Rather, in terms of describing the organisation of talk, a 'story' comprises the tied and sequential utterances of inviter-teller-inviter, as outlined in pattern (ii); and this pattern can itself be taken as a 'natural unit' of talk. Its shape – the fact that it has a beginning, a middle and an end – is manifestly generated by the interactional collaboration of the parties involved. It is a unit of talk which demarcates who can properly talk and who should properly await a suitable completion point before gaining the right to hold the conversational floor. Furthermore, as we have noted earlier, not only does the organisation of a 'story' organise as a unit a number of turns, including opportunities to talk extendedly, but it can itself be seen to be incorporated into an even wider organisation of talk, namely, a 'round' of stories. Research has shown that the availability of a 'round' in talk – an organisation that has to be interactionally achieved by the parties to the talk – affords the parties further resources for both anticipating and producing orderliness concerning speakers and speaker change (Sacks, 1970; Atkinson, Cuff and Lee, 1978).

Clearly, several of these sequential features are to be found in interactions which are heard differently – for example, as rounds of question-answer sequences. However, we naturally have no interest in whether these materials are stories in any definitive sense, or in attempting to exhaust the bases for our own hearing of the materials as stories. This hearing merely provides us with one particular analytical purchase, and any warrant for that starting-point lies in what the analysis can yield. For example, we consider the ways in which particular utterances may be sensitive to problematic analytical issues, such as achieving a completion in story telling, and demonstrating understanding of a story, whilst maintaining and serving to constitute not just a round, but a round of 'invited stories'.

Thirdly, the candidate nature of the children's stories in Stage 3 might be read from the fact that, of the seven contributions, only one story, the seventh, appears to be clearly oriented to producing what can be heard as a possible closing of the story (i.e. 127. Kevin: (N) – I was lonely). In the other stories, regardless of their length and complexity (*vide* Paul's story, utterances 109-124 *passim*), the teacher can be taken effectively to produce a closing in terms of both providing a topical, relevant ending and also of effecting a change in speakers by means of reiterating the substance of her initial story invitation and by nominating next-speaker, i.e.

86/88.	Colin's story	. . . and then you felt lonely . . . Yes (Sarah) when did you feel lonely
90/92.	Sarah's story	and you felt lonely on your own . . . What about you Wendy
104.	Wendy's story	and you felt lonely – – Yes Melanie
109.	Melanie's story	Oh I see – – what about you Richard have you ever been lost or felt lonely – – – – never what about you Paul

124.	Paul's story	and-that's-when-you-felt-lonely what about you Kevin

In this way, the teacher provides what can be taken as a story ending/ closing and thereby displays her hearing of what has been said by the children as something which has appropriately met the terms of her invitation/request. An apparent exception in this round is her reply to Melanie which might indicate her inability (as well, possibly, as readers' inability) to follow this story and to find in it anything which can be heard to proffer a story about being lonely, although it should be noted for future reference that the teacher could be seen to be accepting Melanie's production as at least a 'story'.

There are some further features of the utterances closing off each story which are of interest. With the exception of the talk to Melanie, the teacher's closings partake of some of the conventional linguistic features of story endings, although appropriately transformed (e.g. I → you). In addition, however, they can be viewed as particularly sensitive to their location within an invited story format. For such utterances appear to display an orientation to this format in serving, by their very production, to help to constitute and maintain this format. We noted earlier that a potentially problematic issue in story telling is in achieving a completion, and that completions to invited stories present different interactional requirements from completions to volunteered stories. As completions, utterances like 'and then you felt lonely' are continuations of the talk in two senses: first, as linguistic constructions; second, as developments in a chain of events. In these ways, they would appear to be particularly economical devices which build on previous talk in such a way as to recognise such talk as leading to a proper possible completion and also themselves to constitute a completion to an invited story.

There is a further facet to these utterances as economic devices which is of interest. As continuations to a chain of events, they display monitoring and understanding of the previous talk. To a certain extent, it can be argued that such utterances do more than claim an understanding (as in 'Oh I see'), but go on actually to demonstrate some understanding by their use of the previous materials (as in 86: 'You stayed in the tent on your own – and then you felt lonely'). We noted earlier that a major member's method of demonstrating understanding is to produce a 'second story'. To do so, however, might lead the parties to the talk to constitute the occasion not only as other than a round of invited stories, but might also generate problems of 'agenda control', 'topic control' or even 'class control' for the teacher. Later, we will illustrate these points when we briefly address ourselves to the organisation of Stage 4 of the talk. In Stage 4, it appears that the ways in which the round of stories is generated resemble pattern (i) *as well as* pattern (ii); that the teacher aborts her own attempt to set up a new round of invited stories (128: 'Were you – well does anyone know – – of anybody that lives on their own perhaps') by producing an extended utterance (136 and 139) which can be heard as a 'first story' about how she and her son, Daniel, help the man next door; that Paul thereupon volunteers what can be heard as a 'second story'; that further 'second stories' are produced; and that at least one child, Paul, can be seen to be orienting to a different organisation of talk in so far as he volunteers a further extensive story in this stretch of talk.

To return, however, to our detailed consideration of the round of invited stories in Stage 3, we are drawing attention to the economical features of teacher-initiated utterances which can serve not only to conclude a particular story, but also to help signal the imminence of a next story in a continuing round of stories. Thus utterances like 'and-that's-when-you-felt-lonely what about you Kevin' (124) can simultaneously discharge these functions, show understanding and continue to constitute the occasion as a 'round of invited stories about loneliness'.

Although we note the economical nature of these productions, the basic format of which is 'and then you felt lonely' plus nomination of next-speaker, we must also draw attention to the fact that the teacher usually provides even more materials for the production of the stories. For example, Colin's offer of a candidate closing (85: 'and I stayed in the tent') is incorporated and extended in the teacher's closing and recycling to a new speaker (86: 'You stayed in the tent on your own – and then you felt lonely'). Here it appears that staying in a tent is not of relevance until it is made explicit that being on one's own is involved. Thus 'and then you felt lonely' serves as a continuation/completion to Colin's-story-as-developed-by-the-teacher. In short, the 'previous talk' which is being brought to a completion and for which understanding is being displayed is, in part, the teacher's talk.

Considerations such as these lead us to suggest that at least the first six of the stories in Stage 3 can be seen to display, as an integral aspect of their production, the feature that they are joint productions in a very strong sense. Although, clearly, any story produced in natural conversation might reasonably be described as a joint production, in the sense that it has been collaboratively achieved and also generates resources for subsequent talk (as described earlier and schematised in patterns (i) and (ii)), these stories accentuate this feature.

One aspect of this feature is that the children might be heard to be producing candidates for continuation and completion by the teacher's anticipated next utterance, i.e.

85.	Colin:	and I stayed in the tent
93.	Wendy:	Well uh – I got lost / / (one day)
123.	Paul:	. . . and no-one was in the 'ouse =
125.	Kevin:	. . . and then I went in the river
		(0.5)

These utterances can provide possible resources for a teacher take-up of the 'and then you were lonely' type, although the teacher does not always take up this option immediately. More obviously, these stories are joint productions in that the teacher does not only provide the invitation which specifies what the story should be about, but she also produces additions to and completions for the stories.

At this point, let us briefly pull together some of the issues addressed so far. On the basis of our observation that story telling seemed to be a major feature in the transcription, we outlined some aspects of what we take to be potentially applicable work on stories: the work of Harvey Sacks. Having noted that Stage 3 of the transcription seemed to have as its distinguishing characteristic (as regards story telling) the presence of a series of invited stories, we then considered some research into this class of stories. The possible relevance of that research in providing for features of Stage 3 was discussed, although it was pointed out that the broader organisation of the talk as a round of invited stories should also be attended to. We have argued that particular utterances produced by teacher and children can be seen to be occasioned by (i) the orientation of participants to these stories as invited stories, and (ii) the orientation to an ongoing round of such stories. In their details, certain utterances provided solutions to potentially problematic matters, given these orientations. In particular, we discussed how such utterances might be precisely attuned collaboratively to achieving completions and demonstrating understandings. Through providing such solutions, participants ongoingly constituted and maintained the occasion as an orderly round of invited stories. An integral feature of this accomplishment is the way that these stories can be seen to have the characteristic of joint production in a strong sense.

It can also, of course, be suggested that potential problems for the teacher of, for example, 'agenda control' and 'topic control' are in part provided with solutions by means of this feature of joint production. One story which amply illustrates the strong sense of joint production which we have been discussing is Wendy's story.

92. T: What about you Wendy
93. Wendy: Well uh – I got lost / / (one day)
94. C: KATHY
95. T: Yes
96. Wendy: and uh – – and – – I can't remember (the rest)
97. T: You got lost did w– were you going shopping
98. Wendy: Uhm – yes I (was with) Mummy ( ) a– a–
no I wasn't going shopping with ( )
and uh she uhm she was in the shop and I went
down and no she wasn't in the shop
99. C: hahhhh
100. Wendy: and I went and looked in the shop and she wasn't
there ( ) and she (caught) up ( )
101. C: hahhhhh
102. T: and did you think for a moment you'd been left
on your own
103. Wendy: Y (hhh) es
104. T: and you felt lonely – – Yes Melanie

Here the teacher undertakes fairly extensive interactional work by way of continuers/questions to assist in the generation of a recognisable story and an appropriate story. Our points concerning joint production might be seen to be extendable into issues of competence. It could be argued that the joint production of this story is not only a consequential feature, given Wendy's 'inadequacies' as a competent story teller. We suggest, however, that such an argument on this point would be premature. Competence in terms of talk production is presumably a situated hearing and accomplishment. Hearings of utterances are, of course, made in terms of their location in the ongoing talk, in the immediate particulars of the sequential organisation of the talk. Hearings are also made, however, in terms of more general orientations to the talk, deriving from the parties' background knowledge and experience concerning what the setting is and should be. In making this point, we are reinvoking the occasioned nature of the talk in our materials; it is talk which does not simply occur 'in' story time, but, in occurring, effectively constitutes story time, for what it is.

IV

The background knowledge and experience of the parties, which we gloss as their 'general orientations', afford them valuable resources for generating appropriate talk and activities which can occasion the here and now of this particular setting. Consequently, we turn to a consideration of the parties' common-sense knowledge of what is involved in story time and how such knowledge can provide a resource for making sense of particular utterances and activities.

First, the parties know that what they are doing is 'story time' and characterise the activity in this way. It is a scheduled occasion in the school day and is signalled by means of such utterances as

8. T:	Anyway – it's time for your story now . . .

and

10. T:	. . . the story I'm going to tell you today is about . . .

In our materials, we do not find the children responding to such utterances in ways which suggest surprise; we find no utterances by the children which indicate that what is happening is anything other than routine. Part of this routine is knowledge that story time is commonly scheduled at the end of the school day and is therefore a non-extendable activity. Of relevance here is the following teacher's utterance which occurs towards the end of the transcription:

201. T:	Well that's nearly the end of our story time about the little donkey – the lonely little donkey – and perhaps you might think about people . . .

This talk appears to have at least two functions: it marks the coming to an end of story time; and it emphasises in retrospect what is projected as a central theme of the occasion (i.e. being lonely). It also draws attention to another and second feature of story time to which the parties possibly orient as a matter of routine everyday knowledge

– in addition to their orientations to the temporal scheduling and location of story time. This feature consists of the knowledge that story time is more than the telling of a story by the teacher; it often involves the children in more activities than listening and displaying their monitoring of the teacher's talk; and it involves the teacher in doing more than telling a story and doing an occasional check on the children's monitoring. The teacher's utterance (201) seems explicitly to encapsulate this feature, since her telling of the story about the lonely donkey finished some considerable interactional time previously, but she is only now drawing 'story time' to a close.

More implicitly, we also draw attention to the ease with which the parties to the talk accomplish transitions between the various stages or episodes of story time as a further means of documenting the 'oriented to' nature of story time and the various activities and temporal scheduling it entails.

Thirdly, we suggest that a further 'oriented to' feature of story time derives from the background knowledge that it is not only a temporally scheduled and temporally delimited occasion, and an occasion for doing more than monitoring the teacher's story, but also that it is an occasion with an 'agenda' (Anderson, 1979). Routinely, the 'agenda' is made up of a story introduced and then told by the teacher, and also it is made up by some post-story work. By the use of the term, 'agenda', clearly we do not intend to indicate that story times are pre-planned or predictable to any degree of specificity of details over their entire course. We do not even suggest that the teacher has planned or prepared what will occur in post-story work. After all, the whole time might be taken up with the story, the bell may go before it has been finished, given the routine possibility of delays, disruptions and the like which can occur in the infant classroom. What we do intend the term 'agenda' to mean, as regards what participants standardly know, is that there are recurrent formal features of story time which make up an 'agenda' in terms of what might routinely, typically, standardly be expected to occur.

Fourthly, it is a part of the parties' background knowledge that not only is there temporal scheduling of story time and a range of possible activities, an 'agenda', but they also know that there is someone, the teacher, who is assigned responsibility for attending to and taking the initiative on these matters. Of course, such knowledge is no more than a commonly available resource for interaction; it does not, and cannot, *per se*, prescribe what particular exchanges and activites will, in fact, occur. Activities, agenda, responsibility have all to be achieved in the then-and-there of that particular occasion; the occasion has to be brought off in, by and through the talk in a localised (utterance-by-utterance) manner; it is not produced by automatons, robots and the like. Thus, background knowledge that the teacher is 'oriented to' as responsible for the schedule and the agenda does not indicate 'classroom consensus', automatic co-operation and an absence of interactional troubles. Rather, it provides a resource which can be used for either avoiding or creating troubles, but, whatever the outcome, it is the product of the situated interactional work of the parties to the talk.

V

The discussion of background knowledge leads us into making an important methodological point which is germane to any scrutiny of our materials in terms of the imputed competence of the parties to the talk. It will have been noted that we have studiously avoided referring to transcription ST 2 as 'the data', preferring to refer to it as the 'materials'. The reason for this apparent circumlocution is simply that the transcription does not 'speak for itself'. In order to make sense of any particular utterance, not only do we have to utilise sequencing considerations, but also we have to trade off our common-sense, background knowledge of how the social world is organised – e.g. the ways of infant schools, the nature of infant-adult relationships, the fact that parents collect their children from school at the end of the school day, etc. Similarly, the parties to the talk in our materials have to use such knowledge to bring off their social world through their talk. In short, 'the data' for analysis consists of common-sense knowledge, and members' methods of organising and deploying such knowledge, which are made available for description and analysis by means of a transcription of a bit of the everyday social world. Here the bit of the social world in which we are interested is the naturally occurring activity of story time in an infant classroom.

In particular, we are addressing the question at this point as to how parties to the talk can display their competence by constructing talk in such a way that it is recognisably a post-story production. We suggest that the teacher does precisely this in her story invitation:

79. T: Have you ever felt lonely have you ever felt lonely

Our hearing, and, we would argue, the parties' hearing, relies on some aspects of what we presume to be known as commonly shared knowledge about story time. Parties know, at least, that post-story work (i) routinely commences with the teacher initiating some activity for the children; and (ii) not only will questions routinely be asked by the teacher at this point, but also these questions will have a strong thematic relationship to the story that has just been told. In turn, it might seem that children can produce talk properly constitutive of post-story time by means, in part, of using as a resource their knowledge that such talk should have strong thematic links with what the teacher has extracted as relevant themes from the story. We would mention, however, that, on these grounds alone, a number of the children's productions might be viewed as somewhat incompetent. In particular, we note, for later return, Paul's story (utterances 111-123).

Apart from thematic considerations, we suggest that the children can routinely draw on their knowledge of post-story time as a place in the talk for telling *their* stories. In other words, the sort of business that follow-up work to *the* story commonly consists of for the children is having to, or having some licence to, produce some stories. Our specific focus earlier was on a characterisation of the immediate post-story talk as a round of invited stories. We argued that, in various ways, teacher and pupils displayed an orientation to an ongoing round of such stories, but considered aspects of the production of these stories with particular reference to their status as invited stories. Here, we further suggest that, through the inviting of and production of these stories, the parties constitute the setting as recognisable post-story work in a story time. Through their talk, the parties constitute the occasion as recognisable to themselves and others as a specific part, a stage, of the life-as-usual agenda to be got through during story time. Our particular focus in no way denies the observation that such talk serves to constitute the occasion as 'life-in-an-infant-classroom', 'teacher-doing-story-time-with her-pupils', etc. Rather, we are trying to focus on and draw out some aspects of the occasioned nature of the talk, namely, that it is story time and, moreover, it is a 'part' of story time.

Utterances 82–86, involving Colin, include what we hear as the basis of a story, in so far as he reports a sequence of events leading to what the teacher is able to recognise as a state of feeling lonely. The fact that Colin produces what he does, at this point, involves him in using as a resource his knowledge about story time to provide a suitable hearing for the teacher's previous utterance.

Wendy's 'Well uh – I got lost / / (one day)' (utterance 93) would appear to be precisely on target in terms of thematic relevance, since being lost is presumably a good basis for the possibility of feeling lonely. It rapidly becomes clear, however, that, for the teacher at least, her utterance is insufficient and, we would argue, its insufficiency lies in its not being recognisable as an 'adequate' story – i.e. it does not give an account, a sequence of events culminating in getting lost, where such an account is interactionally occasioned. In short, it is less than an 'adequate' story in not being even a recognisable story (Sacks, 1972), although it might be adequate elsewhere as a story preface and here as an answer to a question. Its inadequacy, therefore, appears to stem from its inappropriateness as a recognisable story in response to an invitation to tell such a story. Of course, the teacher could continue and complete with 'and you felt lonely' and it is not difficult to imagine circumstances which might warrant such action for herself, e.g. her identification of Wendy as a 'very shy child', as 'someone who has done well to produce even that talk', etc. In fact, in our materials, she goes on to invoke the sort of common-sense knowledge that an adult can employ to find the sort of situation in which a six-year-old child could get lost. In other words, the teacher provides, as a possible prompt, an example of what Wendy is required to do: locate the sequence of events leading to being lost and thus produce a story. The fact that the teacher's 'You got lost did w– were you going shopping' (utterance 97) provides Wendy with problems in her next utterance should not prevent us from noting that in Wendy's utterance, although parts are untranscribable, the pupil is very much in the business of constructing a sequence of events which can be heard to lead to getting lost. Utterance 98 can be contrasted with Wendy's previous talk in utterance 96, 'and uh – – and – – I can't remember (the rest)' in which she might be attempting to build on the story which she has not yet achieved.

Wendy's story can be interestingly contrasted with a later story in this round of invited stories, namely, the one produced by Paul (utterances 111-123). It may be that the materials of Paul's story come off as largely irrelevant *vis-à-vis* the teacher's invitation, whereas, as we have noted, Wendy's first utterance has strong topical coherence. Yet Paul appears to display a recognition that a story is called for and he is also able to maintain the floor by constructing it in terms of an extended sequence of events which can be heard to culminate in a proffered candidate for conclusion and completion. We further note that he is able to embed within this sequence of events a story funny enough to evoke a response from his peers and that this funny story seems to have been touched off by the talk of a previous child about ice-cream. In addition, we can speculate about Paul's interest in maintaining the conversational floor, and his role of 'joker' (see his further story in Stage 4, utterances 180–191), and also about the dual directionality of his talk in that he appears to be addressing two audiences, his peers and the teacher. The central feature of Paul's talk is that he can construct stories, and story time has, as one of its routinely possible occurrences, a time within it for the production of such stories by the children. We suggest that the post-story work for story time is in part constituted as such by the ways in which children are able to construct coherent stories, in the sense that such stories are made up of a recognisable sequence of events. That certain of these stories seem to us as hearers to have minimal bearing on the themes nominated by the teacher may not be a central issue, if competence is viewed in terms of acquiring methods of telling stories rather than the ability to produce an appropriate utterance or story in terms of topic. As noted much earlier, even Melanie's production during Stage 3 would appear to be accepted by the teacher. It would also appear that it is less important for Wendy to tune into the topic as defined by the teacher than to produce something that can be heard as a recognisable story during this stage of story time.

VI

In the round of invited stories, the children's productions are usually recognisable as stories, though in some cases it requires joint production in the strong sense to transform them into appropriate stories. We have noted that, in Stage 3, the organisation of the talk is such as to build in joint production in a strong sense as a central feature. As a consequence, we hear the teacher/inviter as usually able to incorporate the children's productions as not only topically coherent, but also as being on the same topic.

By contrast, in Stage 4, we appear to have a different sort of organisation to the round of stories. Although the production of stories appears to continue as a focal activity, the interactional resources available to teacher and children have changed somewhat, as reflected in this different organisation of talk. This different organisation incorporates features which, we would suggest, in part account for and serve to sustain what we hear as the teacher's problems in maintaining 'topic control' and, possibly, 'class control'. We will briefly focus on one of these features of the talk in Stage 4, in order to provide some basis for this argument. It should be noted that this discussion develops some points made earlier in Section IV.

The teacher's utterance at 139 provides for the possibility of, and receives, what can be regarded as a 'volunteered second story' from Paul. Paul's story is followed by what can be heard as further 'second stories' from other children. In Section II of this paper, we referred to some of the features of 'volunteered' second stories and particularly stressed their potential for demonstrating understandings of a previous story in terms of topical coherence and structural similarities. Topical coherence, however, does not necessarily entail talking about the 'same' topic, and, as a series of stories develops, the parties may be provided with a growing body of materials from which further stories can be built. Thus, in Stage 4 of our materials, we can find some seemingly obvious topical relationships. For example, Paul's starter (142), 'Old people old people can get co:old by their doors . . .', appears to build on an item from what we are taking as the teacher's 'first story', in which she notes that old people may feel tired and like to rest (see utterance 139). Paul's story can be heard eventually to attempt a closing by tying back to 'the door' and old people feeling cold. The very next story can be seen to have been touched off by some of the references in Paul's story, in so far as it concerns someone lying on the floor in the cold (see utterance 160). It is Paul again, however, who can be heard to manipulate a variety of topically coherent items, whilst seeming to provide a story which is unconcerned until the very end with themes expressed by the teacher (see utterances 180–191). To illustrate, we point to his use of 'seeing someone lying on the pavement' (utterance 180) and 'looking for a cake' (utterance 186), which both tie back to previous stories. In addition, this story can be found to be completed in utterance 191 with '. . . you get too much wind really for old people' and, as we already know, old people get tired, get cold, and are clearly a matter of some concern for the teacher. We find it interesting that not only does the teacher accept Paul's candidate closing, but also decides at this point to reinvoke her earlier question, i.e. 'Well what about Marianne do you know anybody that's alone' (utterance 192).

As a very general gloss on Stages 3 and 4, we would argue that, in Stage 3, the invited stories, as joint productions in a strong sense, come off as generally 'on the same topic', whereas, in Stage 4, the stories do not come off in this way, although they are topically coherent in various respects. It can be argued, however, that, in Stage 4, the talk is so organised as to provide more resources for the children to produce 'their own stories' and that these further resources are generated by the children (or Paul, at least, in the first instance) hearing the teacher's previous talk as a 'first story' from which 'second stories' might properly follow (see pattern (i) outlined in Section II).

This more open organisation of talk (pattern (i)) may be valued by the teacher if she is concerned with the generation of recognisable stories rather than with tighter topic control. Certainly, teacher and pupils collaborate in the production of this stage of story time and appear to have no problems in recognising what they are doing to be a proper part of post-story (i.e. post-*the* story) work.

Thus, regarding our earlier reference to the possible issue of competence at talk production which might be seen to be raised by a scrutiny of our materials, it should be clear that, in some respects at least, a proper consideration of this issue requires consideration of the occasioned nature of talk. Such consideration is required to focus on the localised sequential organisation and structures of talk and, also, on how such talk shapes and is shaped by what the parties commonsensically know about the routine activities of their everyday world (such as 'story time'). Our focus in this paper, in terms of illustrative analyses, has been on some features of these structures of talk and on the ways in which they organise and are organised by commonsense knowledge of the social world.

Transcription Conventions

//	talk overlapped at this point by next utterance
wh–	word started but not completed
yes-I-know	words run together quickly
– –	untimed pause, duration shown by number of – –
(1.0)	timed pause (of one second)
=	next utterance starts immediately
( )	something said but not transcribable; amount indicated by length of bracket
(yes I know)	transcriber thinks 'yes I know' was said
((laughter))	description not transcription
<u>yes</u>	underlining indicates emphasis

YES	capitals indicate loud volume
:	indicates prolongation of syllable
(hh)	indicates aspiration – usually laughing sound in a word
x x	syllables in a name – omitted for anonymity
T	teacher
C	unidentified child
CC	unidentified children speaking together

Figures in margin indicate utterance number.
Entries in top left hand margin are tape codes (here 'ST 2').

References

Anderson, D.C. (1979). 'The Formal Basis for a Contextually Sensitive Classroom Agenda'. *Instructional Science*, January

Atkinson, M.A., Cuff, E.C. and Lee, J.R.E. (1978). 'The Recommencement of a Meeting as a Member's Accomplishment'. In J. Schenkein (ed.), *Studies in the Organisation of Conversational Interaction*

Cuff, E.C. and Francis D.W. (1978). 'Some Features of "Invited Stories" about Marriage Breakdown'. *International Journal of the Sociology of Language*, 18, pp. 111-33

Garfinkel, H. (1967). *Studies in Ethnomethodology*. New York: Prentice-Hall

McHoul, A. (1978). 'The Organization of Turns at Formal Talk in the Classroom'. *Language in Society*, 7, pp. 183-213

Mackay, R.W. (1974). 'Conceptions of Children and Models of Socialization'. In R. Turner (ed.), *Ethnomethodology*

Payne, G. (1976). 'Making a Lesson Happen: An Ethnomethodological Analysis'. In M. Hammersley and P.E. Woods (eds.), *The Process of Schooling*. London: RKP and Open University

Sacks, H. (1964-72). Unpublished Lecture Notes. Mimeo. University of California, Los Angeles and Irvine

— (1970). 'Aspects of the Sequential Organization of Conversation'. Unpublished MS

— (1974). 'On the Analysability of Stories by Children'. In R. Turner (ed.), *Ethnomethodology*

—, Schegloff, E.A. and Jefferson, G. (1978). 'A Simplest Systematics for the Organisation of Turn-Taking for Conversation'. In J. Schenkein (ed.), *Studies in the Organization of Conversational Interaction*

Schenkein, J. (ed.) (1978). *Studies in the Organization of Conversational Interaction*. New York: Academic Press

Turner, R. (ed.) (1974). *Ethnomethodology*. Harmondsworth: Penguin

8 CHILDREN'S USE OF ADDRESS TERMS

A.J. Wootton[1]

Within the sociolinguistic literature on address terms the focus has been on disclosing those features that are systematically associated with the application of a particular term from the set of possible terms. Much less attention has been paid to the precise placement of these terms in ongoing dialogue, a matter that is of some interest given that they are clearly not used in all talking turns, and that their attachment to an utterance does not appear radically to alter the meaning of the utterance. There is an assumption that the use of such terms is especially prevalent within certain types of speech sequence, like greetings,[2] but even a casual inspection of transcripts reveals their occurrence within a wide range of sequence types, and that suggests that the work that is done through the use of such terms may be characterisable in some way or ways which are non-sequence-type specific. In the child language literature such a characterisation often appears to be presumed. Shatz and Gelman (1973), for example, take it that the use of a recipient's name by a four-year-old functions as an 'attention getter' and then go on to compare the extent to which the use of this device, and others, is associated with the age of the recipient relative to the speaker and the kind of situation interactants are engaged in.[3] Rather than make such a presumption, this article seeks to clarify, from the way in which they are used, the job of work that is done through the use of such terms by young children.

In the usage that I have examined[4] of four-year-old children to their parents, the address terms 'mummy' and 'daddy', or dialect equivalents (e.g. 'da') or abbreviations of these terms (e.g. 'mum'), are those overwhelmingly used. These forms are characteristically, though not exclusively, employed in three positions; first, as a summons (see p. 155 for transcription conventions):

(1) Wa:M:19

→	C:	Mummy
		(1.3)
	M:	Fit
	C:	I want (somethin)

secondly, in utterance initial position:

(2) Ta:E:40
→ C: Mam ↑tel 'im ↓t'<u>go::</u> [(away)
M: [Leslie
get through oot the hoose till I get you washed
(6.7)
→ C: ↑Ma (•) how is he gettin on tha one

thirdly, in final utterance position:

(3) To:M:84
((fantasy play with dolls))
→ C: A::w he's forgotten his boots mummy:
M: Oh: dear
C: ( )
(1.5)
C: He'll get so co:old

On sequential grounds, among others, the summons class can be kept distinct as they constitute the initial turn of a three-turn sequence. The initial summons sets up an expectation for a particular type of next turn, not just an answer but an answer designed to inform first speaker that he should go ahead and say what he had to say. So, if the answer is done with 'yes' or 'mm', it is characteristically in question intonation, though often the answer is in the form of a question, e.g. 'what' (in (1) it is the dialect equivalent 'Fit'). This displays both an expectation that the summoner will talk again, and a preparedness to monitor his talk. These and other properties of summons-answer sequences have been examined by Schegloff (1968) and will not be touched on further here. In these sequences, however, the use of the address term, where such a term is used as a summons, is treated by potential recipients as a check on their availability for talk; 'attention' is not presumed simply by virtue of the summons item being delivered; in fact, the absence of an initial answer is generally taken to imply that the potential recipient is either unwilling or unavailable to engage in talk.

The initial focus of this paper will be on final position address terms, cases like (3). For various reasons, the 'attention getting' characterisation fits this class least easily. As they are final position items, they appear to assume that the recipient has monitored, and in this sense given attention to, the words occurring before. Furthermore, they can be used in this position where no other person than the recipient is present, so they cannot exclusively be next-speaker selection techniques, even though we may want to allow for the possibility that, in some circumstances, that may be an interactional problem for which they are a solution.[5] My argument will be that, in this position, address terms function as solicit mechanisms, and that, by virtue of this, they have a particular affinity with objects like question tags.

The first kind of evidence for this is loosely consistent with the argument rather than compelling. It is that, where children produce utterances which have an appended address term, but which are not adjacency pair first parts,[6] an on-topic next turn is nevertheless usually taken by the recipient, one which addresses the remark just made by the child ((4)–(7)):

(4) To:M:62

C:	I'm getting on ↑mummy:
→ M:	Yer ↑gettin o:n
C:	Ye:es
M:	Goo:d

(5) To:M:66

	((discussing the picture of a teddy bear))
C:	A little te::dy: •hh ↓with a little <u>too</u>thy: mummy =
→ M:	= ↑Oh: ye:s (•) so it is

(6) Ta:E:86

	((discussing toenails))
M:	( ) they just break off theirse::lves
Younger C:	They brak ↑a:ff
M:	Mhmm
C:	We::ll mine didna brak off ma:m
→ M:	They must be harder nails

(7) Mi:M:14

	((C. is painting; after long pause sings Ali Bali Bee))
C:	↑I said Ali Bali Bee ( ) mummy::
→ M:	Did you
C:	Ali Bali Bee sitting on her mummy's knee

This minimally suggests that appended address terms are associated with the occurrence of next turns where the design of the initial does not explicitly set up a constraint on recipient to produce a next turn.

That there may be a constraint on next-turn production at such points in conversation is more strongly suggested by the pattern of children's turn organisation post non-response to turns with appended address term which are not adjacency pair first parts. Following non-response to such turns, a regular pattern is for the child to produce another turn which recognisably solicits a response to the prior ((8)-(11)):

(8) Ta:E:89

	((sounds of exertion))
C:	I-I'll gie ye'it ma:m
	(2.2)
→ C:	I'll gie ye'it ma:m (•) right óh
M:	( )

(9) Ta:E:10

	((reference is to something on the TV))
C:	°A (0.5)$^{\phi}$ A lady's got a ↑ca:t ↑ma::m
	(4.2)
→ C:	A lady's go' a ca:: 'as shi
M:	Aye:

(10) To:M:135

C:	A'have to take the:se with mi [ma::m
Younger C:	[((·))
	(2.0)
→ C:	O:K::?
	(0.7)
M:	Where to::

(11) To:M:85

C:	Have to cut the:se mummy
	(1.3)
→ C:	Won't we mummy
	(1.5)
C:	Won't we
M:	Yes

In (8)–(11) the solicit character of the remedial turns is displayed through the inclusion of explicit adjacency pair first part components: 'right oh' in (8), ''as shi' in (9), 'O:K::' in (10) and 'won't we' in (11). That such turns solicit, specifically, responses to the unanswered prior is displayed through repetition – in (8) 'I'll gie ye'it ma:m', in (9) 'A lady's go' a ca::' – or elliptical reliance on the prior turn for their sense. These fragments suggest that initial utterances with appended address terms are looking for a next by-recipient, and they raise as a possibility that the appended address terms may not just be associated with the occurrence of a next-turn constraint but that they may actually carry that aspect.

The appended address term may also be used as a remedial device post no answer to an initial remark by children, and it is this mode of use which constitutes the third, and perhaps most persuasive, part of the evidence concerning my claim that appended address terms function as solicit devices((12)–(16)).[7]

(12) Ha:M:21

	C:	(Will) I buy you new little wee ones
		(5.5)
	M:	A new little wee what?
		(1.2)
	M:	Eh?
	C:	A new little wee toothpaste
		(0.5)
	C:	OK
		(1.5)
→	C:	OK Mummy
	M:	°Yes

(13) Ta:E:72

		((TV reference))
	C:	Look a'tha:: ma::nie
		(0.5)
→	C:	↑Look at tha ma::n mum
		(1.0)
	M:	Aye

(14) To:M:4

	C:	Which one are (•) which ones are ye fi::ndin
		(2.5)

→ C: Eh mummy =
M: = I'me just having a look through pe::t

(15) Ta:E:57

((referring to recording jacket))
C: Mum I: could tie: it righ:: ↑could a
((M coughs)) (1.5)
→ C: Could a' ma::m
M: Ah
C: Look at tha(t)
M: Oh: aye

(16) To:M:168

(('this' = a xylophone on the TV))
C: What's [this fo:r
Younger C: [(Da)
Younger C: Dada
(·)
Younger C: ↑Dada
→ C: Wh[at's this fo:r ma::m
Younger C: [Dada
Younger C: ↑D[ada
M: [Making music

Subsequent to no answer, or no relevant next action (as in (13)), post an initial utterance children can attempt to secure the absent action by combining a final position address term with an initial component which explicitly seeks that action.[8] In some cases the initial component is a repetition of the unanswered initial – in (13) the words 'Look at that man' are repeated; in (16) the words 'What's this for' – but, more characteristically, elliptical remedial formats are employed – in (12) 'OK', in (14) 'Eh', in (15) 'Could a'. In elliptical remedial formats the address term is often appended to a solicit item which did not occur in the initial unanswered turn – in (14) 'Eh' is such a solicit item – but there is a clear set of cases where, post the failure of the first part of an adjacency pair to elicit a second part, the sole component added to the repetition of first part components is the address term. In (12), after 'OK' has not solicited a response to the request, then, after a pause of (1.5), a 'mummy' is appended to the item which has just failed to get a next, 'OK'; similarly in (15), after 'Mum I: could tie: it righ:: could a' has not solicited a response, then, after a pause, a 'mummy' is appended to 'Could a'. And these remedial techniques do produce a relevant next from recipients, 'Yes' in (12), 'Aye' in (13), and so on.

My argument, then, is that the most adequate general characterisation of final position address terms, as used by these children, is as devices for soliciting a next turn from the named recipient. Given that they constitute a technique for transforming an utterance, at its potential completion point, into one which carries a stronger constraint on recipient to take a turn, they bear some resemblance to question tags. In fact, we have some evidence in these fragments for these devices being used in ways that seem interchangeable; in (9), the initial 'A lady's got a ca:t ma::m' does not receive a reply, and in the remedial turn the question tag ''as shi' is substituted for the address term; in (15), the failure of the question tag 'could a' initially to get a reply leads to the supplementation of that component with an address term, 'ma::m', in the remedial 'could a' ma::m'. There are also, however, important differences between final position address terms and questions tags.[9] The question tag explicitly selects the type of next utterance that the speaker is looking for, whereas the appended address term is empty of meaning in that the recipient is required to analyse the words that preceded the address term for the kind of action being sought in next turn by the speaker. So, in fragments (8)–(11), the question tags used in the remedial turns, post parental non-response, appear to clarify the nature of the initial turns. For example, in (8), the 'right oh' makes the utterance into something more readily treatable as an offer, and, in (10), 'O:K::' turns the issue more clearly into a permission request sequence. That they do this implies that the first turn, which was not replied to, can be thought of as a less direct, and perhaps more guarded, way of doing that action on the part of the child. In (10), for example, the child could have chosen at least three ways in which to handle the matter of taking the things with her to a friend's. She could have not mentioned it at all, she could have informed/announced that she would be taking them, or she could have asked if she could take them. To inform/announce stands to be taken as presuming that she can do the relevant action, whereas to ask if she can do it is to display that as problematic in an explicit way. 'A'have to take the:se with me ma::m' appears to stand somewhere between the two alternatives; it does not stand as presuming that the child can take the things with her, given that the 'ma::m' sets up a next-turn constraint, but nor does it explicitly ask if she can take them. It broaches the issue in such a way that it can be checked out by the parent while not making it formally into a requestable matter.[10]

Earlier, I gave some reasons for not characterising appended address terms as 'attention getters', and further support for this is contained in those sequences in which the address term is used as a remedial device post non-response to an initial ((12)-(16)). In a few cases like (13) and (16), the appended address term is associated with a full repeat of the prior, but in the majority of cases it is one component of an elliptical solicit utterance. Two points can be made off these fragments. Firstly, given that the use of the address term as a remedial is often embedded in ellipsis, then that displays a presumption by the child that recipient has monitored, and given attention to, the child's prior turn. Secondly, the appended address term, where used as a remedial, is not exclusively associated with any particular account of what happened to the initial unanswered turn. The full repeats in (13), 'Look at the ma::n mum', and (16), 'Whats this fo:r ma::m', are consistent with the view that the child may be treating the parent as having not attended the prior unanswered turn, though the elliptical remedials rely on the recipient's having monitored the prior turn. Whereas final position address terms, when used as remedials, appear to be non-exclusively associated with any particular treatment of the unanswered prior, such an association does appear to operate with the use of initially positioned address terms.

When an utterance of the child's gets no response from the parent, then the child can attempt to secure a response with a turn which employs an address term in initial position ((17)-(22)):

(17) Ca:M:4

C:	Is it ↑yours
	(1.4)
→ C:	Mummy is it yours
M:	Yes sweetheart

(18) Ha:M:14

C:	↑Why does the ma:n give you tha::t ba::ck
	(2.2)
→ C:	Mummy why does the ma:n gie' •hh gi:ve ye'it ba::ck for

(19) Mu:M:122

	C:	Do you need cold water in thi::s
		(1.0)
→	C:	Mummy do ye need cold water for the ve:::getables
	M:	[Ye:s I must have cold water

(20) Ga:E:81

		((discussing toy soldiers))
	C:	No: theyre fa:s:t'asl ↑↑ee::p
	(M):	( )
→	C:	(Mum) the ↑soldiers ↓fa:st asleep =
	M:	= Well go an'make sure that the . . .

(21) Ma:M:7

	C:	°hh You 'aven't got a big spoon have you
		(1.0)
→	C:	°hh You (°) uh Daddy ↑you: haven't got a big [( )
	F:	[I've finished mine love

(22) Ma:M:62

		((C. draws father's attention to bus on back of cereal packet))
	C:	Daddy look at a double decker bus
		(2.0)
→	C:	Dad look at the double decker bus
	F:	Mm its more than a double decker that.

Where such a turn is employed, it is never, within my corpus, an ellipticised version of the prior unanswered turn; it is a self-sufficient unit which is either a repeat of the prior turn or one which, while employing repeat items, also includes non-elliptical substitutions or elaborations of words in the prior. In (17), for example, the remedial turn takes the form of address term + repeat, 'Mummy is it yours'; in (19), it takes the form of address turn + repeat + elaborated noun phrase, 'Mummy do ye need cold water for the ve:::getables'. In none of these cases is there anaphoric tying back into the unanswered prior; in fact, the tendency, in this sequential position, is to make the utterance more explicit than the prior. So, in (19), the pro-term 'thi::s' in the first turn is replaced by 've:::getables' in the remedial turn; in (20), 'they' is replaced by 'the soldiers'. The self-sufficiency of the remedial turns with initial address terms holds even where initial address terms were employed in the prior unanswered turn (see (22)), though, if an ellipticised remedial design is used, then the address term is either absent from the remedial turn (as in (23) below) or, in a small but significant number of cases, we find a switch in positioning of the address term from initial position in the first unanswered turn to final position in the remedial turn (as in (24) and (25)):

(23) Ta:M:96

C:	Mum •hh are ye ↑nae gan ti mak the'supper
	(1.2)
→ C:	↑Are you nae::
M:	No
	(1.3)
M:	I'm away to make the dinner

(24) Ta:E:57

	((also example (15)))
C:	Mum I: could tie: it righ:: ↑could a
	((M. coughs)) (1.5)
C:	Could a' ma::m

(25) To:M:100

C:	Mummy can I – can ↑I:: spread it o::n
	(1.4)
C:	Can I mummy

The use of initial address terms (in remedial designs) seems, then, to be associated with an exclusive treatment of the unanswered prior in that, where the initial address term is used, it always treats the prior as missed.[11] As the remedial turns are constructed as potential initiations of the matter in hand, they exclusively remedy the non-response through *reinitiation.*[12]

Because the initial address term, where used as a remedial, treats the unanswered prior as missed, and because it is associated with the work of initiating, the very 'initialness' of its positioning within the remedial turn is crucial for the work that it does. As further evidence of that, one can note that, where that initialness could be potentially lost, then children take active steps to secure it. In (21), the child, in the remedial turn, could have relied on the presence of the turn initial 'You' and constructed the turn as follows '•hh You (•) uh Daddy haven't got a big (   )', but instead she duplicates the item 'you' which occurs prior to the address term – '•hh You (•) uh Daddy ↑you:' thus making 'Daddy' into the potential turn initial item. Similar designs can also be found where the use of the initial address term does not occur in a remedial context, post no response to a prior. In (26) below, for example, the turn could have been constructed as 'When we've woken up (•) mummy is Audrey comin over', but instead the items occurring prior to the address term are duplicated – 'When (we've woken up) (•) mummy when (we've woken up) up is – is Audrey comin over?'.

(26) Mi:E:65

C: When (we've woken up) (•) mummy when
(we've woken up) up is – is Audrey comin over
M: (   )

In these ways the initialness of the initial address term is a feature attended to through the design of turns by children, and this contrasts with final position address terms which do not, through their organisation, demonstrate the same exclusive affinity with final utterance position. Thus, although they are mainly situated in final position, there are a number – as in (27) – which occur prior to a final item in the turn ('OK' in (27)) where that final item seems integral to the over-all character of the utterance and the way it is treated by recipients:

(27) To:M:82

((C. is involved in an activity with stamps))
→ C: One hasnt got stuck through mummy •hh OK?
(0.8)
C: One hasnt got stucky stamps mummy
M: [Ye::s I know

In the usage of these children, therefore, initial address terms are exclusively associated with turn constructions which do not place reliance on recipients having monitored either just prior returns (as in (17)-(22)), or just prior items within the same turn (as in (21) and

(26)). From their use as remedials, the initial address terms appear to provide a solution to the problems of recipient having missed, not monitored, the prior. They, specifically, are solutions, given that, in many cases (such as (17), (18), (21) and (22)), it is their inclusion which is the sole significant feature of utterance redesign to be found in the remedial turn. As remedials, they instruct recipient to monitor the words that follow. I use the description 'instruct recipient to monitor' rather than, say, 'get attention', because, although getting the attention of the recipient may be one interactional basis for the use of the initial address term, it is not the only one. In extracts like (17)-(22) it is the case that the use of the initial address term, as a remedial, treats the unanswered prior as non-attended by the intended recipient and seeks to ensure attention to the remedial turn, but in other cases the attention of the recipient, in this sense, seems to be ensured, yet we still find the use of initial address terms. For example, in (28), the parent is engaged in talk with the child immediately preceding the use of the address term, while, in (29), the parent has actually solicited the turn in which the address term is used. In these cases, the address term again pre-figures units of talk which are not constructed such as to rely on priors for their sense; in fact, they initiate what appear to be thematic[13] departures from the prior line of discussion.

(28) Ma:M:42

	((initially discussing the recording jacket))	
C:	Its a bit heavy =	
M:	= Yes I know its heavy	
	(•)	
→ C:	Mummy could I ask •hh go over an ask Mar:ti:n	

(29) Ca/M

M:	The:res a do::g up the:re	
	((looking out of window))	
C:	Whe::re	((moving at same time))
	(•)	
M:	↑Look	
	(2.3)	
	↑See it	((C. now close to mother))
→ C:	Yes (•) mummy •hh look here's one of the dollie's mums has come to see ye loo:k	

In (28), the 'Mummy' initiates a switch of topic from the recording jacket to a request to play with a neighbour's child, Martin. In (29), the 'mummy' occurs as an initial to both a switch of focus (from the view outside the window to something(s) in the vicinity of the child) and a switch of topic. Here the address terms are not being used as remedies to problems which have occurred in the discourse prior to their use; they are being used prospectively either simply to mark the beginning of some unit which is thematically discontinuous with what has gone before, or to mark the subsequent words as being in special need of monitoring by the recipient. Either way, the initial address terms here do not seem to originate from the problem of gaining recipient's attention, as they did in (17)-(22), and for this reason 'getting attention' is best reserved as one of the possibly several interactional problems for which the use of these initial address terms can act as solutions.

From the organisations of turns in which they are employed, it appears that the work accomplished through the use of address terms by these children is closely associated with where they are positioned in discourse. In arguing this, some weight has been placed on the usage of these terms in explicit remedial sequences – that is, post no response to some child initial turn – and it has been shown that the initial address term is associated with a distinctive treatment of that non-response. Presumably, the choice to treat the non-response in some specific way, as a product of non-monitoring, for example, is systematic in some form, but from audio-materials alone little light can be shed on the nature of this systematicity. The occurrence of address terms in these remedial sequences, however, only accounts for a fraction of their over-all incidence; more often, they occur where there is little evidence of some breakdown having occurred in the talk. In these more 'normal' situations of use, by deploying otherwise remedial devices, children indicate to recipient that, and what, trouble was anticipated, and can thus be saying something about the interaction and/or the relationship. Through high frequencies in the use of these terms in certain families,[13] the children display the securing and activating of recipients' (parents') involvement to be an ongoing and pervasive interactional problem, one which has some special salience in their management of interaction with their parents. To know whether that is generally the case would require an extensive analysis in other families of those turn components which function in equivalent ways to address terms.[15]

Transcription Conventions

Underlining (I cant)	emphasis on that word (or the underlined part of the word)
capital letters (PLEASE)	loud in volume
( )	unsure transcription or words not transcribed
°	words spoken softly (cancelled by $^{\phi}$)
/ ¬_	pitch contours
↑ ↓	mark an utterance, or part of an utterance, as lower or higher in pitch than either that speaker's last turn, or their 'normal' pitch or prior component of same turn
:	extension of the prior sound
(°)	pause of under half a second
[	marks point of overlap in speech or speakers beginning their utterances simultaneously
–	slight perturbation of speech rhythm
•hh	audible inbreaths
(hh)	audible outbreaths or breathiness in words
=	no gap between two speakers' turns or between units within one speaker's turn
C	always the four-year-old, who is also always the first-born child in the family

Notes

1. I would like to acknowledge and thank Dr Gail Jefferson for her extensive detailed comment on an earlier version of this paper.

2. One of the ways in which Brown and Ford collected data on address terms was to ask business executives 'to write down for each person listed the exact words that he (the informant) would customarily speak in greeting that person for the first time each day' (1964, p. 235). For a more general sociolinguistic approach to address terms see Ervin-Tripp (1972).

3. Sociolinguistic analyses of the use of address terms in different contexts (speakers, situations, etc.) have built-in limitations. The sheer correlation of the use of such terms with, say, the number of speakers engaged in a conversation may suggest certain interactional problems for which such terms are solutions, but the correlation in itself does not demonstrate that to be the case in any satisfactory way. It leaves open the question of which a number of conceivable problems associated with contexts may have been resolved through the use of

such terms, and it does not pay adequate attention to the possibility that a use, supposedly characteristic of one context, can be found in other contexts. The latter suggests that uses are not in some way tied to contexts, but rather to forms of conversational organisation within contexts, forms of conversational organisation which can occur in a variety of contexts. The focus here is on locating the use of such terms in the context of conversational organisation, though clearly any such analysis should produce conclusions which are at least consistent with known sociolinguistic variations.

4. The article is based on a scanning of over 500 instances of the use of address terms by children in eight families, though special attention and transcription effort has been made with specific classes of occurrence – notably their use post non-response to an initial child remark. The children concerned were all aged within one or two months of four years exactly, and the conversations were recorded in the homes of these children, with the aid of a radio-microphone, in Aberdeen, Scotland.

5. For a discussion of next-speaker selection see Section 4.12 of Sacks, Schegloff and Jefferson (1974). In that next speaker selection is accomplished through the use of address terms in all three positions that have been mentioned in the text, then speaker selection is unlikely to stand as an adequate description of the specific work that the use of these terms accomplishes by virtue of differential positioning.

6. Adjacency pair is a general term used to refer to those utterance combinations in which a first utterance, the first pair part, sets a constraint on what should be done in next turn. Invitations, requests, greetings and questions are examples of first pair parts, and their relevant seconds are acceptance/decline, granting/rejection, greeting and answer. For a more detailed discussion of the properties of adjacency pairs, see Schegloff and Sacks (1973). Final position address terms *can* be used by these children with adjacency pair first parts, and where no other potential recipient is present; for example:

Ga:M:67

C: Does thi:s go on he:re mummy

7. It may be of relevance to note that, in (12), the child and the mother were the only people present in the home, while, in (14), only mother and child were in that room at that time.

8. Two observations, however, argue for final position address terms being weaker next turn constraints than the initial components they accompany in this type of remedial turn: (i) the address terms, as remedials in this type of sequence, are *only* used in combination with initial components such as question tags: (ii) the initial components that they accompany can constitute complete remedial turns in this type of sequence (e.g. the child's third turn 'Won't we' in fragment (11)). So, in cases like (14), 'Eh mummy', there seems to be a within turn transition from stronger to weaker solicitation devices.

9. A crucial and distinctive property of address terms *vis-à-vis* question tags is their relative syntactic freeness; this makes possible, for example, their final position use in sentences where tags, say, would be inappropriate (e.g. at the end of 'wh' questions). Furthermore, even in those cases where a tag would have been syntactically possible, an address term in final position may work better to solicit the particular kind of response that a child is seeking, where that response is not simple agreement/disagreement. The child's 'A::w he's forgotten his boots mummy:' in (3), for example, could have had a tag on the end (i.e. 'hasn't he') but it would have worked less well to produce a parental expression of sympathy in next turn.

10. It so happens that, in (10), no response is immediately forthcoming from the parent, and that remedial work is engaged in. That this happens is immaterial to the argument that has just been elaborated.

11. There are, of course, a variety of possible remedial designs post non-response to an initial, and through the design of the remedy they display that speaker's proposed analysis of the problem that they are remedying. There is an especially wide variety of remedies which appear to presuppose that recipient has monitored the unanswered prior. Fragments (10), (11), (12), (14), and (15) contain some examples, though a further two types can be illustrated off the following sequence:

To:E:144

((C. wanting to cut out a character in a comic))
(19.4)
(1) C: How d'ye cut ou::t
(4.2)
(2) C: ↓That
(4.0)
(3) C: How d'ye cut
(1.6)
(4) C: Around here – ↑there
(2.1)
(5) M: Tha:ts the way

(2) (perhaps accompanied by a gesture) appears to clarify precisely what it is that the child is hoping to cut out, thus treating the silence post (1) as arising from potential ambiguity in (1) itself; (4) is also elliptically reliant on its prior but presupposes a possible response to that prior which pins down and restricts the class of response required from the recipient. The great variety of elliptical remedials makes it all the more interesting that the initial address term is not associated with these elliptical designs. The reinitiations which accompany the use of initial address terms can also be taken as opportunities to carry out other remedial work on the unanswered prior, as in fragments (19) and (20), types of remedial work which can be found in elliptical remedials (e.g. clarifications). To this extent the remedial turns in (19) and (20) contain multiple remedial devices.

12. In cases like (17), (18), (21), (22) and (23) – which consist of remedials constructed as repeats of the unanswered priors – it is worth noting that the repeats do not appear to display, through their intonation contour, that they are repeating. Jefferson (personal communication) writes that 'the repetition can be done as a recognisable "repeat" in which the intonation contour clearly indicates that this is not the first time the utterance was done. Or, the repetition can be done as an initial; the display then being that the proposedly not-heard initial did not, for interactional/sequential purposes, occur. This, of course, in independence of whether recipient did hear the initial, and whether or not speaker takes it recipient did or did not hear it.' For a more general discussion of repetition in child discourse, see Keenan (1977).

13. I am avoiding a term like 'topic' as there are instances in which children appear to use the address term to initiate new lines of development within what might be considered to be topically tied conversation. A new topic, therefore, is just one kind of thematic departure.

14. The use of these terms by children is highly variable in sheer frequency. At the extremes, in a four-hour recording, one girl used the terms about 25 times to her parents whereas another girl used them about 200 times. No explanation or account of this variation in frequency is offered here.

15. In the course of the article various equivalents to final position address terms have been suggested. For an outline of various mechanisms which may constitute equivalents to initial address terms, see McTear (forthcoming).

References

Brown, R. and Ford, M. (1964). 'Address in American English'. In D. Hymes (ed.), *Language, Culture and Society*

Ervin-Tripp, S.M. (1972). 'Sociolinguistic Rules of Address'. In J.B. Pride and J. Holmes (eds.), *Sociolinguistics*

— and Mitchell-Kernan, C. (eds.) (1977). *Child Discourse*. New York: Academic Press

Hymes, D. (ed.) (1964). *Language, Culture and Society*. New York: Harper and Row

Keenan, E.O. (1977). 'Making it Last: Repetition in Children's Discourse'. In S.M. Ervin-Tripp and C. Mitchell-Kernan (eds.), *Child Discourse*

McTear, M.F. (forthcoming). 'Hey! I've Got Something to Tell You: A Study of the Initiation of Conversational Exchanges by Preschool Children'. *Journal of Pragmatics* (forthcoming)

Pride, J.B. and Holmes, J. (eds.) (1972). *Sociolinguistics*. Harmondsworth: Penguin

Sacks, H., Schegloff, E. and Jefferson, G. (1974). 'A Simplest Systematics for the Organization of Turn-Taking for Conversation'. *Language*, 50, pp. 696–735

Schegloff, E. (1968). 'Sequencing in Conversational Openings'. *American Anthropologist*, 70, 6, pp. 1075–95

— and Sacks, H. (1973). 'Opening Up Closings'. *Semiotica*, 8, 4, pp. 289–327

Shatz, M. and Gelman, R. (1973). *The Development of Communication Skills* (Monographs of the Society for Research in Child Development, 38). Chicago: Chicago University Press

9 THE CLARIFICATION REQUEST SEQUENCE IN CONVERSATION BETWEEN MOTHERS AND THEIR CHILDREN

David Langford

It happens as a routine occurrence within conversations between children and their caretakers that the caretakers can locate particular utterances produced by the children as troublesome, by means of the production of what have been termed contingent queries or clarification requests. My aim here is to provide a preliminary analysis of those conversational sequences which are generated between children and their caretakers when the child's utterance is located by the caretaker as troublesome. What seems to be involved is a specific type of conversational activity that has a distinctive structure in its performance. The data transcripts upon which the analysis is based are taken from recordings of naturally occurring conversations between caretakers and their four-year-old children, in the home, with no observer present.[1]

Before providing my own preliminary analysis of this conversational activity, I should first mention, as a basis for possible comparison, analyses of the same phenomenon which have been provided by Corsaro (1976) and by Garvey (1978).

Corsaro isolates three forms of clarification request as used by the adult in interaction with the child and pairs four functions with these three forms. The three forms he isolates are:

1. minimal form clarification request markers such as 'what', 'huh', etc.;
2. whole or part utterance repeats with rising intonation;
3. initial utterance expansion.

The four functions that are served by these three forms he suggests are:

1. elicitation of an utterance repeat on account of a failure to hear, which function is generally served by the minimal form clarification request marker;
2. elicitation of an utterance repeat or clarification on account of a failure to understand, which function is generally served by the utterance repeat or expansion form;

3. conversational turn filling, which function is generally served by the simple utterance repeat form;
4. expression of surprise on account of the unexpectedness of an utterance, which function is generally served by the simple utterance repeat form.

Corsaro argues that the production of a clarification request by an adult in interaction with a child serves as a marker of a suspension of what Cicourel (1973) termed 'interpretive procedures' and that the suspension of these procedures occurs in such interactions because in them there is an absence of background cues (vocalisations, nods and other gestures), there is an absence of shared cultural interpretations, and there are clear status differences between the interactants.

Garvey's report is based on an analysis of interactions among children but suggests that it would hold equally for adult-child interactions. She describes the phenomenon as a 'contingent query' and argues that what is involved is an embedded speech act, crucially similar to the speech act type 'request for information', in that its intended perlocutionary effect is the elicitation of information not known by the utterer who must, however, presume it to be known by the intended hearer.

This embedded speech act has a three-step sequence:

1. the occurrence of a troublesome utterance;
2. a query which can take a variety of forms;
3. a response to 2.

The second item in this three-step sequence exercises both a selectivity function with respect to what might be problematic in the first step and a determining function with respect to what is required as a response in the third step. Thus, for example, if 'what' is produced as the query, then it is non-specific in its selection of what might be problematic in the first step and it determines that a repeat of the first-step utterance will be produced as an appropriate response.

My own analysis differs from the two just described in certain crucial aspects which I hope will become clear in what follows.

A first problem for the intended recipient is to display the fact that what he has heard did not or could not have communicated what was intended. Where the intended recipient does not determine this for the benefit of the child then the child has work to do in eliciting such a determination for himself. Having arrived at a determination of what is problematic, the child must then in some way make it unproblematic. Finally, the intended recipient must display that what was hitherto problematic is no longer so. Thus, in the paradigmatic case, the clarification sequence will comprise four components:[2]

1. there is a child's utterance which is troublesome;
2. there is the clarification request itself;
3. there is the child's response to the clarification request;
4. there is a display by the adult to the effect that, by virtue of the child's response to the clarification request, what was troublesome is no longer so.

The following examples are illustrative of the general shape which the clarification sequences under discussion take (the conventions of transcription set out on page 173, at the end of this chapter):

(1) Ga:E:395

C: Come and see Captain Flack
(4.0)
M: Pardon
(5.0)
C: I see Captain {(F)/(V)}lack
M: Huh. Huh.

(2) Mu:M:033

C: (   )
(4.0)
F: What did you say
M: I dunno Harry
F: I couldn't make it out either
C: Butter
M: Buttered
C: (   )
F: Oh ya you want your toast buttered
C: Yes =
M: = Well ask for it properly pet.

(3) To:M:343

C: ↑Mu:m ↑(.) ↑is there one for me: ↑
M: One what
C: Is is this one for me
M: Yes

(4) Mu:M:099

C: ( ) Is this the one we (after) the roo:dboat
M: A roadboat
C: No a roo:d one
M: A roodboat
C: Yes a roo:dboat
M: A rowingboat
C: Yes
(1.0)
One we s one we went on to Britain
M: Oh a carferry boat
C: Ye::s
M: A carferry boat the one we went on to te the continent
C: Yes we went to the continent an with a car.

(5) Mu:M:694

C: An keep it to have a (tuv) to for his holiday to have to be a fi:re
M: Oh: (is) goin to be a fire on his holiday. Oh what a holiday
N: Y//eah::
C: (ne) No no mon no he holiday goin' to be fire not him
M: Oh a the his holiday goin' to be on fire// (did) ya mean the house where he's goin' to stay for his holiday
C: Yes
C: Yes
M: Oh dear

Taking the first two components, as given, it seems that, once the clarification request is produced, the subsequent components obligatorily follow.

Consider, for example:

(6) To:M:139

C: ↑The front door's not coming out for. ↑
M: What
(1.0)
M: Pardon

In this case, the adult's expectation of a child's response to an initial clarification request has been frustrated and, though nothing seems to hang on the matter documented in the child's utterance, the issue is pressed. Consider next:

(7) Ca:E:059

C: He's gonna buy eight yoghurt
M: Eight
C: Yes (0.5) ↑Is that a lot↑
M: What else is he gonna buy.

(8) Ca:E:068

C: No (°h) a bit (.) ↑knocks down trees (.h) an they come into pla:n(ts) ↑.tree
F: They make the trees into (.) what
C: °Plan
F: ↑Plants↑
C: Yeah
(1.0)
↑Plants↑
F: Planks of wood
C: No (.) pl_a_nts that grow
F: ( ) into plants
C: Ya could take out the roots to n n knock it down, then when no more roots left (.) make a plant.
F: Oh. I see. And make a tree into little bits.
C: Yes
F: And plant them.
C: Yes
F: I see

What I want to illustrate off these examples is the way in which the child seems to expect a display of understanding immediately post his response to the clarification request. Thus, in example (7), the child, after a 0.5-second gap in which no display of understanding is forthcoming from the adult, himself makes an issue of the possibly troublesome nature of his initial utterance. Similarly, in example (8), there is a 1-second gap post the child's utterance 'yeah' where one might expect to find a display of understanding from the adult. In the absence of this display, the child does what would have been a relevant first response to the initial clarification request and the sequence does not finally close until a strong display of understanding has been produced by the adult.

The four components of the clarification request sequence can take a variety of forms. With respect to the first component, it is clear that, where an issue is made of the communicative efficacy of a particular utterance, a variety of factors can have occasioned it. Thus, if we consider the first five examples cited, the first component of example (1) was an utterance to which the intended recipient was perhaps inattentive. The first component of example (2) involves a phonetic indeterminacy; that of example (3) involves the referential opacity of a deictic element contained within it; that of example (4) involves a lexical novelty; whilst that of example (5) involves syntactic irregularity. However, it seems that characterisation of a trouble in linguistic terms does not determine what form of clarification request will follow or even that any will.

With respect to the second component, a variety of devices can be used by the intended recipient of the first component to bring off a display that an utterance which constituted that first component is the occasion of some trouble. Thus, such displays can be brought off with (i) a free-standing minimal form clarification request marker, such as 'what', 'pardon', etc., having level or rising intonation, (ii) expansions of the child's utterance, (iii) repeats of the whole of the child's utterance, usually with rising intonation, (iv) partial repeats of the child's utterance, again usually with rising intonation, (v) isolation of specific items in the child's utterance with interrogative proterms such as 'what', 'which', 'who', etc.

The third component, i.e. the child's response to the clarification request, can take the form of: (i) a confirmatory/disconfirmatory item, (ii) partial or whole repeat with attendant modulation of pitch, stress or volume, (iii) a reformulation of the initial utterance.

The fourth component, the function of which is to display the fact that a state of mutual understanding with respect to the initially problematic item obtains, can take the form of an overt display item such as 'Oh I see' or an on-topic continuation of the initially problematic utterance, which continuation could, of course, be achieved through a variety of speech act types, depending on the speech act type realised in the first component.

What I want to do now is to provide a more detailed analysis of the second component of the clarification request sequence, i.e. the clarification request itself.

As has been noted, a first problem for the intended recipient of an utterance that is troublesome is to display that such an utterance did not or could not have communicated what its utterer intended. The devices available for bringing such a display off are more or less specific in their determination of just how what was said did not or could not have communicated what was intended (cf. Garvey, 1978). The least specific device available is the free-standing clarification request marker such as 'what' or 'pardon'. Where the clarification request marker is used the child has as clear an indication as he could have that there is some trouble with his immediately prior utterance. It might be supposed, as Corsaro has argued, that, where the minimal form clarification request marker is used, what is at issue is that what the child has said was not or could not have been heard with sufficient precision to allow for adequate interpretation. On several counts this appears not to be the case. Firstly, it is very rare for utterances which take minimal form clarification request markers as immediate seconds to be untranscribable by the analyst. In the one case which I have found in which whole utterance phonetic indeterminacy was clearly the issue the more specific form 'what did you say' was used to display that fact. Secondly, children's seconds to caretaker's minimal form clarification request markers can be overlapped by caretaker's utterances which can be such as to indicate that what was originally said was, in fact, deciphered at the phonetic level:

(9) To:M:268

C: Mummy that's the baker at the end of the road
M: Pardon
C: That's the baker at the end of the // road
M: Now you can just wait here until the baker comes up.

Finally, and perhaps most significantly, in the general case the child seemingly interprets the minimal form clarification request marker not as a display of a simple failure to hear but as a display of some other difficulty, though in the particular case it can be that the child supposes there to have occurred a simple failure to hear. My evidence for these claims is just that children tend to reformulate what was said prior to the caretaker's production of a minimal form clarification request marker immediately subsequent to such a production rather than doing such things as a straightforward repeat or making use of exaggerated articulation. Thus:

(10) Ca:E:055

1. C: Is Derek a nice boy
2. M: Pardon

3. C: Is Derek a bad boy

(11) Ga:M:380
1. C: I see S for Shona
2. M: I beg your pardon
3. C: I see red ↓S for Shona↓

(12) Ca:E:048
1. C: Here's a man coming (.) with a pick
2. M: Pardon dear
3. C: The man's coming with a pick

(13) Ca:E:037
1. C: En whose gonna spea who gonna (.) to speak his ↑<u>o</u>ther end
2. M: Pardon
3. C: Who gonna speak the ↑other e://n

(14) Mu:M:099
1. C: Mummy who built the one we seen on Sunday
2. M: What
3. C: (   ) Is this the one we (after) the roo:dboat.

(15) To:M:019
1. C: I had sore gums when daddy was upstairs
2. M: Pardon
3. C: I had sore .h teeth

In each of the foregoing examples some form of modification of the utterance to be clarified is effected by the child.

In example (10), there is a substitution of 'bad' for 'nice'. It seems that the child here is satisfied that his mother has attended to what was said and that what was said was phonetically in order and so must monitor his own utterance for some other source of trouble. The one term in his utterance which he assumes could be problematic is the evaluative term 'nice'. Over all, it seems that he takes his mother's production of a clarification request marker to be faulting the evaluatively favourable attitude to the referent Derek which his utterance implies. In example (11), the modification involved in the child's second utterance is such as to provide for a more specific identifying description of the referent 'S'. It is perhaps interesting to note that, in this example, as is the case in example (15), there is some hesitation on the part of the child in the production of his reformulating utterance. Thus, in (11), there is a repetition of the personal pronoun 'I' and a marked drop in pitch level towards utterance termination point, whilst, in (15), there is an inbreath prior to the part of the utterance which contains a reformulation. I take the occurrence of such hesitation phenomena to be indicative of the child's being engaged in a search for some form of words which will render unproblematic what the clarification request marker has displayed as problematic in a situation where the character of the problem has not been indicated. In example (12), the reformulation achieves greater specificity by substituting the indefinite article related to 'man' with the definite article. In example (13), it seems that the child assumes the communicative inefficacy of his first utterance to be largely a matter of syntax and so edits out the 'to' of the infinitival form 'to speak' and achieves more appropriate specificity of reference with the substitution of the definite article for the possessive 'his' in the phrase 'his other end'. In example (14), the child attempts in his reformulation to provide a description which will be more precise in its capacity to aid the mother in locating the informational needs of the child expressed in his first utterance. In example (15), the child's initial utterance contains an adverbial subordinate clause and it is perhaps interesting that the child locates the problematic feature of that utterance in his main clause even though, as the sequence unfolds, it turns out to be the content of the subordinate clause which is an issue for the mother.

Thus it continues:

(15a) M: had sore teeth (.) when
C: when daddy was down
M: when daddy was down (1.0) down where
C: uh down here h' sitting on hi on his chair

It may be that, where statements containing subordinate clauses are followed by minimal form clarification request markers, the child follows a principle of locating the problem in the statement's main clause. In this example, he locates the problem as having to do with the formulation of mouth disorders which are relevant to dental treatment (his father has just left for a visit to the dentist) and so substitutes 'teeth' for 'gums'.

The characteristic feature of all these examples is that some form of reformulation occurs in each subsequent to the caretaker's production of a minimal form clarification request marker and this seems to be me to be evidence of the strongest kind for such markers not being treated by the children as displays of simple failure to hear.

A second form of clarification request is the expansion of the child's initial utterance. Usually in the literature the notion of a caretaker's expansion of a child's utterance has been defined as an utterance which adds functors to the content words of the child's telegraphese so as to render the child's utterance grammatically well formed (e.g. Brown, 1973). Thus, a child's utterance comprising just the content words 'Milk gone' might be expanded to 'The milk has all gone'.

My use of the notion expansion differs somewhat from this paradigm since the children whose talk is the source of my data have already achieved a fair degree of expressive mastery of the functors of their language. I have isolated two sorts of expansion. In the one case, the expansion involved a syntactic rearrangement of a syntactically deviant utterance so as to make that utterance syntactically well formed and, in the other, it involves doing an alternative predication of the topic of the child's prior. An example of the first sort appeared in fragment (5) above:

(5) Mu:M:694
C: An keeping it to have a (tuv) to for his holiday to have to be a fi:re
M: Oh: (is) goin to be a fire on his holiday.
Oh what a holiday.

An example of the second sort is:

(16) Ca:E:067
C: Well
(2.0)
This is a door that opens
F: The door (.) to let the man into the tractor

The use of expansions as initial displays of concern about some trouble with prior utterances is rare when compared with the other forms available. This rarity of use may derive from the fact of expansions not being specific with respect to the problematic nature of the prior utterance. Clearly, any utterance could be expanded in a variety of ways, given the constraints of the two sorts of expansion

I have isolated, and any one of the possible expansions might be heard as a relevant production, even though the state of affairs it relates to might not be precisely the state of affairs originally envisaged by the child and documented in his utterance. Given the inherent variability of possible expansions, an issue is just how does the child hear them as displays of concern about the communicative efficacy of his prior utterances and not as routine topic continuations. That he does is evidenced by the fact that the child's characteristic responses to them are markers of confirmation or disconfirmation rather than topic builders marked by some such device as a conjunction, which tends to suggest that he treats expansions as hypotheses about what he has just said. The formal basis which the child probably has for so treating the utterances is the retention in the expanded utterances of major elements of the child's utterance and the absence of an explicit appreciation as the caretaker's immediate second to the child's utterance. This perhaps has the effect of displaying in the caretaker's utterance that the caretaker at that point in the conversation wants attention to be focused on the child's prior utterance *qua* linguistic production not *qua* topic contribution.

Let me now consider whole utterance repeats as displays of concern about some similar trouble with a prior utterance. Whole utterance repeats are similar to expansions in that, by definition, they retain major elements of the prior utterance but crucially different in that they involve no rearrangement of elements or alternative predications. It is precisely because of this difference that they are more specific than expansions in their capacity to display what might be problematic about the child's prior. For, if the caretaker is mistaken about what was said, then the fact that he is will be immediately obvious to the child, since what he is hearing purports to be an echo of what he originally said. As was pointed out earlier, expansions have a greater licence with respect to their relevance. On the other hand, if whole utterance repeats are accurate reproductions, as they tend to be, they are weak in their capacity to focus the child's attention on just what was problematic in the child's prior utterance. In the sequences I have so far transcribed, in which whole utterance repeats seemingly display a concern about some trouble with a child's prior, they occur, unlike part utterance repeats, after priors which evidence some form of hesitation phenomena. Thus:

(17) Ca:E:65

C: This is a different (.) this is a different <u>ja</u>cket.

(0.5) This is a different↑ one
F: This is a ↑different one↑

(18) Ga:E:223
C: (We) just playin' with (1.0) pastry
F: (e) playin' with pastry. Baking

(19) Ca:E:068
C: The egg ones (.) the (.) to push away things
(0.2)
(en the it push ra:)°h
It pushes down trees
F: It pushes down trees

But compare:

(20) Ca:E:059
C: He's gonna buy eight yoghurt
M: Eight

(21) Ca:E:057
C: He wants some oil
M: Oil

It seems to me that what the whole utterance repeats in these clarification sequence initial positions are doing is to display a recognition that the speaker has had difficulty in constructing his message and to exhibit the problematic utterance for inspection by both parties as a basis for its eventual repair by either party. It seems not to be assumed that any necessary repair is exclusively the responsibility of the first speaker. This is a wholly reasonable assumption on the part of the caretaker, in view of the hesitation phenomena displayed in the child's initial utterance. This idea of shared responsibility for repair in whole utterance repeat situations is well evidenced in examples (18) and (19), if we consider the continuation of these sequences:

(18a) C: (We) just playin' with (1.0) pastry.
F: (e) playin' with pastry. Baking
C: No: (.) just playing with pastry//not baking
F: Oh: :uh not baking. I see.

(19a) C: The egg ones (.) the (.) to push away things
(0.2)
(en the it push ra:)°h
It pushes down trees
F: It pushes down trees
C: An they come in// (   )
F: Oh its a tractor with a digger is it

In (18a), the caretaker offers a repair immediately post his whole utterance repeat but immediately accepts the child's rejection of that repair with his next, overlapping utterance. In (19a), the child's second utterance is overlapped by the caretaker's utterance at a point where it can be apparent to the caretaker that the child's utterance will not be one that effects a repair but rather one that straightforwardly continues the topic. As can be seen, the caretaker's utterance proposes a lexically more precise description of the object which the child has been attempting to describe.

Part utterance repeats, however, appear to locate responsibility for repair as a problem for the child in that they function as invitations to self-correct.[3] This can be seen to be the case, for example, by consideration of the eventual outcomes of sequences (20) and (21).

(20a) Ca:E:059
1. C: He's gonna buy eight yoghurt
2. M: Eight
3. C: Yes (0.5) ↑Is that a lot↑
4. M: What else is he gonna buy

(21a) Ca:E:057
1. C: He wants some oil
2. M: Oil
3. C: Petrol
(2.0)
4. M: Has he no petrol

That there are clarification request objects which project either co-operative or self-correction by the child argues against Corsaro's suggestion that they are markers of the suspension of interpretive procedures and against Garvey's suggestion that they are analysable in speech act terms as a species of request for information. For, in so far as they project co-operative correction, what is implied is that no assumption that the recipient knows what an adequate response would be is being made; whilst, in so far as they project self-correction, precisely that assumption is being made. It cannot, therefore, be argued, for such cases at least, that there is an awareness of an absence of shared cultural knowledge or that the utterer intends to elicit information by production of the clarification request which the utterer does not know but which is presumed to be known by the recipient.

The final form of clarification request that I want to comment on is the partial repeat which includes an interrogative proterm such as 'what' or 'who'. As clarification requests, these forms would appear to be highly efficient in locating the problematic nature of a prior utterance. Surprisingly, however, they seldom occur, at least in the data available to me, and this despite the fact that where they do occur they seem to be appropriately processed by the children involved, as is evidenced in the following sequence:

(22) Ca:E:055

C: He an ugly face
M: ↑He's a what↑
C: An <u>ugly</u> face
M: He hasn't an ugly face He's a pretty face

(23) Ga:E:212

M: Its supposed to be a a space 'h h
C: Cane:t
M: A space what darling
C: Space Canet
M: Can<u>e</u>:t
C: Yes a space canet
M: Ahh

Each of the forms of clarification request that I have isolated can occur as the second utterance of a four-utterance sequence and so as the initial and only display of a concern about some trouble with a prior utterance. It can happen, however, that clarification request sequences extend over more than four turns when the initial clarification request is ineffective in eliciting a response that is sufficient to resolve the issue of communicative inefficacy. What happens in such cases is that other forms of clarification request are introduced and are sequentially so ordered as to move towards increasing specification of the problem at hand. We can see this ordering operating in the following two examples:

(24) Ca:E:055

C: Is Derek a nice boy
→ M: Pardon
C: Is Derek a bad boy
→ M: Who
C: Derek
M: No

(25) To:M:179

C: What a rate yer in Mummy
→ M: Pardon
C: Look what her rate (.) yer i:n
→ M: ↑Pardon↑
C: What a rate yer in
→ M: What a what
C: What a rate yer in
M: What a rate am in. What a ↑hurry↑ am in
C: Ye::s
M: Am I

I hope to have shown that the clarification request sequence instances a distinctive conversational activity, engagement in which requires specific competencies on the part of both caretaker and child. Different forms of the clarification request have different implications for what can occur as nexts. It would be interesting to explore these implications and how they arise, in particular to see how asymmetries of knowledge amongst participants can occasion the use of particular forms of clarification request and how different conversational contexts (e.g. request sequences, informative sequences, fantasy sequences) exhibit particular forms.

Transcription Conventions

M.	mother
F.	father
C.	child
N.	other child

:	indicates the prolongation or 'stretching' of a sound
underlining	indicates emphatic stress
↑	indicates that an utterance is raised in pitch height
.h	indicates an inbreath
(.)	indicates a micropause
(3.0)	indicates the duration of a pause in seconds
(we)	indicates that the utterance is unclear and hence the transcription tentative
( )	indicates that the utterance is very unclear and hence untranscribable
//	indicates that a turn at talk overlaps with the next, and the point at which the overlap begins

Notes

1. Many of the data upon which this chapter draws come from a large number of tape-recordings made by Dr Tony Wootton, to whom I am grateful for access.
2. Jefferson (1972), in her discussion of 'misapprehension sequences', treats interactional matters, similar in some respects to what are here being called 'clarification request sequences'.
3. See also the contribution by Drew in this volume, on 'invitations to self-correct'.

References

Brown, R. (1973). *A First Language*. Boston: Harvard University Press

Cicourel, A.V. (1973). *Cognitive Sociology*. Harmondsworth: Penguin

Corsaro, W.A. (1976). 'The Clarification Request as a Feature of Adult Interactive Styles with Young Children'. *Language and Society*, 6, pp. 183–207

Garvey, C. (1978). 'The Contingent Query: A Dependent Act in Conversation'. In M. Lewis and L.A. Rosenblum (eds.), *Interaction, Conversation and the Development of Language*. New York: Wiley

Jefferson, G. (1972). 'Side Sequences'. In D. Sudnow (ed.), *Studies in Social Interaction*. New York: Free Press

10 SOME COMMENTS ON CLARIFICATION REQUESTS: A RESPONSE TO LANGFORD

David Hustler

Langford's paper is, in part, a contribution to the developing body of literature which suggests that, by quite an early age, children orient to a range of conversational rules. The work of Garvey, in particular, from a speech act perspective, has documented aspects of this competence as it relates to the handling of multi-utterance sequences by children over 3.6 (Garvey, 1975). Keenan and Klein's (1975) research suggests that, even before they are three years old, children can be seen to be working to achieve coherent dialogue; that, over a series of exchanges at talk, they construct their utterances with reference to the other party's previous turn and that, more generally, the talk of young children displays a central feature of coherent conversation: that of 'recipient design'.[1]

The interest in the development of conversational competence has led, amongst other things, to new perspectives on old observations about children's talk. Keenan's (1975) analysis of the uses of repetition in children's discourse is probably only one of the earliest of many studies to come, which will readdress such observations. Indirectly, Langford's paper provides an additional argument for the value of considering items such as 'repeats' in terms of their location and function in ongoing conversational exchanges. There is, however, one methodological issue which bears on the embeddedness of utterances in discourse, which I will touch on now and return to briefly later on. Where multi-utterance sequences such as clarification request sequences are being considered, we often find the analyst making suggestions as to the possible 'hearings' that participants are arriving at. The analyst attempts to warrant these with reference to other components in the identified sequence; further warrant is often sought by means of the natural strategy of offering for inspection a large number of examples of the same sort of sequence. I intend no criticism of this necessary strategy, but would note that, where clarification sequences, for example, are themselves embedded in conversational structures, the analyst needs to consider the possible implications of that embeddedness. Where the concern is, let us say, with the hearing that a child makes of the 'clarification component' itself, then the detachment of the sequence from its conversational environment cuts the analyst off from the resources which the child may be making use of. An extremely interesting paper which takes up such issues is one by Schegloff (1977), where he discusses how participants' orientation to the location of a particular utterance in two different sequential structures initially generated a case of ambiguity, but also provided the resources for the participants to resolve that ambiguity. It so happens that Schegloff's particular analysis centres around one participant's hearing of an utterance as a request for clarification. Collating examples of particular sequence types and focusing on these in isolation from the surrounding discourse may, in addition, not only hinder our understanding of the ways in which young children might be orienting to sequencing, but may also involve us in imputing problems to conversationalists which they might be seen not to have.

This brief response borrows very loosely from some of the work done in 'conversation(al) analysis'.[2] More generally, my interest here is in the interactional strategies which children and adults might be said to be pursuing through their talk, and how those strategies seem to display an orientation to the rules of conversational conduct. The clarification request sequence is here just a vehicle for some rather speculative comments which cannot receive rigorous analytical attention here, and which are certainly marginal to the central issues raised in Langford's paper. To begin with the most marginal and most speculative side-issue: it happens to involve making a start with the first component in the clarification request sequence – i.e. the 'communicatively inefficacious' utterance. Langford notes that caretakers can make an issue of communicative efficacy, and my initial comments rely on the possibility that, in certain cases, there may not be so much of an option as his paper implies. My speculation is that, on occasion, children may make use of linguistic malproductions as interactional resources. It is, however, the issues raised in my arriving at this as a possibility which are of more interest than the speculation itself.

Apart from noting that children are capable in various ways of participating in coherent discourse, capable of handling multi-utterance structures, capable of maintaining sustained dialogue, many studies on child discourse provide interesting examples of children using complex verbal strategies to accomplish interactional goals. In discussing his own and Garvey's work, Dore comments that certain choices children make in conversation 'might not be characteristic of an "ideal co-operative conversationalist", but . . . would certainly make for an "ideal Machiavellian conversationalist" ' (1977, p. 162).

I take it that, just as clarification request sequences are routine occurrences in interaction between children and their caretakers, so it is a routine occurrence that children have problems in obtaining speaking rights (and that adults may at times wish to deny them speaking rights). Sacks (1974) has noted the prevalence of utterances such as 'You know what mummy?' from children of about three and four, and has suggested some ways in which such an opener might be a particularly nice solution to the problem of obtaining proper access to conversation. His argument rests on pointing to a few aspects of conversational sequencing: in particular, that such a question has a question as its appropriate answer, which, should the child receive it, obliges the child to continue whatever 'what' might be.

Should such a strategy succeed, then the child has not only managed to raise what he wished to raise, but has done so on invitation; in so doing, the child has also, we could say, achieved one aspect of being a proper child – i.e. that of displaying his recognition of who's in charge. Let me introduce and briefly comment on a fragment of conversation which raises similar themes.[3] Although the previous conversation is of relevance to an extended analysis, I reproduce the data only from the point when the child attempts, for the second time, to break into the ongoing conversation between her parents:

(1) C: 4 years 10 months
1. M: That was all really–oh she walk taking about – –erm
Julie and
(1.0)
2. C: Mu (mmy
(
3. F: (Julie – – Julie and (who
(
4. M: (Chris
5. F: (Julie and who
(
6. M: (Julie and Chris
(1.0)
7. M: ((and) – – and
(
8. C: (Got to tell you some (thing
(
9. F: (Julie ((high rise))
10. M: Julie Smith 'n Chris

11. F: Mmm
→ 12. C: (This is funny
(
→ 13: M: ('n Pat 'n
(0.5)
14. M: ((Just a minute Sally I've told you before)
(((low volume))
15. C: (((inhales noisily)) ermm – – Mummy have you got any
16. of that decorated paper what's under the Christmas tree
17. M: Not at the moment. No I'm not moving (at the moment
(
18. C: (but you ( )
19. M: No:o
20. C: ('Cos) want to wrap this up
((and M continues))

There are a number of interesting features in this extract: one, for example, being the observation that, at no point, does the child actually begin an utterance whilst the other participants are talking, apart from line 18, where we would still seem to have a possible completion point. The child's first utterance in the extract could be said to occupy another's pause, but it is a lengthy one. However, the particular utterance I wish to single out for a moment is on line 12. This utterance can be viewed as a 'story preface', and perhaps quite an appropriate one in the sense that its content seems to promise more news of the sort that parents might be interested in than the similar item at line 8 and the earlier 'mummy' (line 2). This progression from what might be viewed as less powerful to more powerful starters is in itself a noteworthy feature of these data. Work by Sacks on story prefaces suggests that they can, in part, be seen as designed to handle the problem of achieving an extended turn at speaking, where such an extended turn may include within it a number of possible completion points – i.e. possibilities for other participants to disrupt the hoped-for extended turn. Story prefaces request invitations to proceed, and we can note both the parallel with the analysis of 'Do you know what, Mummy?' (Sacks, 1974) and (with reference to these data) that silence might be viewed as such an invitation.

A relevant aside is that it might be what children of about four could on occasion fruitfully do with setting up extended turns. This is because they would then create for themselves the opportunity not only to make a request of some sort, but also to provide within the same turn the grounds for that request; the point being that such a strategy might allow them to avoid getting involved in the complex syntactic constructions, and other devices, which would avoid possible completion points.

There are further features of these data, which I believe support a more rigorous analysis along these lines: for example, it so happens that the child does, in different turns, produce a request and some grounds for that request; the child makes use of a conventional paralinguistic resource for starting a story (line 15); whereas the previous attempts by the child to gain the floor receive no response from the parents, her 'This is funny' does get a response; the child is eventually allowed to talk without interruption in her next utterance. That an issue is not made of the apparent lack of a story, let alone a funny story, could probably relate to the parents' recognition that 'This is funny' is the fourth in a progressive series of attempts to gain the floor (this probability at least demonstrates the relevance of attending to the conversational environment of sections of talk, particularly where possible 'hearings' are to be proposed by the analyst). However, the general concern in the above is with the interactional problems facing children which their verbal strategies may provide possible solutions for, and this leads me to a restatement of my earlier speculation. This consisted of the notion that, at times, children may make use of syntactic irregularities, semantic incongruities and phonological malproductions, as interactional resources.[4] I reproduce a brief set of utterances which presumably can be viewed as a clarification request sequence:

(2)	C:	4 years 6 months	
	C:	C'n I have a ba	
	F:	((a ba–)	
		(	
	A:	(ba	((high rise))
	C:	ba heheh	
	F:	a bath you want a bath	
	C:	Yes please I (( )	
		(	
	F:	(Now I told (you)	

As orientation, I should note that this child had previously pronounced 'bath' (in fact 'baf') on numerous occasions, and that, somewhat prior to this exchange and the visitor's arrival, the child had made a series of unsuccessful requests for a bath. I should also note that the first utterance could be regarded as a starter and that it filled a pause in the ongoing adult–adult conversation. There are, of course, a number of perspectives which could be brought to bear on these data: one might involve a reliance on characteristics such as children being shy in the presence of relative strangers. I see no reason, however, for not being speculative in another direction. The interactional resource could be not so much the phonological malproduction, but rather the child's orientation to sequencing routines such as the clarification request sequence. The outcome is that what could be viewed as a dubious topic is finally established by the father, and established in a manner which the child rapidly builds on. I certainly do not want to make any claims for this casual comment on the above extract. The perspective which leads to it is of more relevance, but I would like to raise one further possibility for analysis which stems, in part, from the above.

Of interest is the fact that the above exchanges took place in a multi-party setting, as have a number of 'do you know what' openers with this same child. The issue is raised as to the ways in which young children may construct their utterances with some regard to the setting as a multi-party setting, and with regard to 'overhearers' in conversation. As apart from constructing utterances which invite repair (where reparative attempts provide possible speaking options for all parties to a conversation), it could be that some children orient to the possibility that parents may not want to be seen to be unconcerned about their children's capacity for language, or be seen to be uninterested in the unknown news that their children might have to tell. Where the initial utterance is constructed as a question, then the caretakers may find themselves that much more constrained to request a clarification. Hence, my initial comment to the effect that the caretaker's option to make something of a communicatively inefficacious utterance may at times not be so much of an option.

It could be suggested that the most one can get out of the above speculations is a fleeting but amusing vision of child language researchers arriving at inferences as to levels of linguistic competence (e.g. the child's phonological system), where those inferences are based on phonological malproduction samples which contain some *interactionally occasioned* malproductions. What the extracts do point to, however, and this is probably as much as should be made of them here, is the relevance of some attention being paid to features such as, at least, the sequential implicativeness of the communicatively inefficacious utterance. Such contextualisation seems to be of importance where the analyst is engaged in proposing possibilities as to children's and adult's 'hearings' and 'orientations'. It is the last of the above-mentioned features which I now wish to consider in more detail – i.e. the sequential implicativeness of the communicatively inefficacious utterance.

Implicit in earlier sections is a reliance on some aspects of the work on 'adjacency pairs' (e.g. Schegloff and Sacks, 1973). Adjacency pairs have a number of properties, but one central rule of their operation is that, once a first part of a pair has been recognisably produced, then, at first possible completion, the next speaker should commence with a second part to that same type of pair. Examples of adjacency pair types would seem to be 'question–answer', 'greeting-greeting', 'offer–acceptance or refusal'. Having provided an invitation, you expect to find, as a next, an utterance which can be seen to bear some relationship to that invitation as an acceptance, or an offer. Garvey's (1977) work suggests that, by the age of three, children are sufficiently familiar with such conventions to be able to make use of sequential implicativeness as a resource for verbal play with each other. As one general but brief comment, I would note that, where the analyst has an interest in the issues participants can make of communicatively inefficacious utterances and the work that may follow them, it seems important to be prepared to distinguish between initial components which are possible first pair parts, and initial components which do not appear to have that status. Not allowing for that distinction may conceal or blur the sort of work that children are putting into conversations with their caretakers. In particular, the oriented-to status of the initial component is likely to have implications for what resuming or continuing the conversation will involve. The work of Jefferson (1972) on 'side sequences' and Schegloff (1972) on 'insertion sequences' is of relevance here. An initial inspection of some of Langford's data suggests that, in some cases, the initial components may be oriented to as first pair parts, and I wish finally to apply some of the observations made in this response to one fragment of those data:

C: Come and see Captain Flack
(4.0)
M: Pardon
(5.0)
(F)
C: I see Captain (V)lack
M: Huh. Huh. (Langford, example (1), p. 161)

It is suggested by Langford that, in this particular case, the first 'component . . . was an utterance to which the intended recipient was perhaps inattentive' (p. 164) (although it might be seen that in certain respects this fragment bears a close resemblance to examples (10) to (15), in that the second component might, as in those examples, be taken not as a display of the recipient's 'failure to hear' but as a 'display of some other difficulty' *via* the reformulation of the initial item post the clarification request). At an earlier point in this response, I noted that detaching sequences from their conversational environment may lead the analyst to impute problems to conversationalists which they might not be seen to have: in similar vein, Langford, rightly in my view, is somewhat critical of Corsaro's argument to the effect that a simple minimal form clarification marker (e.g. 'what', 'pardon') is used to note that one interactant has not clearly heard the previous utterance, and is interpreted as such by the child. Nevertheless, in the case of this specific fragment, he suggests that the issue may be one of hearing – i.e. inattention.

There are probably a variety of possible analyses of the particular extract and I wish briefly to propose one. The intention here is not to provide a competitive version, but loosely to pull together (if somewhat implicitly) some of the themes touched on earlier. The child's initial utterance could be said to partake of at least some of the properties of a first part of an adjacency pair. As such, and reading it loosely as a request for action, we might expect the child to inspect any next for its relationship to that request. The silence which does in fact follow, plus that silence and the eventual 'pardon', could be heard by the child as 'refusal-implicative' – i.e. looking to the possibility that a refusal is on its way.[5] As an initial basis for this as a possible 'reading', we can note, first, that the child does not respond immediately to the 'pardon', which itself makes a particular type of response sequentially relevant and, second, we find an extensive reformulation: certainly extensive in terms of a change in sequential implicativeness. In brief, it might be suggested that a negotiation process has taken place, by means of which an outright refusal has been avoided, and that both participants have achieved this state of affairs through their talk (and absence of it) without that being made explicit.

This short analysis clearly relies on various common-sense notions as to what are routine goals and problems for children and their caretakers in their interaction with one another. The analysis does not, however, require the importing of decoding problems; rather, it assumes adequate communication at this level, and it credits the child with what probably appears to be somewhat overbuilt competence – i.e. that the child not only recognises the possibility of refusal, but is able to construct an utterance which, on the one hand, destroys the continuing sequential implicativeness of the initial utterance and, on the other hand, builds on that first utterance in such a way as to be able to be potentially heard as treating the 'pardon' as in fact a request for an object such as a repeat. In common with the rest of this response, the general direction for looking at the talk produced by the child is to consider the interactional problems that such talk might be viewed as a solution to. Where those solutions seem to suggest as their basis a fairly sophisticated grasp of aspects of the social organisation of conversation, I see no reason for not living with that as a possibility to be investigated by means of more rigorous analyses.

Notes

1. For an expansion of the notion of 'recipient design', see Sacks *et al.* (1974). The term originally encompassed the variety of ways in which talk, in conversation, is so constricted as to display orientations to co-participants to that talk, and thus serves to constitute any occasion of conversation as this particular, here-and-now occasion. Drew and Wootton in this volume also specifically address features of recipient design.

2. By 'conversation(al) analysis', I am referring to the body of work centring around researchers such as the late Harvey Sacks and Emanuel Schegloff. This approach is (some would say 'was') grounded in certain principles associated with 'ethnomethodology'. For an introduction to ethnomethodology, and a brief location of conversational analysis within it, see Turner (1974). See also Wootton, in this volume (Ch. 6), for an account of conversation(al) analysis.

3. The basis of data presented here consists of tape-recordings of adult-child interactions in the home setting. The transcript notation has largely been borrowed from the system developed, in particular, by Gail Jefferson. Briefly:

(1.0)	one second elapsed
(and)	sound is poor, but probably 'and'
(( ))	double brackets enclose transcriber's comment
really –	a 'cut-off' production
– –	pause
(Julie and (who ((Chris	overlap. 'Chris' starting as 'who' starts
(Julie and . . . ((Julie and . . .	simultaneous start
underlining	stress
:	elongated syllable

4. For analysis of linguistic malproductions as interactional resources, see Jefferson (1978).

5. For a developed analysis of, among other things, how disagreements, rejections and refusals may be prefaced, see Pomerantz (1975). By 'refusal-implicative', it is meant here that a refusal is likely to be the outcome of his request.

References

Dore, J. (1977). ' "Oh Them Sheriff": A Pragmatic Analysis of Children's Responses to Questions'. In S. Ervin-Tripp and C. Mitchell-Kernan (eds.), *Child Discourse*

Ervin-Tripp, S. and Mitchell-Kernan, C. (eds.) (1977). *Child Discourse*. New York: Academic Press

Garvey, C. (1975). 'Requests and Responses in Children's Speech'. *Journal of Child Language*, 2, pp. 41–63

— (1977). 'Play with Language and Speech'. In S. Ervin-Tripp and C. Mitchell-Kernan (eds.), *Child Discourse*

Jefferson, G. (1972). 'Side Sequences'. In D. Sudnow (ed.), *Studies in Social Interaction*

— (1978). 'What's in a "Nyem"?' *Sociology*, 12, 1, pp. 135–9

Keenan, E.O. (1975). 'Again and Again: The Pragmatics of Repetition in Child Language'. *Pragmatics Microfiche*, 1, 5, p. A3

— and Klein, E. (1975). 'Coherency in Children's Discourse'. *Journal of Psycholinguistic Research*, 4, 4, pp. 365–80

Pomerantz, A. (1975). 'Second Assessments: A Study of Some Features of Agreements/Disagreements'. Unpublished Ph.D. thesis, University of California, Irvine

Sacks, H. (1974). 'On the Analysability of Stories by Children'. In R. Turner (ed.), *Ethnomethodology*

—, Schegloff, E. and Jefferson, G. (1974). 'A Simplest Systematics for the Organization of Turn-Taking for Conversation'. *Language*, 50, pp. 696–735

Schegloff, E. (1972). 'Notes on a Conversational Practice: Formulating Place'. In D. Sudnow (ed.), *Studies in Social Interaction*

— (1977). 'Some Questions and Ambiguities in Conversation'. In W. Dressler (ed.), *Current Trends in Text-Linguistics*. New York: de Gruyter

— and Sacks, H. (1973). 'Opening up Closings'. *Semiotica*, 8, 4, pp. 289–327

Sudnow, D. (ed.) (1972). *Studies in Social Interaction*. New York: Free Press

Turner, R. (ed.) (1974). *Ethnomethodology*. Harmondsworth: Penguin

Part III

ADULT-CHILD INTERACTION AND DEVELOPMENTAL ANALYSIS

11 TOWARDS A MODEL FOR ANALYSING CONVERSATIONS INVOLVING CHILDREN

Michael F. McTear

Introduction

A few years ago, Roger Brown remarked that 'all over the world the first sentences of small children are being as painstakingly taped, transcribed and analysed as if they were the last sayings of great sages' (Brown, 1973). Now, five years later, as the emphasis has shifted from the construction of children's grammars to studies of their conversational competence and the interactional contexts in which their utterances occur, not only children's utterances but whole sequences of interactions involving other interlocutors and, usually with the help of film or video-recordings, gestures and other non-verbal accompaniments of speech are being recorded, transcribed and analysed. It is the third of these activities which raises the most problems. Vast amounts of data are being collected in various parts of the world. But how are these to be analysed? The absence of a fully adequate model of conversation has impeded work on the development of conversational competence and those working in this area are well aware of the difficulties in developing a model capable of accounting for their data.

It is to problems such as these that the present paper is addressed. The first part of the paper is concerned with general issues related to models of discourse:

1. What are the criteria for a fully adequate descriptive model?
2. If the model is to be applied to children's conversations, can it show where development takes place?
3. Can the model be used to explain the processes of development?

The second part of the paper deals more specifically with the components of such a model and looks at the units of discourse necessary for the explication of informal conversation. These are the individual acts accomplished by a speaker's utterances in a discourse and the way these combine into larger, sequentially related units.

Finally, I look at some currently unresolved problems in the analysis of discourse as articulated by several investigators in the field.

I

Criteria for a Model of Conversation

One important requirement for any model of discourse is that it should be able to account for the data. Work on conversational analysis by ethnomethodologists has provided extremely useful insights into aspects of conversation such as openings (Schegloff, 1968), closings (Schegloff and Sacks, 1974), side sequences (Jefferson, 1972), etc., but the main problem with this work for discourse analysts is that it focuses only on those parts of a text which are considered interesting and revealing for the authors' purposes and which, in many cases, do not necessarily coincide with those of the discourse analyst. Two recently published models of discourse seek to provide a comprehensive system of analysis capable of handling a whole text (Sinclair and Coulthard, 1975; Labov and Fanshel, 1977). The authors of both models envisage generalisability to forms of discourse other than those which they analysed. In addition to being able to handle a complete text, both these models aim to provide an explicit means of analysis, which is a primary aim of most linguists. Rules are specified to account for how particular grammatical configurations can be heard as particular discourse functions or speech acts. For example, both models provide explicit procedures for explaining how an utterance in declarative form such as

(1) The door is open

can be heard under certain specifiable conditions not as a statement but as a request for action (i.e. to open the door). This contrasts again with the work of the ethnomethodologists which avoids premature formalisation but which is open to the criticism that its descriptive categories cannot be explicitly defined for use by other researchers.

I would now like to look at some problems which have arisen from attempts to generalise these models to other forms of discourse, focusing on the Sinclair and Coulthard model where most of the work has been done. One immediate problem is that several of the acts described in their model are classroom specific. Other acts have to be added to account for different types of interaction and especially for the possibility of non-compliance between participants, which is not envisaged in the original model. Several of such alternative lists of acts have been reviewed by Burton (1978). This is, however, a fairly minor problem. We would expect that different types of acts would occur in different speech events and it seems to pose no problem to incorporate new acts into the model.

The more substantive problem which has faced other analysts concerns discourse structure – that is, how acts combine into larger units. The Sinclair and Coulthard model sees acts (or more specifically, moves) as combining into exchanges which consist of an initiation and a response (plus a feedback move in some forms of discourse, e.g. classroom discourse in teacher-eliciting exchanges). Initiations are prospective – they look forward to a following move and set up expectations about its appropriateness. Responses are retrospective – they provide a response from the options made available by the preceding initiation. However, when we examine transcripts of informal discourse, we find it is often not possible to decide which utterances are initiating and which are responding. In fact, many seem to fulfil both functions simultaneously:

(2)		
	1. Heather: do you like his big brother?	Initiation
	2. Siobhan: what?	?
	3. Heather: do you like his big br – her big brother?	?

Line 2 is clearly some sort of response to line 1, though not the expected or 'canonical' response. Rather, it is a request for repetition. It does, however, take account of the preceding initiation. Line 3 is a response to this request but at the same time functions to request a response. Thus, it would be possible to double-code lines 2 and 3 as simultaneously responses and initiations. In other words, they are retrospective and prospective at the same time. The same problem arises in discourse consisting of series of statements where each utterance takes account of a preceding utterance but is, in turn, responded to by a subsequent utterance:

(3) B: ah we moved ourselves
S: squatted we squatted
B: we did not indeed squat
S: we did
we squatted
B: when you're a squatter you've no rent book . . .
(from Milroy and Milroy, 1977)

The point of these examples is to show that different speech events can give rise to different discourse structures. The structures proposed in the Sinclair and Coulthard model seem to work only for certain types of discourse and are not generalisable, except with widespread modifications, to those types, in particular, where non-compliance is possible or to various speech events such as teasing, banter, performed narrative, etc. (McTear, 1978a). Thus, problems arise when we try to meet the criterion of descriptive adequacy, where a model can account for a total text but only within limited sets of speech events.

In this respect the Labov and Fanshel (1977) model might be perhaps less susceptible, as the rules it proposes are more abstract and apparently thus more generalisable. However, the problem does arise here that the authors find no way of relating their more abstract categories such as *challenge, insult, retreat*, to linguistic forms and so run the risk of failing to provide an explicit means for analysing these. In addition, they avoid the problem of discourse structure by not attempting to make structural statements, i.e. about what type of act can follow what. Instead they focus on sequential relations between actually occurring utterances. That is to say, they provide a list of speech actions which can be performed by participants A and B but do not suggest which combinations are possible and which are not (1977, p. 61).

To conclude this section, I would like to introduce one further issue. Most models of discourse try to account for the exchange of referential or propositional content in conversational interaction. Halliday (1977), for example, proposes that, in dialogue, participants enact reciprocal roles of either giving or demanding, if initiating, or receiving or supplying, if responding, where the basic commodities are either goods and services or information.[1] However, there are some instances of discourse in which neither goods or services nor information are being exchanged or, in other words, where there is no referential or propositional content, as, for example, in children's sound play (Keenan 1974; Garvey 1977b). One example from my own data will illustrate this point:

(4) Heather: horrible smell
it's not my shoes
Siobhan: it's not my shoes
Heather: it's not my shoes
Siobhan: uh?
Heather: it's not my shoes
Siobhan: it's not my sandals

Heather: ⟨ they're ⟩ not my sandals
Siobhan: it's not my bottie
Heather: it's not my bottie (both laugh)
Siobhan: it's not my head
Heather: it's not my head
Siobhan: it's not my um nose
Heather: it's not my nose
Siobhan: it's not my mouth
Heather: it's not my mouth

Here the content is virtually irrelevant. This interaction gains its structure from the basic initiate-respond/repeat pattern which is reinforced prosodically by identical intonation contours (high falling tone and heavy accentuation on the final substituted word) as well as isochronous timing, where the children exploit the basic stress patterns of the English language in order to produce identical frames into which new words can be substituted. Both children orient to this mutually constructed pattern and, when it threatens to break down, at a point just beyond the cited extract, Heather takes the initiative and sets the activity in motion again with further substitutions. In fact the sequence continues for a further twenty-seven turns. The fact that Heather is able to do this and that Siobhan immediately assumes the responding role, suggests that both are orienting towards the structure of this speech event. The sequence can be described in terms of initiation-response exchanges but it gains its cohesion not from propositional content but from its prosodic characteristics. A model of discourse would have to be extended to account for such a speech event and to differentiate it from those in which the main commodities to be exchanged are goods and services or information.

Criteria for a Developmental Discourse Model

The second main requirement for a model of discourse which is to be applied to children's conversations is that it should be capable of indicating where development is taking place. As in all developmental work, the basic problem is whether to start from a model based on adult competence, the presumed goal of the child's development, and show how the child progresses from immature to more mature forms, or whether to start with a child-based model, i.e. one which reflects what the child seems to be doing and which is constructed on the basis of the child's own system and not in relation to the adult system. However, although it is possible that children and adults operate with different discourse systems, we must assume some correspondence, otherwise communication as well as development would hardly be possible. For this reason, it seems that perhaps a compromise between the two positions is preferable, where we seek to specify the child's system on its own terms but at the same time try to relate it to the adult model, i.e. the end-product of development. This position is adopted in the following attempts to show the development of conversational competence.

One line of approach has been to show that children, as they develop, become more able to produce contingent or related discourse. This work is generally conducted implicitly, if not explicitly, against the background of Piaget's theory that pre-school children's speech is predominantly non-social or egocentric, in that it fails to take account of other interlocutors (Piaget, 1959). Work by Keenan (1974), Mueller (1972), Garvey and Hogan (1973) and others has shown that, for their samples at least, children produce discourse which is, for the most part, socially adapted. Nevertheless, very young children are less able to maintain discourse. Bloom, Rocissano and Hood (1976) found, for example, that two-year-olds did not sustain the topic initiated by adults, whereas, at age three, the children could sustain successive turns by adding new information to an adult's utterance. Garvey (1977a) found that slightly older children could sustain more extensive sequences. Thus, it should be possible to show how children develop from an initial inability to sustain a topic or produce contingent talk to a stage where they produce extended sequences of contingent talk. Similarly, their basic ability to respond to questions, commands and statements as well as their awareness of the discourse expectations of these should be expected to develop with age. Some of these concerns are being addressed in my current research (McTear, 1978b).

The second approach I would like to describe derives from Halliday's (1977) model of dialogue and is currently being developed at Bristol (Wells, Montgomery and MacLure, 1978a and 1978b). Basically, this involves viewing children's linguistic behaviour in terms of options which are fairly general at the earlier stages but become more differentiated with development. In other words, as children develop, they add more options to their linguistic potential and make more delicate distinctions within these options. This approach allows comparability between children. Some work has already been done on a limited sample, showing how two children of the same age differ in respect of the options they have available to them, as manifested in their performance in two brief interactions. The discourse systems, which I have reproduced below, illustrate how Mark's system is more developed than Thomas's in terms of more options and greater differentiation within options. For example, Mark and Thomas both have the means for receiving information and goods and services but Mark has the further options for accepting or rejecting these and, if accepting, of simply acknowledging or accepting more positively (agreeing). In addition, Mark possesses the ability to request repetition and clarification which Thomas has not yet developed.

Figure 1.1: Discourse Systems

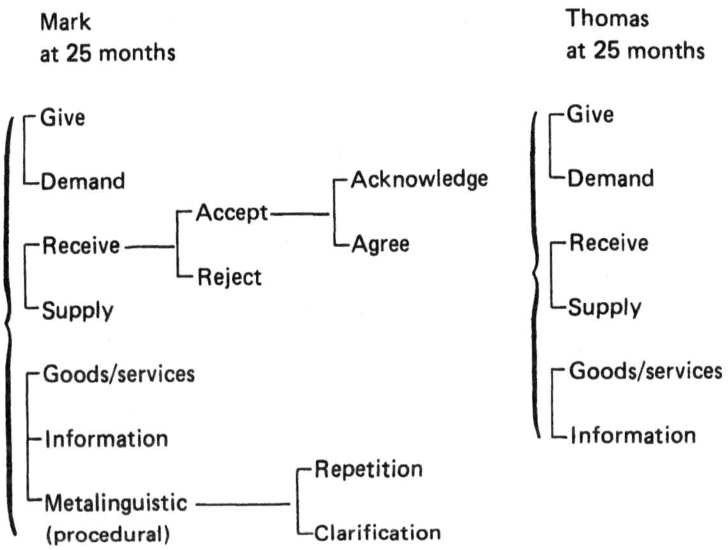

Source: Wells, Montgomery and MacLure, 1978a, p. 34.

This approach permits comparisons between the same children at different stages as well as between different children across samples. One further refinement might involve examining increases in the use of options, though the problem here, as with any measures of linguistic behaviour, is that selection of a particular option derives from various contextual factors which it would be difficult to hold constant, especially in a naturalistic observational study.

Criteria for an Explanatory Model of Developmental Discourse

Present work at Bristol is being directed towards investigating the hypothesis that children's language develops through their participation in linguistic interaction and, furthermore, that variations between children in their rate of development can be related to variations in the quality of this interaction (Wells, Montgomery and MacLure, 1978a). Halliday stresses the crucial role of language in the transmission of the cultural order to the child as a result of interaction between the child and other human beings, at first his family and later his peers. What remains to be done now is to show the interactive processes which explain this development. This depends, in the first place, on the development of an adequate model for the description of interaction. In order to illustrate this point, I will briefly describe two investigations which apply a model of discourse to the description of linguistic interaction as a means of explaining language development.

Cole, Dore, Hall and Dowley (1978) investigate the factors which determine situational variability in children's use of language by recording children in two settings – in a fairly free setting in a supermarket with a peer and a research assistant, who was minimally interactive, and in a more formal setting at school with a teacher, who questioned the child about the supermarket visit. They found that, where variability was produced, this was a result of changing the relative frequency with which certain speech acts occurred in the corpus. For example, in the supermarket setting the children produced more descriptions, whereas in the school setting they produced more responses to WH-test questions. In other words, they had greater freedom to initiate sequences in the supermarket setting and this gave rise to a wider display of their linguistic competence. These findings are reached following a fine-grained analysis of the functions of the utterances of the adults and children, using a model of discourse developed by Dore.

Wells, Montgomery and MacLure (1978b) set out to identify different strategies of interaction which might have an effect on children's learning as a result of habitual participation in such interactions. They examine two samples of discourse involving the children referred to above, in interaction with their mothers, and find differences in the degree of reciprocity in these interactions. One mother tends to support her child's utterances by acknowledging them and extending them, whereas the other mother tends to ask questions to which she herself knows the answer and corrects the form and content of his responses. The former mother seems to show greater conversational co-operativeness and encouragement in her dialogue and it is hypothesised that the child's habitual participation in such dialogues would have beneficial consequences for his learning in comparison with habitual participation in the type of interaction displayed by the second mother.

This work is still very much at the exploratory stage but the line of investigation is most promising. What still remains to be done is to develop a rigorous method for evaluating and comparing modes of interaction, in terms of dimensions such as effectiveness, utility, co-operativeness, support, etc. Some of the discourse features described in the analysis suggest how this might be done. Secondly, in order for this hypothesis to have explanatory power, it is necessary to show in what way and to what extent the interactive patterns of the first mother affect her child's learning, in comparison with those of the second mother. Is the effect on the child's linguistic forms or on his communicative use of language and how are these, especially the latter, to be measured? Finally, we need to stress the phrase 'habitual participation', as one or two isolated instances of minimal or less encouraging interaction could be ascribed to various factors such as tiredness, lack of time, etc. This point can be illustrated anecdotally by reference to my own research on child-child interaction, where my role as investigator was to play as minimal and unobtrusive a part as possible, the aim of the research being to investigate the extent to which children could structure their own interaction without the support of a conversationally more mature interactive partner. Consequently, I tended either to ignore or to give minimal responses to initiations which the children addressed to me. This might appear to provide evidence of non-supportive interactive patterns. However, these arose under special circumstances. Moreover, it could also be claimed that the children, in order to secure my participation, had to develop more fully their resources for getting my attention and securing my response, which are some of the basic prerequisites for initiating talk (McTear, 1978c).

To sum up, any explanation of language development, in terms of interactive patterns, requires an adequate model for the description of interaction. The two studies which I have described here have shown how such a model can be effectively employed by identifying the types of speech acts employed by children and adults in particular settings and showing how various sociolinguistic factors, such as status of participants, setting, perception of task or nature of interaction by participants, etc., can determine the type of speech acts which occur in the interaction with possible effects for the child's learning. It is, indeed, ironic that, if children's own initiations and descriptions, which occur in a setting where the adult is more supportive and less dominant, are more qualitatively beneficial than their responses to test questions, for example, and these give rise to a greater display of linguistic potential, nevertheless the type of language typically elicited from children in formal classroom and experimental settings is in response to such test questions, which would seem actually to minimise the potential complexity of the child's linguistic performance.

II

Components of a Model of Discourse: Acts

By now, fairly general agreement has been reached among discourse analysis that the smallest unit of discourse is the *act* (although this is variously named within different systems of analysis). The act represents the function of a speaker's utterance in discourse. Work on discourse acts derives mainly from work on speech acts by philosophers of language (e.g. Austin, 1962; Searle, 1969), where typical speech acts are requests, promises, threats, warnings, etc. The main problems with work on discourse acts are that there is a tendency to produce infinite lists of acts which often overlap and that different authors suggest similar acts but with different labels, thus giving rise to considerable terminological confusion. I follow the suggestion by Wells, Montgomery and MacLure (1978b) that what is required is a finite list of basic acts which can be further subdivided into more delicate options. Thus, many of the functions proposed in the Bristol *Coding Manual* (Wells, 1975) could now be seen as more delicate options of more basic acts. Interestingly, other writers are also moving in this direction, for example Dore (1978), who proposes four basic types of conversational act: metalinguistic *regulative* acts, which are devices for organising conversation and include boundary markers and attention-getting devices, *requestives*, which solicit specific kinds of responses and include various question types, action and permission requests, suggestions, etc., *assertives*, which supply information and establish facts, and *responsives*, which supply solicited information or additional information related to preceding requestives or assertives. Sinclair and Coulthard (1975) propose somewhat similar acts. For example, their three main initiating acts are *elicitation*, which is a request for a linguistic response, *directive*, which is a request for action, and *informative*, which functions to supply information. Their scheme has the additional advantage that it shows how other acts can be subsidiary to these three main acts. In other words, the three main acts occur at the head of initiating moves but can be supported by acts such as *nominations, prompt, clue*, etc. Their scheme also permits more delicate options for the three main acts. For example, directives could be further subdivided into suggestions, entreaties, commands, etc.

The main criterion for discourse units such as acts is that they should be discrete and identifiable and that they should be motivated by the text. In earlier models, Dore (e.g. 1977), for example, proposed two types of assertives: *descriptions*, which express observable or verifiable facts, and *statements*, which express facts, rules, attitudes, feelings, beliefs, etc. Yet it is sometimes difficult to see how these can be kept separate, although, perhaps, reference to the more detailed categories in the coding scheme might help. However, it is not clear how these distinctions are motivated, i.e. whether on linguistic grounds (e.g. is there a difference in realisation between the two types?) or on discourse grounds (e.g. does the selection of one option have any effect on the subsequent discourse by constraining the range of options available to the next speaker?). Similarly, there is a class of acts labelled *performatives*, which accomplish facts by being said. But it is difficult to see how an utterance such as 'stop', which would be coded as a *protest*, is to be distinguished from *action requests*, which by definition 'solicit a listener to perform (or cease to) an act (or process)'. Various conditions are specified which enable us to distinguish protests from requests for action, but this might be conceptualised more economically by considering protests as a more delicate distinction within requests. The main problem, anyway, with the category of performatives is that it obscures Austin's (1962) insight that all illocutionary acts perform an act as well as encoding content. It is difficult to see how categories such as *protest, tease, joke, warning*, etc. do this to any greater extent than *requests, descriptions*, etc.

Once a taxonomy of discrete and well-motivated acts has been established, the next problem for the analyst is to be able to identify instances of these in texts. This is especially problematic with children's utterances, particularly at the earlier stages where the utterance has little or no grammatical structure to aid identification. This problem is discussed by Wells, Montgomery and MacLure (1978a) in relation to the identification of children's requests. How do we know, for example, if a child's utterance 'ball' is intended as a request or as some sort of informative act? The authors are unable, as yet, to present a set of criteria for disambiguating such indeterminate utterances, in terms of how they are likely to be responded to, and point out that intonation and other prosodic features do not appear systematically to provide the means for doing so. The possible approaches suggested are, firstly, to identify possible reinitiations of requests which might then aid in the retrospective identification of an utterance as a request and, secondly, to examine how the child's interlocutors respond to the utterance.

Dore has proposed a decision procedure for the identification of conversational acts (see, for example, Dore, Gearhart and Newman, 1978). The first step is to identify the grammatical form of the utterance, which will, in unmarked cases, aid identification of the act – for example, an imperative is the unmarked form of a request for action. However, as is clear from work on indirect speech acts (e.g. Searle, 1975), there is no necessary direct relationship between grammatical form and discourse function. These have to be systematically distinguished by specifying the conditions under which particular forms can represent particular functions. Ultimately, one would hope to be able to show that the linguistic form of an utterance, where this is taken to include its syntactic form as well as prosodic features such as intonation, voice quality, etc. (and probably also non-verbal accompaniments), has some bearing on its meaning in a particular context and its effect on subsequent discourse.

Bearing this crucial distinction in mind, further steps involve examining the literal semantic reading of the utterance, its conventional illocutionary force, its relation to other utterances in discourse, marked illocutionary devices, its relation to more global features such as the interactional task served by the discourse and, finally, gestures and non-verbal features.

The importance of this decision procedure can be seen when we examine utterances of the type 'I want X', which notoriously cause problems in coding. At the grammatical level this is a declarative, which, in unmarked cases, realises a statement of desire. Take, for example,

(5) I want to go to bed early

which expresses the speaker's desire to go to bed early. However, under certain specifiable conditions, this utterance can function as a request for action, for example, if it is spoken to B with the intention of getting getting B to leave, not to visit at that particular time, etc., and B is able to infer this intention. This is then an indirect request for action expressed by a declarative form. We can go further and examine the relation of the utterance to preceding discourse. If it occurs in the following sequence

(6) A: Would you like another drink?
B: I want to go to bed early

then B's utterance is seen as a response to A's offer of another drink. In order for A (and the discourse analyst) to see B's response as relevant, he has to locate an underlying proposition either in the preceding discourse or from his background knowledge of local culture and B's characteristic way of life, to the effect that B's wish to go to bed early affects his decision as to whether or not he wishes to have another drink (see, for example, Labov and Fanshel's 'Rule for Implicit Responses', 1977, p. 99). In isolation, it would not be possible to decide here whether B is refusing another drink or accepting one, but hinting that this ought to be the last one.

One further example will illustrate the application of a subsequent step in this decision procedure. The following 'I want . . .' utterance

(7) I want to clean the table

is coded as a request for permission because of the relation of the utterance to the task at hand. The evidence is based on three sources:

1. the teacher responds to it as a request – the justifications given in her response would not be warranted by an assertion of desire;
2. the conversation preceding the utterance is concerned with participation in, and allocation of, tasks, where others have implied their desire to wash by issuing direct requests;
3. the form of the utterance makes explicit the sincerity condition on requesting (Dore, Gearhart and Newman, 1978).

In this way elements of the task can be employed in the recognition of the conversational-act status of an utterance.

There are also cases where utterances have to be double-coded for function because more than one meaning appears to be in operation. The most common cases appear to be interrogative forms which can be used simultaneously to request information and to request an action, e.g.

(8) Child: can you fix this needle?

In isolation, this utterance could be coded as either a request for information about the addressee's ability or as a request to the addressee to fix the needle. In fact, in the actual sequence, the first meaning was intended by the speaker but the second meaning was assumed by the addressee:

(9) Child: can you fix this needle?
Adult: I'm busy
Child: I just wanted to know if you can fix it
(from Coulthard, 1977, pp. 71-2)

We need to be able to account for the two meanings which were available to the recipient of the utterance in order to explain the misunderstanding.

In fact, we can go further and suggest, with Labov and Fanshel, that 'most utterances can be seen as performing several speech acts simultaneously' (1977, p. 28). In some cases, they propose at least six acts for a single utterance, though these are at different levels of abstraction and involve not only reference to the actual text, but also paralinguistic cues, relevant factual information from preceding and subsequent discourse and shared knowledge. Here the concern is with the way the text is grounded in social interaction. Others wish to show how the text sheds light on the cognitive and operational capacities of children (Shields, 1978), how the text indexes the task at hand (Dore, Gearhart and Newman, 1978), etc. Some analysts prefer to operate at the level of the utterance and its immediately adjacent utterances. How far one wants to go with the meanings of an utterance seems to depend on the aims of the analysis. One important constraint should be that any interpretations made by an analyst need to be somehow motivated by the text if the analysis is to remain rigorous and objective. For example, if participants respond or orient to or formulate one of the meanings proposed, then this could be taken as evidence that this meaning was available.

Sequencing in Discourse

The second main issue in conversational analysis is how utterances combine into larger units. Here there is considerable terminological as well as theoretical confusion and at this point my suggestions will have to be tentative and exploratory. Various units have been proposed which seem to overlap in some cases but not in others. Sinclair and Coulthard (1975) propose the *exchange* which consists minimally of two moves by different speakers, one of which initiates the exchange while the other responds. Typical cases would be elicitation-reply, directive-react exchanges. The various types of exchange which occurred in their classroom data are presented as structural statements. This type of structure fulfils the criteria proposed by others for sequences, e.g. '. . . a series of conversational acts which share a topic and a reciprocal illocutionary domain and which accomplish some interactional purpose' (Dore, Gearhart and Newman, 1978), '. . . a stretch of conversation having unitary topic and purpose' (Wells, 1975). Wells (1975) shows how subsequences (or exchanges) can be embedded within a sequence, where, for example, within a control sequence (request for action) there can be embedded a procedural exchange to get the addressee's attention, accounts, justifications, etc., but where the dominant topic and purpose remain the request for action. Clarification sequences would similarly be seen as embedded structures within a sequence. In these cases we can suggest that we have series of exchanges which combine into larger units, which we can call sequences. In cases where there is no embedding, however, exchanges and sequences are structurally identical.

One problem arises with definitions of terms such as 'topic'. Topics can be rejected, as in non-compliant discourse. If a participant refuses to comply with a preceding request or rejects all or part of its content, then this utterance, in addition to being a response, can in turn be subject to a further response. We then have to decide whether the further response is elicited or whether structure is given retrospectively by virtue of the response having been made. Consider the following example:

(10)	1. Heather:	waken up	directive
	2. Siobhan:	no	refuse
	3.	cos I have to go to sleep	comment
	4.	I'll waken up in the morning	comment
	5. Heather:	no	reject
	6.	waken up now	directive

Utterance 2 is a response to the directive in 1. It is followed by two comments, where comment is a superordinate term for justifications, qualifications, elaborations, etc. Utterance 5 responds to 4 by rejecting it, and 6 reinitiates the directive.

The problem here is to decide on the exchange boundaries. (The sequence itself continues for a further few turns until, in fact, Siobhan complies.) Utterances 3 and 4 are linked to 2 in providing a justification and a promise of compliance, so these could be coded as part of the response. But 5 is a response to 4. The question is whether we code 4 as being simultaneously part of the response to 1, as well as the occasion of 5. If so, do we wish to say that 4 has elicited 5 in the sense that, if 5 had not occurred, its absence would have been noticeable (Sacks, 1968)? This hardly seems justifiable. From Siobhan's viewpoint, this interaction could have concluded with 4. Heather extends the interaction by opting to contribute further to the topic at hand. Her response has retrospective significance in that it responds to a preceding utterance, but it doesn't seem to be the case that 4 has prospective significance in that it expected a response, although it is the case that it sets up constraints on the form and function of a possible next response.

Another possibility would be to say that 1 and 2 constitute an exchange and that 3 is a new initiation (informative). This would, however, raise the problem of an artificial separation of 2 and 3 which are semantically linked, 3 being a justification of 2. The line could be drawn between 3 and 4, but the same objections apply. There would also be problems in the case of implicit responses, where the refusal is not stated explicitly but reference is made to one of the preconditions of the act performed in the initiation, e.g.

(11)	Heather:	now would you give me that?	request
	Siobhan:	don't have to give you my plasticine	refusal/comment

Here the refusal is achieved by rejecting the precondition on requests that the recipient of the request is obliged to carry out the requested action. While this refusal is obviously a response to the request, it changes the topic and introduces a proposition which could, in turn, be subject to a response. This process could then continue for several turns so that we would still have coherent discourse but no means of drawing the lines to indicate exchanges consisting of initiations and responses. In other words, each utterance would respond to a preceding utterance and the structure would be provided retrospectively. This would also seem to apply to series of statements, as in example 3 above. With this type of discourse, it hardly seems justifiable to speak of a tightly defined exchange structure. Instead, what we seem to have is a series of extended exchanges with initiations, responses and extending moves, where, as in Dore's most recent formulation, extensions 'elaborate on either the same topic introduced by the initiating C-act (conversational act) or the illocutionary conditions underlying the imitating or responding C-acts' (1978). These extended exchanges thus develop into larger units, which I would then call sequences.

As far as the notion of topic is concerned, sameness of topic can be defined as preserving the primary sentence constituents (i.e. subject, verb, object, adverbial phrase, etc.) in the propositions which form the content of utterances in an exchange or sequence. Any change in a primary sentence constituent or any new request would give rise to a new exchange/sequence, e.g.

(12)	Adult:	see, these are the fruits we have	
	Child:	(pointing to different objects)	
		an' these are the fruits?	new exchange

Here we are defining topic with reference to the propositional content of an utterance (Keenan and Schieffelin, 1976) rather than more broadly as something like 'topic or subject of conversation'.

The preceding considerations have both theoretical and practical significance. As far as the theory of discourse is concerned, we need to be able to show how successive utterances combine into larger units. This involves first of all deciding what these larger units are to be – that is, specifying their structure. But, apart from these considerations, we have the problem, when examining children's conversations, of showing that children acquire the ability to produce these structures in coherent discourse. In order to do this, we might wish to be able to show that, at early stages, they respond less frequently and that frequency of responses increases with age. In this case, we have to be able to score utterances in terms of whether they respond to preceding utterances or not. An accurate statement of discourse structure is required here, as it is not the case that every utterance has to respond to a preceding utterance. We have to allow for those utterances which quite clearly initiate by introducing new topics and which are often clearly identifiable by boundary markers such as 'right', 'now', etc. This was the main problem with the Garvey and Hogan (1973) scheme, which simply scored utterances in relation to preceding and subsequent discourse without allowing for initiations. This could result in an adverse score of responsiveness for children who nevertheless successfully accomplish initiations at appropriate occasions in an interaction.

A second possible approach to development would be to compare exchange and sequence structure at different stages of development. Here, of course, it is essential that we can appeal to rigorous definitions of these units.

I would like to conclude this section by looking at the notion of prospective discourse structure. Utterances which initiate in discourse set up expectations for a response. If this response is not forthcoming, then its absence is noticeable (Sacks, 1968). It is informative to investigate the extent to which children develop expectations concerning their initiating utterances. One method which I have proposed is to examine their behaviour following non-responses or unsatisfactory responses to their imitations, i.e. whether they reinitiate or not (McTear, 1978c). It is also possible to examine the options available to participants in particular types of sequence and to examine the extent to which children evidence an ability to construct and orient towards such sequences, for example as shown by their ability to reinitiate or effect repairs. The two types of sequence most fully developed in the literature are the request sequence and the clarification sequence. For requests, Labov and Fanshel (1977, p. 111) show that, following a request by A, B has the following options:

1. comply with the request;
2. put off the request with or without giving a justification;
3. refuse the request with or without a justification.

Wells, Montgomery and MacLure (1978a) propose a similar structure which they represent in a flow chart. They also allow for an attention-getting prefatory sequence and recursion within the sequence, i.e. *repeats* following non-responses and *persists* following *refuses* or *stalls* (put-offs). Given such a structure, it is then possible to examine the extent to which children have acquired the various options available, the length of repeat and persist cycles in relation to age, etc. Similar investigations have been carried out on the structure of clarification sequences and aspects of their acquisition (Garvey, 1977a; Corsaro, 1977). What remains to be done is to identify other types of sequence in discourse where the categories can be sufficiently motivated by the text and can be reliably identified by subsequent investigators and then to show the relationship of the various sequences to each other. For example, clarification sequences are generally embedded within other sequences. This relationship would have to be accurately specified in order to show their differential status in discourse structure.

Conclusion

In conclusion, I would like to summarise the main points and then refer to some problems.

A suitable model of discourse has to be able to account for a complete text in an explicit manner. It also has to be able to account for different types of text arising in different speech events. Otherwise, no means of comparison between different types of speech event or between children at different developmental stages are possible. Explicit rules are necessary so that studies are replicable. In addition, functions need to be related to their linguistic and non-linguistic realisations, otherwise we cannot explain why one particular form has been chosen rather than another. Speakers, after all, do tend to converge on which particular set of linguistic items and which set of non-verbal signs (within a particular culture) are most appropriate to express which set of meanings. The model should also be explicit to the extent that the categories can reveal where development is taking place and permit an analysis which can suggest explanatory hypotheses about the relation between features of the interaction and children's development and use of language. The more detailed examination of components of such a model, in the second part of the paper, indicates some of the reasons why it is necessary to establish a taxonomy of finite, discrete items such as acts and then to show how these relate in a coherent discourse structure.

Finally, some problems:

1. Wells, Montgomery and MacLure (1978b) cite an adult-child interaction, which is partially reproduced here, in which, despite surface marks of agreement, little common ground appears to be reached:

(13) 1. Mother: Are you doing the elephant or not?
2. Child: Yes, I'm doing an elephant.
3. Mother: What colour?
4. Child: Red
5. Mother: You don't do elephants red
6. Child: No it's blue
7. Mother: You don't do elephants blue
8. Child: No, it's purple

(1978b, pp. 17-18)

We can divide this sample into two part exchanges with initiations and responses, although we might wish to say that at 6 and 8 the child agrees (i.e. responds) to the mother's initiation but also adds new content to which she responds in 7. However, whichever way we analyse this sample at the local discourse level, we will find structure. Yet this analysis does not account for the impression we get that little successful communication has taken place. Certainly, there is little of the interaction between two minds which is normally taken to be the result of dialogue (Shields, 1978). How are we to characterise this type of discourse which probably occurs frequently in conversations involving immature conversational partners and also in various pathological cases such as thought-disordered schizophrenia, and how can we differentiate it from more successful communication?

2. Related, perhaps, to the previous point is the issue of how the discourse structure of a text reflects some higher-level organisation such as the task at hand, where a discourse model can be used to show how grammatical forms are chosen to convey illocutionary intentions in the service of accomplishing social interaction (Dore, Gearhart and Newman, 1978). In other words, what is the relation between text and task, where task can be understood as the goal of the interaction, whether this is formally organised, as in a classroom lesson, or quite informally, as in desultory conversation? To what extent do we have to go beyond the local discourse structure to examine and categorise the interaction which the discourse accomplishes?

3. In developmental studies there is the problem of deciding whether the child is operating with the same categories as the adult. (We assume, perhaps wrongly, that the adult and analyst operate with similar categories.) Moreover, the child's categories are subject to change over time and what has a certain function in a child's system at one stage may be employed in a different function at another stage, or alternatively the same function may have different realisations at different stages. Wells, Montgomery and MacLure (1978b) point to the problems of assigning communicative values to the child's intonation patterns when these are still in the process of development.

An example from my own data shows how a child tended to repeat questions addressed to her and then either responded or failed to respond. When she didn't respond, she seemed to be using the repeated question as a device for reassigning the question to its initiator, i.e. refusing to accept the role of respondent. Later this device was replaced by 'don't know', which was likewise followed either by the appropriate response or by no response. Thus, the same function had different realisations at different stages (see McTear, 1978b). An obvious danger would be to assign forms such as 'don't know' to their conventional adult meanings when clearly these were not intended by the child. Bearing this problem in mind, how then do we determine a child's discourse categories and, if they are subject to change over time and also tend to be idiosyncratic, what means have we for comparisons between children?

The present paper has attempted to examine some of the problems involved in developing a discourse model to account for children's conversations and has reviewed some approaches to these problems. The exploratory nature of some of my suggestions and the tentative tone I have hoped to convey indicate that many of these problems have yet to be properly formulated, let alone resolved, and that much work remains to be done on the vital question of how human beings talk to one another and how children learn to use language to talk to others.

Notes

1. See also Wells and Montgomery, in this volume.

References

Austin, J. (1962). *How to Do Things with Words*. London: Oxford University Press

Bloom, L., Rocissano, L. and Hood, L. (1976). 'Adult-Child Discourse: Developmental Interaction Between Information Processing and Linguistic Knowledge'. *Cognitive Psychology*, 8, pp. 521-52

Brown, R. (1973). 'Development of the First Language in the Human Species'. *American Psychologist*, 29, 2

Burton, D. (1978). 'Dialogue and Conversation: A Study of Discourse Analysis and Modern Drama Dialogue'. Unpublished Ph.D. thesis, University of Birmingham

Campbell, R. and Smith, P. (eds.) (1978) *Recent Advances in the Psychology of Language: Language Development and Mother-Child Interaction*. New York: Plenum Press

Cole, M., Dore, J., Hall, W. and Dowley, G. (1978). 'Situation and Task in Young Children's Talk'. *Discourse Processes*, 2, pp. 119-76

Cole, P. and Morgan, J.L. (eds.) (1975). *Syntax and Semantics III: Speech Acts*. New York: Academic Press

Corsaro, W. (1977). 'The Clarification Request as a Feature of Adult Interactive

Styles with Young Children'. *Language in Society*, 6, pp. 183-207

Coulthard, R.M. (1977). *An Introduction to Discourse Analysis*. London: Longman

Dore, J. (1977). 'Children's Illocutionary Acts'. In R. Freedle (ed.), *Discourse Production and Comprehension*

— (1978). 'Outline of the Conversational-Act System of Discourse Analysis'. Paper presented at Discourse Analysis Symposium, 5th AILA Congress, Montreal, August 1978

—, Gearhart, M. and Newman, D. (1978). 'The Structure of Nursery School Conversations'. In K. Nelson (ed.), *Children's Language, I*

Freedle, R. (ed.) (1977). *Discourse Production and Comprehension*. Hillsdale, New Jersey: Erlbaum Press

Garvey, C. (1977a). 'The Contingent Query: A Dependent Act in Conversation'. In M. Lewis and L.A. Rosenblum (eds.), *Interaction, Conversation and the Development of Language*

— (1977b). *Play*. London: Fontana

— and Hogan, R. (1973). 'Social Speech and Social Interaction: Egocentrism Revisited'. *Child Development*, 44, pp. 562-8

Halliday, M.A.K. (1975). *Learning How to Mean*. London: Edward Arnold

— (1977). 'Language as Code and Language as Behaviour: A Systemic-Functional Interpretation of the Nature and Ontogenesis of Dialogue'. Mimeo. (To appear in S.M. Lamb and A. Makkai (eds.), *Semiotics of Culture and Language*)

Jefferson, G. (1972). 'Side Sequences'. In D. Sudnow (ed.), *Studies in Social Interaction*

Keenan, E.O. (1974). 'Conversational Competence in Children'. *Journal of Child Language*, 1, pp. 163-83

— and Schieffelin, B. (1976). 'Topic as a Discourse Notion: A Study of Topic in the Conversations of Children and Adults'. In C. Li (ed.), *Subject and Topic*. New York: Academic Press

Labov, W. and Fanshel, D. (1977). *Therapeutic Discourse*. New York: Academic Press

Lewis, M. and Rosenblum, L.A. (eds.) (1977). *Interaction, Conversation and the Development of Language*. New York: Wiley

McTear, M.F. (1978a). 'Is Conversation Structured?: Towards an Analysis of Informal Spoken Discourse'. To appear in *5th Lacus Forum*. California: Hornbeam Press

— (1978b). 'Repetition in Child Language: Imitation or Creation?' In R. Campbell and P. Smith (eds.), *Recent Advances in the Psychology of Language*

— (1978c). 'Hey! I've Got Something to Tell You: A Study of the Initiation of Conversational Exchanges by Preschool Children'. Paper presented to 5th AILA Congress, Montreal, August 1978. (To appear in *Journal of Pragmatics*)

Milroy, L. and Milroy, J. (1977). 'Speech and Context in an Urban Setting'. *Belfast Working Papers in Language and Linguistics*, 2, 1

Mueller, E. (1972). 'The Maintenance of Verbal Exchanges Between Young Children'. *Child Development*, 43, pp. 930-8

Nelson, K. (ed.) (1978). *Children's Language, I*. New York: Gardner Press

Piaget, J. (1959). *The Language and Thought of the Child*. 3rd edn. London: Routledge

Sacks, H. (1968). Unpublished Lecture Notes. Mimeo

Schegloff, E.A. (1968). 'Sequencing in Conversational Openings'. *American Anthropologist*, 70, pp. 1075-95

— and Sacks, H. (1974). 'Opening up Closings'. In R. Turner (ed.), *Ethnomethodology*. Harmondsworth: Penguin

Searle, J. (1969). *Speech Acts: An Essay in the Philosophy of Language.* Cambridge: Cambridge University Press

— (1975). 'Indirect Speech Acts'. In P. Cole and J.L. Morgan (eds.), *Syntax and Semantics III: Speech Acts*

Shields, M. (1978). 'Some Communicational Skills of Young Children: A Study of Dialogue in the Nursery School'. In R. Campbell and P. Smith (eds.), *Recent Advances in the Psychology of Language*

Sinclair, J.McH. and Coulthard, R.M. (1975). *Towards an Analysis of Discourse.* London: Oxford University Press

Sudnow, D. (ed.) (1972). *Studies in Social Interaction.* New York: Free Press

Wells, C.G. (1975). *Coding Manual for the Description of Child Speech.* Revised edn. University of Bristol School of Education

—, Montgomery, M.M. and MacLure, M. (1978a). 'The Development of Discourse: A Report on Work in Progress'. Mimeo. University of Bristol

—, Montgomery, M.M. and MacLure, M. (1978b). 'Discourse and the Development of Language'. Paper presented at Discourse Analysis Symposium, 5th AILA Congress, Montreal, August 1978

12 ADULT-CHILD INTERACTION AT HOME AND AT SCHOOL

Gordon Wells and Martin Montgomery

Introduction

We begin with two propositions: firstly, that the knowledge and values a child comes to draw upon in his dealings with the social and physical world are learned largely through his interactions with other members of his culture, particularly his parents and teachers; and, secondly, that such interactions are achieved to a very considerable extent through linguistic communication. These two propositions together delimit a broad and complex field for investigation, although differences may arise with respect to the selection of specific areas to focus upon and in the theoretical approaches that are adopted.

Our own work starts with the analysis of texts of particular interactions and, on that basis, attempts to identify 'styles of interaction' and to relate these to larger issues, such as differences between the 'language of the home' and the 'language of the school' and the different opportunities these two interactional contexts provide for children to develop control of the resources of linguistic communication and to use these resources to learn about the world in which they live. In this paper, we shall present three extracts taken from recordings of one of the children in our longitudinal study, in order to illustrate certain aspects of the method of analysis and to provide a basis for a discussion of some of the more general issues that are raised by this sort of approach.[1]

In the first extract (A), Rosie (aged 4 years 10 months) is at home with her mother. They are in the middle of carrying out the daily routine of household tasks.[2]

Extract A

1.	R:	121 'Mum(v)		
2.		Mum(v) I've picked it 35 'all up there		[Rosie has tidied
3.			M: 4 'Have 22 'you?	the front room]

4.	R:	34 'Yes (soft)		
5.			M: 25 'There's a good girl	
6.	R:	All – there ain't no 24 'bits in there		
7.			M: ⟨ We got to make ⟩ the 243 'beds later on	
8.	R:	21 'Uh?		
9.			M: Make the 121 'beds (soft)	
10.	R:	2 'Come on 31 'then		
11.			M: 2 'Not 343 'yet	
12.	R:	What in a 24 'minute?		
13.			M: 34 'Yeah / in a 45 'minute	
14.	R:	2 'What 2 'what 23 'time clock / 34 'have we got to do it?		
15.			M: 243 'I don't know I'll see how – / We can 24 'wash up first	
16.			What's the 23 'time / by the 34 'clock?	
17.	R:	31 'Uh?		
18.			M: What's the 34 'time? . . .	
19.			M: ⟨ Now ⟩ 3 'what number's 34 'that?	[Pointing to the position of hands on the clock]
20.	R:	3 'Number 34 'two		
21.			M: 2 'No it's 343 'not	
22.			What 34 'is it?	
23.			It's a 3 'one and a 34 'nought	
24.	R:	3 'Nought – / 3 'one and a 34 'nought		
25.			M: 45 'Yeah / well what's 3 'one and a 34 'nought? . . .	
26.			M: What 34 'is it?	
27.	R:	⟨ There's one ⟩		

28.			M: Yeah what 34 ˈis it?	
29.	R:	34 ˈOne / 3 ˈOne and a 35 ˈnought		
30.			M: ~35 ˈWhat's one and a nought?	
31.	R:	33 ˈUm / 34 ˈthat		
32.			M: A 23 ˈten (+ loud)	
33.	R:	34 ˈTen		
35.			M: 3 ˈTen to 23 ˈten	
35.	R:	3 ˈTen to 12 ˈten		
36.		Well 3 ˈshall we 23 ˈwash them / because – 2 ˈthey're not 23 ˈclean enough?		[Ref. to clock]
37.		On the other 242 ˈside he ain't		[M. shakes head]
38.			M: Well you can't wash them 34 ˈinside / he'd 34 ˈbreak	
39.	R:	23 ˈWould he?		
40.			M: ~323 ˈ<u>Mm</u>	
41.	R:	<u>And</u> if – if we wash 343 inˈside would – would – wouldn't – would – would – would – / that 243 ˈthing won't go round		
42.		On the 24 ˈnumbers (+ loud)		
43.		*		
			. . 7 . .	
44.	R:	He got – 2 ˈHe got 42 ˈone		[Comparing clock with timer on recording box]
45.		And 2 ˈhe got 42 ˈone		

The second extract (B) comes from a recording made about eight months later in the middle of Rosie's second term at school. A group of children, including Rosie, are making calendars from old Christmas cards. Another child is trying to gain the teacher's attention, but the teacher is attempting to interact with Rosie alone.

Extract B

1.	C:	1 'Miss(v) I 24 'done it			
2.			T:	Will you 2 'put it at the 23 'top?	[To Rosie]
3.	C:	1 'Miss(v) I 24 'done it			
4.	C:	24 'Look			
				. . . .	
5.			T:	1 'What are 14 'those things?	[To Rosie] [T points with finger at the card]
6.	C:	31 'Miss(v) / I 24 'done it (+ sustention)			[R drops something on floor, picks it up]
				. .	
7.	C:	3 'Miss(v) I 24 'done it (+ soft)			
8.			T:	2 'What are 24 'those things? (+ soft)	[To Rosie]
				. .	
9.	C:	3 'Miss(v) I 24 'done it			
10.			T:	D'you know ˌwhat they're 243 'called?	[To Rosie]
	R:	(shakes head)			
11.			T:	12 'What ˌd'you think he / 324 'uses them for? . . 6 . .	[R takes the card and examines it]
12.			T:	~ It's 23 'very nice (+ˌsoft)	[To C]
13.			T:	2 'After 343 'play / we'll put some	

				34 ˈribbons / at the 45 ˈtop	
14.	C:	23 ˈWhat?			
15.			T:	34 ˈRibbon / at the 34 ˈtop / (+ soft) To 2 ˈhang them 23 ˈup by	
16.			T:	Would you 2 put all the 354 ˈcards together now?	
17.			T:	2 ˈPut the 35 ˈcards together	
18.	C:	34 ˈOh			
19.			T:	⟨ 31 ˈAlright ⟩ (++ soft) . .	[T takes card and points at it again
20.			T:	1 ˈWhat's – 2 ˈWhat are 35 ˈthose? . . .	with finger] [To Rosie]
21.			T:	What d'you think he 35 ˈuses them for?	
22.	R:	~ Go down . . (+ soft)		. .	[R rubs one eye with back of hand]
23.			T:	2 ˈGo 22 ˈdown –	[R rubs both eyes
24.			T:	343 ˈYes / You're 342 ˈright / 12 ˈGo on . .	with backs of hands]
25.			T:	What's the 45 ˈrest of it . .	[T puts down
26.			T:	You have a little 23 ˈthink * / and 3 ˈI'll get er / get the little 354 ˈcalendar for you	card]
27.			T:	~↓ I think you're sitting on ⟨ one ⟩ (+ soft)	[T moves to fetch calendar from

				. .	behind Rosie. R stands up and moves forward]
28.			T:	⟨↓ Right⟩ could you put some 2 ˈglue (+ soft) on the 354 ˈback there	[T points to calendar]
					[R takes calendar from T]
29.			T:	3 ˈHe 243 ˈuses those / to 3 ˈgo 33 ˈdown – (+ loud) . . 5 . .	
30.			T:	Is it a 2 ˈhill or a 24 ˈmountain?	
31.	R:	A 34 ˈhill			
32.			T:	A 34 ˈhill / 45 ˈYes	
33.			T:	And 3 ˈwhat's 24 ˈon the hill?	
34.	R:	34 ˈIce			
35.			T:	354 ˈYes / 23 ˈIce	
36.			T:	2 ˈThey're called ↑12 ˈskis	
37.	C:	243 ˈMiss(v) –			[Interruption whilst T deals with another child] [R shows card to T] [T takes card from R]
38.			T:	2 ˈThat's 34 ˈlovely / and 232 ˈafterwards we'll put some – 23 ˈribbon / What d'you think the 23 ˈribbon's for?	[Points to calendar with pencil]
				. . 6 . .	[Looks directly at Rosie]

39.	R:	For Father 34 ˈChristmas			
40.			T:	↑↑ 31 ˈSorry	[Bends closer to Rosie looking into her face]
41.	R:	For Father 34 ˈChristmas			[R looks down and away from T]
42.			T:	↑↑ For Father 12 ˈChristmas	[T straightens slightly from bending position and looks at the card, pointing at it again with hand]
43.			T:	If 1 ˈyou want to put it up on the 354 ˈwall / you have a 2 ˈlittle piece of 23 ˈribbon / ⟨ long enough ⟩ to hang it 23 ˈup by	

In the third extract (C), Rosie has been reading aloud to a different teacher, and some discussion follows before Rosie puts her book away and starts on another task.

Extract C

					[T holds book open with one hand, pencil in the other. She is pointing pencil at successive items in the reading text]
1.	R:	I / am / tall / said the / –			
				. .	[T looks from text to R. Shapes

		23 ˈTower			lips to indicate
2.			T:	14 ˈChimney (sustained)	sound]
3.	R:	24 ˈChimbley			
4.			T:	↓ It's a 3 ˈbig 243 ˈfactory-chimney 24 ˈisn't it?	[T points at illustration with pencil]
5.	R:	~ I don't like –			
6.			T:	↓ There's a 2 ˈlot of 343 ˈsmoke / coming out of the 343 ˈtop	[T points at illustration with pencil]
7.	R:	I don't 2 ˈlike that one			[R points with finger at the illustration]
8.			T:	You don't 24 ˈlike it	
	R:	(shakes head)			
9.			T:	1 ˈWhy 243 ˈnot?	
10.	R:	I only 2 ˈlike 342 ˈlittle ones			
				..	
11.			T:	⟨ Have ⟩ 1 ˈyou got 1 343 ˈchimney / in 3 ˈyour 453 ˈhouse?	
	R:	(nods emphatically)			
12.	C:	3 ˈAnd 231 ˈme			
13.			T:	D'you have 2 ˈsmoke coming out of the ↑ 21 ˈtop?	
	R:	(nods emphatically)			
				..	
14.			T:	↑↑ 21 ˈMm? (+ soft)	
	R:	(nods head again)			
				..	[T turns page then closes book]
15.			T:	What's 254 under-ˈneath the chimney then / that 3 ˈmakes the 354 ˈsmoke	

				come out?	
16.	C:	2 ˈI know 24 ˈfire			
17.			T:	↑ 21 ˈMm? (+ soft)	
18.	R:	34 ˈFire			
19.			T:	↑ 21 ˈIs it?	
20.				↑ Is that a 243 ˈfire then?	
21.	C:	21 ˈMiss(v) <u>Can 2 ˈI have 24 ˈthis one?</u>			
22.			T:	<u>Which room's the 34 ˈfire in?</u>	[To Rosie]
					[Shifts gaze to C]
23.				34 ˈYes (+ soft)	[To C]
					[Looks back to R]
24.	R:	in the 34 ˈfront one			
25.			T:	21 ˈIs it / so it 3 ˈkeeps you 34 ˈwarm	
26.				~ ⟨ ˈLovely ⟩	
27.	R:	And 2 ˈI got a 23 ˈbed .			
28.			T:	3 Where's your 34 ˈbed?	
29.	R:	ˈE's 34 upˈstairs			
30.			T:	Anybody 1 ˈelse got a 242 ˈbed in your room?	
31.	R:	Carol got a 321 ˈbed / and 342 ˈKelvin . / and 34 Carol			
32.			T:	↑ 14 Um ˈhum (+ soft)	
33.				What about 23 ˈDonna?	
34.	R:	⟨ Donna was ⟩ we're 13 ˈsharing it			
35.			T:	You're 213 ˈsharing with Donna / 342 ˈare you?	
	R:	(nods head emphatically)			
36.			T:	↓ D'you have a 23 ˈcuddle / at 24 ˈnight?	
37.	R:	ˈYeh / and I –			
38.		~ / When I gets 243 ˈup /			

I creeps in 34 ˈMummy's bed

39. T: For 243 aˈnother cuddle?
40. ~ Ooh that's nice (+ soft)
41. ~ It's nice in the morning when you cuddle

A Model for the Analysis of Discourse

In attempting to describe samples of linguistic interaction of the kind just presented, we consider it important to adopt a dual perspective, seeing language as simultaneously a resource that individuals exploit and a system which constrains particular acts of communication, and in our recent work we have been influenced by Halliday's (1977) paper on the organisation of dialogue which adopts a similar perspective.[2] Rejecting the competence-performance dichotomy, Halliday proposes that we think of language as providing a potential for meaning: the systematically organised resources that define what it is possible to mean in the culture that uses a particular language. For any particular member of that culture, the meaning options that he has mastered, organised in a set of interrelated systems, make up his linguistic repertoire. However, in selecting options from this repertoire as he contributes to sequences of discourse, he is constrained by the socially constituted structures of reciprocation which exist between discourse acts of various kinds, and which make it possible for two or more autonomous individuals to engage successfully in the negotiated construction of shared meaning.

Following Halliday, we take the 'exchange' as the basic unit of discourse and see it as involving two major systems: the first being associated with the 'commodity' that is exchanged, and the second with the 'discourse roles' that are defined by the process of exchange. Combinations of options from each of these systems define the basic communicative acts of Demand (Request + Goods/Services), Question (Request + Information), Statement (Give + Information), Answer (Give-on-Request + Information), etc., as shown in Figure 12.1. More 'delicate' distinctions need to be made within each of these basic communicative acts, as we shall see below, but the extent to which this sub-categorisation is taken will depend on the nature of the data and the purpose of the analysis. The notion of progressively more delicate

Figure 12.1: Basic Systems of Discourse

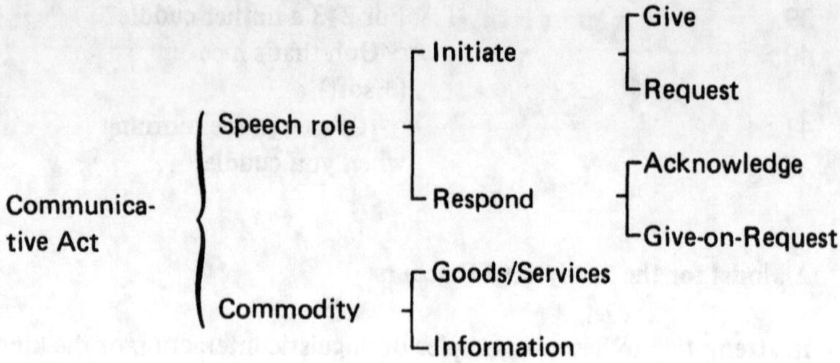

The two types of bracket have the following conventional significance:
{ = simultaneous selection;
[= obligatory selection from mutually exclusive alternatives.

sub-categorisation can also be taken as a powerful hypothesis about the sequence of development. Our initial exploration of this hypothesis, drawing upon consecutive recordings of the same children, suggests that development over time does indeed take the form of the gradual addition of further functions which quite largely correspond to the sub-categorisation that one would make in carrying out a more delicate description of adult discourse. In describing interaction between adults and very young children (e.g. 18–24 months), for example, we have found that very few sub-categorisations are required to describe the acts performed by the children. Their utterances are frequently indeterminate in meaning, even at the most basic level, and to make the sort of fine discrimination that would be appropriate in describing adult speech would be to impute a much more sophisticated ability to participate in discourse than is warranted by the actual data. However, by the time the child reaches school age, he has normally developed a repertoire of options very similar to those of the adults and older children with whom he interacts, and it is possible to describe the conversational contribution of children and adults in terms of the same systems. (For a fuller discussion of the developmental implications of the notion of progressively more 'delicate' sub-categorisation, see Wells, in press.)

Nevertheless, to have a finely discriminated repertoire of options would not in itself be sufficient to participate effectively in discourse, if an individual were not able to select from them appropriately to fill the contextually specified positions in the structure of discourse. At the most basic level, these positions are defined by the exchange roles of Initiation and Response: Giving sets up an expectation of Acknowledgement and Requesting of Giving-on-Request. Indeed, the reciprocal relationship between these pairs of roles is learned pre-verbally in the routines and games that make up so much of early adult-child interaction (Bruner, 1975; Trevarthen and Hubley, 1978); but, with the development of verbal resources, including an increasing repertoire of discourse options, the possibilities become more numerous, allowing for the selection by participants of discourse strategies of various kinds to manage the negotiation of status and power as well as of the ostensible commodities of Goods/Services and Information (Wells *et al.*, 1979). However, the reciprocal relationship between initiating and responding acts of various kinds still remains the basis of discourse structure, and it is upon this that the many variations are built.

Both perspectives – resource and structure – are, therefore, necessary and the advantage of the model presented in Figure 12.1 is that it indicates their complementarity. Working within this framework, we have begun to analyse a corpus of longitudinal data collected from a representative sample of 32 children, spanning the period of development from 15 months to 7 years. In the process, we have had to develop and modify the model in a number of ways in order to take account of the wide range of patterns of interaction we have found in the data, particularly when the children enter school. However, since we have provided arguments for many of these modifications elsewhere (Wells *et al.*, 1979), similar in important respects to those also advanced by McTear (in this volume), we will only mention the most important here.

The first concerns the basic discourse roles that participants can take up. Although it is certainly the case that the articulation of turns within a sequence of discourse depends upon the participants observing the reciprocal relationships of prospectively and retrospectively oriented options, a sharp differentiation between the roles of Initiator and Responder fails to do justice to the status of many utterances, which have simultaneously both a prospective, initiating, and a retrospective, function. For example, when Mother responds to Rosie's justification for washing the clock (A36), she simultaneously rejects the suggestion and gives information about the consequences that would follow if the suggestion were carried out. Similarly, in C39, the teacher's utterance 'For another cuddle?' both acknowledges Rosie's information about getting into her mother's bed and requests further information. Utterances that function both retrospectively and prospectively, in this way, we classify as Continuing options.

Each of the four basic acts is also further sub-categorised. Requests may be either Direct (e.g. 'Put the cards together' (B17)) or Indirect (e.g. 'Would you put all the cards together now?' (B16); Giving, particularly of information, may also be accompanied by a Request for Acknowledgement (e.g. 'It's a big factory chimney, isn't it?' (C4)); Giving-on-Request may take the form of Compliance (e.g. 'Yes' (C23) in response to the request 'Can I have this one') or Refusal (e.g. 'Well you can't wash them inside' (A38)); Acknowledgements may either Accept (e.g. 'Yes' (B24)) or Reject (e.g. 'Chimney' (C2)). Here, the supplying of Substitute information is an Implicit rejection: there is no example of an Explicit rejection in any of the three extracts. Finally, Acknowledgements may also take the form of Evaluation, either Positive or Negative (e.g. 'Lovely' (C26)). This fuller system of discourse role options is shown in Figure 12.2.

The second major modification involves two additions to the Information system of Discourse Commodity. In the first, a distinction is made between information concerning the world of non-linguistic experience – Situational Information – and information concerning the discourse itself. Following other researchers, we refer to this latter category of information as Text-Contingent. From a very early age, children are able to initiate and respond to procedures for dealing with breakdowns in communication and, indeed, it seems possible that such exchanges may provide the child with a particularly useful means of learning about the conditions which are necessary for successful communication (Robinson, in press) and of establishing that 'meta-linguistic awareness', which, it has been suggested, is intimately connected with the development of literacy (Cazden, 1972; Donaldson, 1978). Examples of such exchanges are to be found at A8-9, A17-18, B23, C8, C14, C17-18.

An equally important addition concerns the distinction within Situational between cases where the information exchanged is subject to the normal felicity conditions that govern everyday co-operative interaction (i.e. that in requesting information, A should not be in possession of that information himself but believe that B is (Searle, 1969)) and those exchanges where the information is requested and produced for Display and possible subsequent Evaluation (Labov and Fanshel, 1977). All three extracts contain examples of Display exchanges, although in none of them does the acknowledgement take the form of an evaluation. A paradigm example, based on B33-35, would be the following:

	T:	And what's on the hill?	[Request; Information-Display]
R: Ice			[Give-on-Request; Information-Display]
	T:	Ice, good.	[Acknowl; Accept, Evaluate; Information-Display]

It seems to be a characteristic of Display exchanges that they most frequently occur in situations where there is asymmetry of status between the participants (indeed, in making a Request for Display, the speaker will usually be heard as assuming a superior status on that occasion, even if this is not warranted by his social status relative to the other participant(s)). At the same time, the range of options made available to the respondent is substantially reduced: for example, the selection of the discourse role 'Continue' does not seem to be acceptable, and there is little or no opportunity to adopt any perspective other than that of the initiator. The Display exchange is thus a very clear example of a style of interaction which emphasises the transmission of cultural knowledge and values.

The final addition to the basic model concerns the achievement of thematic coherence in discourse. As well as having syntagmatic organisation resulting from the chaining of discourse role options, successful discourse is characterised by thematic continuity, as (part of) the content of one utterance is picked up and Incorporated in various ways in the utterances which follow. The teacher in Extract C provides some good examples of Incorporating utterances which Extend Rosie's contribution (e.g. 'What about Donna?' (C33) and 'D'you have a cuddle at night?' (C36)). Little attention so far has been given to this dimension of discourse, yet a high level of Incorporation in successive turns seems to be one of the strongest indications of what Grice (1975) is referring to in his discussion of the Co-operative Principle in conversation. It can also be hypothesised to be an important influence on the effectiveness of learning that takes place through linguistic interaction.

With these modifications, then, we propose the system of options set out in Figure 12.2. It must be stressed, however, that this representation of a typical speaker/hearer's repertoire is far from complete. Firstly, as stated earlier, more delicate sub-categorisations are

Figure 12.2: Generalised Linguistic Repertoire (Selected Systems)

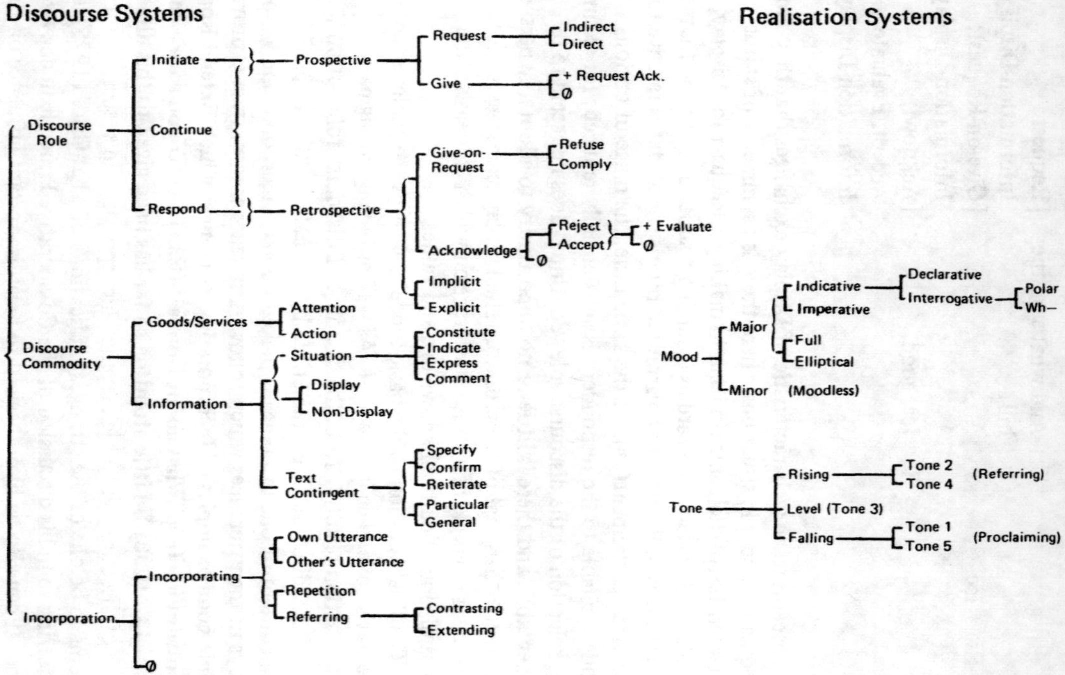

N.B. This should not be treated as the definitive version: development is still in progress.

required when some particular aspect of interaction is investigated in detail (e.g. various sub-categories of Request for Display would be needed if studying teachers' questions (c.f. French and MacLure, 1979)). Secondly, a complete description would also include systems of options concerning the experiential content of utterances (c.f. Wells *et al.*, 1979) and a full account of the systems of lexico-grammar and intonation through which discourse and experiential content options are realised. For present purposes, however, these are taken for granted, since we wish initially to focus attention on the major discourse systems and on the sequential patterns in which options selected from them occur, in order to construct a coherent framework relevant to a wide range of interactional settings and purposes, within which more specific and detailed investigations can subsequently be carried out.

Systems of Realisation

Realisation still presents many unresolved problems in the linguistic study of discourse. These stem from the very predication of 'discourse' as a separate level of inquiry over and beyond lexicogrammar – a predication which rests on the supposition that discourse systems are non-isomorphic with those of intonation, lexicogrammar, etc. By and large, there is no expectation of one-to-one correspondence between categories at one level of description and categories at another; however, there should still be routes – albeit indirect ones – for passing from one level of description to another. Thus, realisation is seen as a way of formally articulating relations at one level of description with those at another.

Such realisation rules are already proposed within linguistics for articulating the lower layers of lexicogrammatical description with phonological features of the substance of language. There is a difficulty, however, in proposing similar rules of realisation for relating discourse with lexicogrammar. For, while the realisation rules that relate form to substance (i.e. lexicogrammar to phonology) are statable in terms intrinsic to the linguistic systems themselves,[4] those that relate function to form (i.e. discourse to lexicogrammar) involve recourse to such extra-linguistic phenomena as situation or 'definition of the situation'. Some such situationally sensitive rules for interpreting the discourse functions of utterances have, of course, been tentatively proposed by Sinclair and Coulthard (1975) and Labov and Fanshel

(1977), amongst others. The acknowledged limitations of such attempts may, however, be ultimately traced to the notion of 'situation' itself, which can easily become merely a technical name for unexplicated common-sense knowledge. There is also a further difficulty, residing in the fact that particular situations or 'definitions of the situation' are partially constituted and brought into being in the very fabric of the language deployed. Accordingly, it would seem to follow that the fullest possible inventory of the formal features of an utterance will not always provide an adequate account of why it serves one discourse function rather than another.

Despite these problems, there are many clear cases where recourse to the formal features of the language can usefully help in disambiguating different kinds of discourse activity. Such possibilities may be illustrated by reference to intonation as it affects the interpretation of utterances C8, 14 and 17, re-quoted here.

7.	R:	I don't 2 'like that one			
8.			T:	You don't 24 'like it	[R points with finger at the illustration]
	R:	(shakes head)			
9.			T:	1 'Why 243 'not?	
10.	R:	I only 2 'like 342 'little ones			
				. .	
11.			T:	⟨ Have ⟩ 1 'you got a 343 'chimney / in 3 'your 453 'house?	
	R:	(nods emphatically)			
12.	C:	3 'And 231 'me			
13.			T:	D'you have 2 'smoke coming out of the ↑ 21 'top?	
	R:	(nods emphatically)			
				. .	
14.			T:	↑↑ 21 'Mm? (+ soft)	
	R:	(nods head again)			
				. .	[T turns page then closes book]

15. T: What's 254 under-ˈneath the chimney then / that 3 ˈmakes the 354 ˈsmoke come out?
16. C: 2 ˈI know 24 ˈfire
17. T: ↑ 21 ˈmm? (+ soft)
18. R: 34 ˈFire

We may comment on the intonation of the three utterances in question in reverse order as follows:

(i) Utterance 17: / ↑ 21 ˈMm / (rising-to-high intonation)
In producing this utterance the teacher is heard as reinstating in some way her original 'request for display' at C15 ('What's underneath the chimney then that makes the smoke come out?'). Rosie's utterance 18 ('Fire') is thus heard as responding to both 17 and 15.

This whole interpretation in fact rests substantially on the prosodic configuration of the teacher's 'Mm' (although the video-recording gives complementary support for it, in so far as the teacher's gaze is directed towards Rosie throughout C15–18). The criterial role of intonation at C17 may be illustrated by way of contrast with other possible configurations. In this utterance 'Mm' occurs with a rising-to-high intonation contour. Possible alternatives would have been a high rising-falling, a high-fall or a mid-fall, which may be glossed respectively as:

High rise-fall	Mm ;	'Yes, that's interesting'	all directed towards C
High-fall	Mm ;	'Yes, that's right'	
Mid-fall	Mm ;	'I see'	

In the event, the 'Mm' with rising-to-high intonation may be glossed as indicating 'Well, Rosie?' The basic contrast carried by the intonation at this point would, therefore, seem to be between positively evaluating or accepting C's unsolicited contribution at C16 (varieties of falling tone) as opposed to what actually happens – the reinstatement of the original question (C15) in order to secure a response from Rosie.

(ii) Utterance 14: / ↑↑ 21 ˈMm / (rising-to-high intonation)
The teacher's utterance at this point supports a similar reading to that

given above for utterance 17. Here she is heard as reinstating C13 ('D'you have smoke coming out of the top?'). Hence Rosie – in nodding her head – is seen as supplying a non-verbal surrogate for 'Yes (we do have smoke coming out of the top)'. Had the teacher employed any of the alternatives offered for 17 above she would have been heard as accomplishing something quite different in terms of the discourse: most probably she would have been interpreted as supplying, herself, a verbal counterpart to Rosie's head-nod and thereby indirectly answering her own polar question (C13) in the affirmative.

Both utterances 17 and 14 may be usefully contrasted in terms of their discourse value and their intonation with the teacher's utterance 32, later in the same extract. This utterance (↑ 14 Umˌhum) with a high wide (rising-) falling intonation is heard as fundamentally retrospective in its function rather than prospective as is the case with 17 and 14.

(iii) Utterance 8: You don't 24 ˈlike it /

As in the previous examples, this utterance sets up relatively strong predictions for a further turn. Here again, the intonation plays a criterial role, but the most important feature on this occasion would seem to be its relative pitch height rather than the specific contour selected. By pitching the repetition high rather than low, the teacher is heard as predicting a further response. If the reverse had been the case, she would have been heard as merely retrospectively acknowledging the previous utterance, but setting up no further predictions.

In this respect, therefore, repetitions involving lexicogrammatical content seem to draw on slightly different features of intonation than 'empty items' such as 'mm', 'mmhum', 'oh', etc. In the latter case, it would seem sufficient for the tone choice to be rising rather than falling for them to be heard as anticipating or predicting a further turn. Repetitions, however, seem capable of realising the same distinction in terms of relatively high fall versus relatively low fall, with relative pitch height being a distinguishing characteristic.

These brief comments on the potential of intonation[5] for realising aspects of the discourse process lead us beyond an emphasis on discourse conceived of in paradigmatic terms as system networks towards a complementary apprehension of it as a linear process unfolding in real time. On this syntagmatic dimension, moves by one speaker set up strong or weak anticipating constraints on the options available to the next speaker and consequently on how we hear or interpret whatever subsequent moves take place. According to this view, the linear relationships of discourse are not syntagmatically binding to the same degree as grammatical structures. They are perhaps best seen as 'guiding principles' for continuous construction/ interpretation rather than as 'mandatory rules'.

The syntagmatic axis of discourse is, of course, more than just an analytic counterweight to the systemically formulated paradigmatic axis. The two dimensions are necessarily interdependent. But, in studying specific dialogues constructed between particular mothers or teachers and children, it is the syntagmatic or sequential patterning of the discourse that is pre-eminently important for the exploration of typical modes of interaction and the variations between them. Moreover, since most language-related learning is essentially interactive, it is also through the study of the syntagmatic structure of discourse that we can expect to find an explanation of the processes through which 'learning transactions' are more, or less, successfully negotiated.

Styles of Interaction at Home and at School

One of our main reasons for developing this model of discourse is to allow us to identify differing styles of interaction and to investigate their consequences for children's learning. Can some of the differences between children in the rate of their initial language learning, for example, be accounted for by differences in the quality of the linguistic interaction they experience? We have certainly found that the speech addressed by adults to more rapidly developing children is significantly different in a number of ways from that addressed to slow developers; in particular, it contains a larger number of acknowledgements of the child's contributions and a larger number of directives and utterances related to the child's current activity or to the joint activity of child and adult (Ellis and Wells, 1980). Some of the differences between adults in the way they interact with their children are no doubt elicited by individual differences between the children in personality, interests and general level of activity, but it also seems that adults have characteristic preferences for particular styles of interaction.

In one comparison of two conversations between mothers and their two-year-olds, for example (Wells *et al.*, 1979), one mother was found to be adopting a 'supportive' style, encouraging her child to develop and extend his initiations, whilst the second mother adopted a 'leading' style, plying her child with questions about a series of visitors and their modes of transport. The two styles of interaction were distinguishable in terms of different patterns of choices from all the discourse systems outlined above: whereas the first mother encouraged her child to adopt a predominantly initiating role by making considerable use of Continuing moves to acknowledge and request further information, the second mother retained control of the discourse herself by making mainly initiating moves, which cast the child in the role of respondent. Secondly, whereas the first mother's questions were mainly designed to help her son extend his initial comment into a rudimentary 'story', the second mother's questions were requests for Display and her son's answers were, on the whole, evaluated as inadequate. As might be expected, therefore, the resulting conversations were quite different in the extent to which they made use of devices of Incorporation in order to achieve thematic continuity. Whilst the first conversation contained a variety of realisations of Incorporation, such as cohesion, ellipsis and rising tone, all of which serve to create and maintain intersubjectivity of perspective, in the second, the mother seemed to insist throughout on her own perspective as the only relevant one, and her son's contributions were never accorded equal status.

Not surprisingly, the first child's contributions to the conversation were much fuller and linguistically more mature, and this could be seen to result, at least in part, from the opportunities made available by the mother's style of interaction and from the fact that the topic under discussion developed from the child's initiation and concerned a matter of immediate interest to him.

Such comparisons are suggestive in a number of ways. Firstly, they demonstrate that different styles of interaction can be identified in terms of recurrent patterns of discourse choices and, secondly, they open up a method for exploring the relationship between rate and style of language learning and the context of linguistic experience in which this learning occurs. Most importantly, however, they suggest a way of studying the learning that takes place through language at home and at school and of investigating the very different degrees of success achieved by different children.

One possible cause of difficulty that has been singled out for attention lies in the different ways in which language may be used in the two settings of home and school. On the basis of a number of descriptive studies (e.g. Sinclair and Coulthard, 1975; Mehan, 1978), 'classroom language' has come to be thought of as essentially constituted of sequences of teacher-initiated three-part exchanges, a style of interaction which, it is assumed, is foreign to many children's experience of 'home language' and which, because of its unfamiliarity, may impede pupils' effective participation in teacher-directed learning. This point of view is made quite explicitly by Mehan: 'To participate effectively in the classroom, students must indeed master academic subject matter. In addition to accumulating this stock of academic knowledge, students must also learn that there are interactionally appropriate ways to cast their academic knowledge' (1979, p. 10). Mehan then goes on to show how effective participation means being able to fill the central slot in the three-part exchange: Initiate-Respond-Follow-up.

However, as a result of studying our longitudinal recordings, which allow comparisons between 'home' and 'school' talk for a considerable number of individual children, we have come to doubt this accepted wisdom. Even if we consider only Display exchanges, where the child is asked a question in order that he may show whether he knows the answer, rather than that the questioner should obtain new information, it is clear that exchanges of this kind occur quite frequently in most children's experience at home. The extract from Rosie at home provides a good example of a Display sequence (A16–37) and the 'leading' strategy adopted by the second mother in the comparison referred to above was implemented through similar exchanges.

What is taken to be characteristic of the Display exchange, and of classroom talk in general, is that it consists of a chain of three moves, where the child has to fill the second slot. But, as we have argued elsewhere (Wells *et al.*, 1979), this is only a particular variant of a fairly common exchange pattern which, although initiated by a Request for Information, may extend over three or more turns. The reason for this is to be found in the nature of the second move, the Give Information on Request. Although it occurs as a response, this option is similar to an initiating Give Information in that it contributes new information to the discourse; it is open to the initiator of the exchange, therefore, to treat it as having prospective force and to respond with some form of Acknowledgement, which may include an Evaluative option. Although there is not a clear example of such an exchange in Rosie's home extract (but c.f. A38–43 for something quite similar), this style of interaction is very characteristic of adult-conversation at home, e.g.:

	Mother: What's he going to buy?
Child: er – biscuits	
	Mother: Mm. What else?
Child: er – meat.	
	Mother: Mm.

It is interesting to note, therefore, that in the second school extract (C22-41) Rosie's teacher manages the interaction in almost exactly this way.

From such comparisons it is clear that there is no sharp discontinuity between the interaction styles of home and school, patterns which are characteristic of one context being equally to be found in the other; although it is certainly true that the relative frequency of particular patterns is different in the two contexts. Where the major difference lies, it seems, is not in the style of discourse itself but in the nature of the information that is being exchanged and its relation to the child's experience. Whereas the vast majority of the talk at home arises out of the child's immediate activities and interests, this is much less obviously true of the classroom. On the whole, the informational content of classroom exchanges is related to 'the curriculum' and this is almost entirely determined by the teacher. This is not to say that teachers are following a detailed and strictly defined curriculum in their moment-by-moment interactions with pupils, particularly in the infant school, but rather that they seek to assimilate almost every object, event or item of information to a frame of reference which is both more abstract than demanded by the immediate situation and with which they happen to be much more familiar than their pupils. The induction/socialisation of children into these broader frames of reference is, of course, one of the main aims of formal education, but too abrupt a transition can be bewildering for children whose pre-school experience has been interpreted largely in terms of personally-initiated practical activities. As Donaldson (1978) points out, the problem is to help children to recognise and cope with problems that are disembedded from their context of practical everyday experience without quenching the personal involvement and creativity that they have developed from success in dealing with contextually embedded problems. The solution to this problem will certainly have implications for the style of interaction adopted, but its achievement requires a permeability of the teacher's frame of reference to those provided by the pupils, rather than just a superficial adjustment in the pattern of conversational exchange.

Beyond Linguistic Analysis

Although a comparison in terms of style of interaction makes it clear that there is no fundamental discontinuity between the language of home and school, there are a number of differences which are brought out by an analysis in terms of the model presented above. Such differences can be stated in purely linguistic terms but, at the same time, it is important to point out that close linguistic analysis, in its systematic attention to the language, can also point to features or phenomena that remain, as it were, beyond or around the edges of the system itself.

The distribution of text-contingent exchanges in the three extracts provides a case in point. Montgomery (1979) notes that, for some children in the earlier stages of development, items such as 'mm', 'eh' with a high rising tone can be a pervasive feature of their talk. As such, they are almost invariably interpreted by the adult as a request for some form of repetition or reformulation of their own (adult) utterance. Their exact status in the child's repertoire is unclear. Initially, they may provide him with a highly economical and simple device for merely prolonging or sustaining sequences of interaction. Later, they may, of course, be manipulated for tactical purposes such as 'stalling' or signalling inappropriateness.

Rosie clearly has the device at her disposal, as may be seen by considering utterances A8 and 17. It is noticeable, however, that she does not deploy such items in either of the two school extracts. We would suspect, in fact, that, in interactions informed by pedagogic purposes, children experience sharp constraints on the deployment of text-contingent options associated with checking the channel or the message.

The reasons for this are not 'linguistic' in any narrow sense. Basically, it would seem that children experience the process of 'being taught' as one in which they are not at liberty to admit that they have not heard something said by the teacher or that they have failed to understand it. This rather speculative point may be developed in various ways. It may be seen as a linguistic reflex of the asymmetrical relationships obtaining in the classroom between the teacher and the taught. It may be seen as related to the teacher's difficulty in negotiating individual encounters in a situation where she is set to interact on the basis of collective characteristics. Or children's reticence in this respect may be related to characteristics of the teacher-talk itself, which presumes continuous availability for response on the part of its recipients and is also somehow presented as indexically transparent and non-problematic. These, of course, are not mutually exclusive accounts but they all direct us beyond the language itself to elements of the social scene for a fuller understanding of linguistically identifiable patterns.

Turning our attention from features of children's talk in the classroom to that of the teacher, one prevalent device deployed by the latter has been discussed already in terms of 'requests for display'. The first school extract is particularly rich in such examples, which we can simply list as follows:

B5 What are those things?
B8 What are those things?
B10 D'you know what they're called?
[Rosie: shakes head]
B11 What d'you think he uses them for?
B20 What's . . . what are those?
B21 What d'you think he uses them for?
[Rosie: go down]
B23 Go down . . .
B24 Yes, you're right. Go on
B25 What's the rest of it?
B29 He uses those to go down . . .
B30 Is it a hill or a mountain?
[Rosie: a hill]
B33 And what's on the hill?
[Rosie: ice]

Finally, at B36, the teacher supplies the required response to her initial request for display with 'They're called skis'.

Linguistic analysis can highlight the prevalence of a particular category in a sequence, or its persistent and cumulative use, but it is difficult to account in purely linguistic terms for why (what emerges retrospectively as) a 'line' of questioning is not abandoned earlier. (Note, for instance, that Rosie indicates, as early as B10/11, that she does not know what the teacher is asking to be told but, none the less, the name 'skis' is not supplied till B36.) Whatever reasons can be adduced for the phenomenon lead once again beyond the language itself. Partly, it would seem to be a matter of the teacher's role as arbiter of 'knowledge' in the classroom. 'Knowledge' may be introduced into the discourse by the teacher in two principal ways: either by 'giving information', or by following up a pupil response with some kind of comment or evaluation.[5] Teachers presently appear to display a preference for the latter and this, in turn, depends heavily on securing manageable responses from the child. But, without responses, no evaluation/comment can be made and 'knowledge' remains uninstated on the sidelines. The teacher is thus reluctant to abandon her line till some kind of workable response has been secured.[6]

There are similarities here with Goffman's (1969) account of 'face-work' done by interactants. During encounters, says Goffman, any person

> tends to act out what is sometimes called *a line* – that is, a pattern of verbal and non-verbal acts by which he expresses his view of the situation and through this his evaluation of the participants, especially himself . . . The term *face* may be defined as the positive social value a person effectively claims for himself by the line others assume he has taken during a particular contact . . .
>
> A person may be said to *have*, or *be in*, or *maintain* face when the line he effectively takes presents an image of him that is internally consistent, that is supported by judgements and evidence conveyed by other participants, and that is conveyed through impersonal agencies in the situation. (pp. 3–4)

The metaphor of 'maintaining face' is perhaps a trifle dramatic but there is a sense in which classroom encounters are relatively public events and both teachers and pupils are to some extent 'at risk'. In such encounters, therefore, there is an important sense in which pupils sustain or support teachers in maintaining face by providing workable responses to the teachers' questions, thus confirming or validating the line adopted. When this validation or confirmation is absent, the adopted 'line' is threatened but can only be abandoned with attendant risk of 'losing face'. Within this framework, the teacher's action in persisting with a series of requests for display to the point of trying out anything that seems likely to secure a response (e.g. B30: 'Is it a hill or a mountain?) may be seen in terms of very basic 'face-work' where almost any kind of response will do in order to validate or confirm the line.

The kinds of interpretive account suggested above are, of course, more subject to discussion and disagreement than the more narrowly conceived linguistic analyses from which they begin. They also represent a movement towards areas in sociological study where such terms as 'knowledge', 'role', 'validation', etc. are themselves currently a matter of debate. In the last analysis, however, we see linguistic analyses of interaction facing two ways: towards, on the one hand, specific verbally mediated encounters for which linguistics offers systematic analytic tools; and towards sociology, on the other hand, for richer and more interpretive accounts of the processes of interaction located within a theory of society.

Rosie: from Home to School

Finally, let us consider the three extracts as a small case study of one child making the transition from home to school Rosie is the youngest in a family of four children. Father is an unskilled labourer, but has been unemployed for a number of years; mother has not been out to work since Rosie was born. The family lives in a dilapidated and sparsely furnished nineteenth-century terrace house in an area of the inner city that has been considerably changed by the building of the motorway. In January 1977, Rosie followed her elder brother and sisters to the local infant school, which is a large, SPA-designated, local authority school, in which white indigenous children are in a minority. The school has a good reputation for its relations with the local community; parents are welcome in the classroom at any time and many of them take up the invitation, particularly at the beginning and end of the school day. When Rosie started school, she joined the younger of her two sisters in a 'co-operative unit' of modern design, where a 'family-grouped' class of some 40 children are taught by two teachers, both of whom volunteered to work in this particular situation.

The first point that strikes one on reading the three extracts is the considerable disparity between them, particularly between the two school extracts. This is all the more surprising as the two extracts are taken from the same recording made during the course of one morning. From the first, one gets the impression of a child who, in spite of her teacher's undoubted efforts, is either unable or unwilling to answer straightforward questions with anything more than an occasional word or minimal phrase. Since this was the form of behaviour observed on other occasions when this teacher attempted to engage her in interaction, it might seem reasonable, on the basis of such samples, to conclude that Rosie is seriously deficient in communicative ability and, given the facts available about her home background, to see her as a clear example of the 'linguistically disadvantaged' child. However, the extract recorded at home makes it clear that this would be inaccurate, as there is no question there of an inability to communicate through language. In reporting completed events, negotiating future activity and considering the consequences of a hypothetical course of action, Rosie demonstrates her ability to deploy her linguistic resources effectively to achieve a variety of interactive ends, both self- and adult-initiated.

As an alternative explanation of Rosie's apparently incompetent performance in the first school extract, it might be suggested that the particular style of interaction that the teacher expected – that of supplying information for Display – was unfamiliar to her. But this, too, cannot be the full explanation for, as the home extract demonstrates, Rosie was successfully, if uninformedly, able to participate in a similar sequence initiated by her mother, and, as we have already seen, such typically 'school-talk' exchanges are by no means uncommon in the pre-school experience of most children.

A clearer understanding of Rosie's strengths and weaknesses emerges when we consider the second school extract, where she is interacting with the other teacher in the unit. Here her behaviour is very similar to that observed at home, and she volunteers information with little need of prompting. However, when we analyse the interaction more carefully, we can see that there are other similarities with the home extract that may account for Rosie's much fuller participation in the interaction. Firstly, there is the topic itself, which, although it arises out of the book which Rosie has been 'reading', is one with which she is familiar and on which she can inform her teacher with confidence. Secondly, the teacher conveys the impression, through various realisations of Incorporation, that she accepts Rosie's utterances as valid contributions to the shared perspective that they are establishing.

It might be suggested that, in behaving in this way, the second teacher is 'not really teaching'. However, this, we would argue, betrays too narrow a view of the forms of teacher behaviour that can promote effective pupil learning. In encouraging her to relate the familiar experiences of her life at home to the less familiar content and activity of reading, the teacher is providing a bridge which may enable Rosie to move into the realm of more 'disembedded' problem solving which is associated with 'curricular' knowledge, without experiencing the defeating bewilderment which the more straightforwardly didactic approach of the first teacher seems to engender.

Just as at home, both 'supporting' and 'leading' parental strategies of interaction provide different, but in some ways complementary, opportunities for learning to use language, so in the classroom, too, different strategies are likely to be appropriate in promoting different educationally valued ends and perhaps also with different children at differing stages in their school careers. In our view, therefore, the further exploration of the constitutive characteristics of such styles and strategies offers a potentially fruitful way of gaining greater understanding of the processes whereby parents and teachers more, or less, successfully facilitate children's learning.

Notes

1. The research reported in this paper is supported by grants from the SSRC and from the Nuffield Foundation.

2. The conventions of transcription are given in Appendix 1. Subsequent reference to parts of these extracts will specify first the extract (A, B or C), and then the utterance number. Thus, A10 refers to the tenth utterance in the first extract.

3. Although not specifically referred to in the following brief account of the model, analyses developed in the 'structuralist' tradition (e.g. Sinclair and Coulthard, 1975) and in the 'conversational analysis' tradition (e.g. Jefferson, 1972; Garvey, 1977) have also influenced our thinking.

4. Though see Labov's work on sociolinguistic marking.

5. Our work on intonation owes much to that of David Brazil (1975, 1978) in the same area. Our comments here are relatively informal and thus should not be taken as representing the full scope of his description. The remainder of the paragraph also bears comparison with his own remarks in his contribution to this volume.

6. We could call these two modes of transference the 'direct' and the 'derived', respectively. One possible reason why the 'derived' mode seems so prevalent in contemporary classrooms relates to doubts amongst teachers and educationalists concerning what really does count as valid curricular knowledge for the infant school child. Where knowledge in this sense remains ill-defined, pupil's responses become grounds for its derivation and it thereby becomes continuously constructed for the occasion.

7. Pursuing a line of questioning is just one of the strategies that teachers adopt in carrying out their pedagogical aims. Limitations of space preclude further discussion of these strategies in detail here, but c.f. French and MacLure (1979) for a discussion of the role of 'preformulations' and 'reformulations' in display sequences, and Wells (1978) for a more general discussion of styles of interaction appropriate to different tasks. Drew (in this volume) offers a good account of differing strategies for correcting children.

APPENDIX 1

Bristol Language Development Programme: Conventions and Layout for Transcription

The speech of the child is set out in the left-hand column. The speech of adult participants is set out in the centre column, with the identifying initials where necessary. Each new utterance starts on a new line. Utterances are numbered consecutively.

Contextual information is enclosed in square brackets [ ] and set out in the right-hand column.

Interpretations of utterances and descriptions of tone of voice, where applicable, are enclosed in round brackets ( ) and included immediately after the utterance to which they apply.

Utterances, or parts of utterances, about which there is doubt are enclosed in angular brackets ⟨ ⟩; where two interpretations are possible, they are both given, separated by an oblique stroke.

Symbols of the International Phonetic Alphabet are used for utterances, or parts of utterances, which cannot be interpreted with certainty. Phonetic symbols are always enclosed by oblique strokes. Except where there is doubt about the speaker's intended meaning, the speech is transcribed in Standard English Orthography.

The following is a list of additional symbols used, with an explanation of their significance. (Stops and commas are not used as in normal punctuation.)

?	used at end of any utterance where an interrogative meaning is considered to have been intended.
!	used at the end of an utterance considered to have exclamatory intention.
'	apostrophe: used as normal for contractions and elision of syllables.
*	used to indicate unintelligibility, for whatever reason. The number of asterisks corresponds as nearly as possible to the number of words judged to have been uttered.
. . .	stops are used to indicate pauses. One stop is used for a very short pause. Thereafter, the number of stops used corresponds to the estimated length of the pause in seconds. Pauses over 5 seconds in length are shown with the figure for the length of

the pause, e.g. . . 8 . .

—— underlining – where utterances overlap because both speakers speak at once, the overlapping portions are underlined.

" " inverted commas are used to enclose utterances considered to be 'speech for self'.

\+ plus mark indicates unbroken intonation contour where a pause or clause boundary might otherwise indicate the end of an utterance.

\- hyphen indicates a hiatus, either because the utterance is incomplete or because the speaker makes a fresh start at the word or utterance.

(v) used to indicate that the preceding word was used as a vocative, to call or hold the attention of the addressee.

Intonation

Some of the transcripts include a representation of intonation, in which case the following additional conventions apply:

/ tone unit boundary. Where an utterance consists of only one tone unit, no boundaries are marked.

ˈ this symbol immediately precedes both prominent and tonic syllables. Prominent syllables[a] take a single digit before the symbol to indicate their relative pitch height. Tonic syllables[b] take two or more digits before the symbol to indicate the onset level, range and direction of significant pitch movement (see 'Pitch Height' below).

↑ ↓ shift of pitch range relatively higher or lower than that normal for the speaker.

↑↑ ↓↓ shift to extra high or extra low pitch.

: lengthened syllable. The symbol follows the syllable to which it applies.

Pitch height the height, direction and range of significant pitch movement is represented by a set of digits corresponding to points on a scale. The pitch range of a speaker is divided into five notional intervals, numbered 1-5 from high to low, thus:

1
2
3
4
5

The following information is retrievable from this coding:

Direction of Movement	Halliday (1967) Tones
Falling: (e.g. 13, 25)	Tone 1
Rising: (e.g. 31, 43)	Tone 2
Level: (e.g. 33)	Tone 3
Fall-Rise: (e.g. 343) or (e.g. 342)	Tone 4 or Tone 2[c]
Rise-Fall: (e.g. 324)	Tone 5

Notes

(a) Prominent syllables are salient with respect to combinations of pitch, duration and intensity.

(b) Tonic syllables carry at least the onset of significant pitch movement. Significant pitch movement in its entirety may, of course, occur on a single syllable or be spread over a number of syllables.

(c) Fall-Rise movements may be of two types, corresponding to Halliday's Tone 2 and Tone 4. They are conventionally denoted in the transcripts as follows: Tone 2 is represented with a higher terminal pitch than its onset (e.g. 342), whereas Tone 4 is represented as having a terminal pitch no higher than its onset (e.g. 232, 354).

Source: M.A.K. Halliday, *Intonation and Grammar in British English* (Mouton, 1967).

References

Brazil, D. (1975). *Discourse Intonation*. English Language Research Monographs, University of Birmingham

— (1978). *Discourse Intonation II*. English Language Research Monographs, University of Birmingham

Bruner, J.S. (1975). 'The Ontogenesis of Speech Acts'. *Journal of Child Language*, 2, 1, pp. 1-20

Cazden, C. (1972). *Child Language and Education*. New York: Holt

Dickson, W.P. (ed.) (in press). *Children's Oral Communication Skills*. New York: Academic Press

Donaldson, M. (1978). *Children's Minds*. London: Fontana

Ellis, R. and Wells, C.G. (1980). 'Enabling Factors in Adult-Child Discourse'. *First Language*, 1, pp. 46-62

French, P. and MacLure, M. (1979). 'Getting the Right Answer and Getting the Answer Right'. *Research in Education*, November 1979

Garvey, C. (1977). 'The Contingent Query: A Dependent Act in Conversation'. In M. Lewis and L.A. Rosenblum (eds.), *Interaction, Conversation and the Development of Language*

Goffman, E. (1969). *Where the Action is*. London: Allen Lane

Grice, H.P. (1975). 'Logic and Conversation'. In P. Cole and J.L. Morgan (eds.), *Syntax and Semantics III: Speech Acts*. New York: Academic Press

Halliday, M.A.K. (1977). 'Language as Code and Language as Behaviour: A Systemic-Functional Interpretation of the Nature and Ontogenesis of Dialogue'. Mimeo. (To appear in S.M. Lamb and A. Makkai (eds.), *Semiotics of Culture and Language*)

Jefferson, G. (1972). 'Side Sequences'. In D. Sudnow (ed.), *Studies in Social Interaction*

Labov, W. and Fanshel, D. (1977). *Therapeutic Discourse*. New York: Academic Press

Lewis, M. and Rosenblum, L.A. (eds.) (1977). *Interaction, Conversation and the Development of Language*. New York: Wiley

Lock, A. (ed.) (1978). *Action, Gesture and Symbol: The Emergence of Language*. New York: Academic Press

Mehan, H. (1978). 'Structuring School Structure'. *Harvard Educational Review*, 48, pp. 32-64

— (1979). *The Competent Student*. Mimeo. University of San Diego, February 1979

Montgomery, M. (1979). 'The Values of Rising and Falling Tones in the Intonation of One Child'. *Bristol Working Papers in Language*, 1, pp. 87-105

Nelson, K. (ed.) (in press). *Children's Language*, vol. II. New York: Gardner Press

Robinson, E.J. (in press). 'The Child's Understanding of Inadequate Messages in Communication Failure: A Problem of Ignorance or Egocentrism'. To appear in W.P. Dickson (ed.), *Children's Oral Communication Skills*

Searle, J.R. (1969). *Speech Acts: An Essay in the Philosophy of Language*. Cambridge: Cambridge University Press

Sinclair, J.McH. and Coulthard, R.M. (1975). *Towards an Analysis of Discourse*. London: Oxford University Press

Sudnow, D. (ed.) (1972). *Studies in Social Interaction*. New York: Free Press

Trevarthen, C. and Hubley, P. (1978). 'Secondary Intersubjectivity: Confidence, Confiding and Acts of Meaning in the First Year'. In A. Lock (ed.), *Action, Gesture and Symbol: The Emergence of Language*

Wells, C.G. (1978). 'Talking with Children: The Complementary Roles of Parents and Teachers'. *English in Education*, 12, 2, pp. 15-38

— (in press). 'Apprenticeship in Meaning'. In K. Nelson (ed.), *Children's Language*

—, Montgomery, M.M. and MacLure, M. (1979). 'Adult-Child Discourse: Outline of a Model of Analysis'. *Journal of Pragmatics*, 3, pp. 337-80

13 ADULTS' CORRECTIONS OF CHILDREN'S MISTAKES: A RESPONSE TO WELLS AND MONTGOMERY

Paul Drew

Wells and Montgomery have outlined the model which they and some of the members of the Bristol Language Development Project have been using to analyse the data they have collected: the data consist of audio- and video-recordings of naturally occurring talk between children and adults. My comments in response are not intended to be exegetal and, therefore, I have not tried to do full justice to the arguments in Wells and Montgomery's presentation, either regarding the details of the coding scheme or its theoretical basis and relevance to the study of linguistic development.[1] Indeed, I shall steer clear almost entirely of the methodological and theoretical issues associated with this model and concentrate instead on empirical aspects of the data which the Bristol Project has been working with. Briefly, I will argue that this kind of model does not take into account the interactional work which is managed in particular turns at talk and the ways in which turns are designed to achieve that work; nor does it fully recognise the importance of the sequential organisation of talk, and the orderliness exhibited in sequences which occur in the data. And it is in these areas that one can expect to find systematic features of talk. To illustrate these points, I shall focus mainly on aspects of the previously circulated data associated with the apparently instructional character of some of the sequences.

The model which Wells and Montgomery outline (Figure 12.2 in their preceding chapter), in common with other recent work in discourse analysis, is an attempt to locate the coherence and orderliness of talk between two or more parties. It breaks with many of the traditional concerns of linguists, not only in taking naturally occurring talk as the object of study (instead of contrived examples), but also in treating the unit of study as being more than single utterances. Where linguists have previously tried to model the competence involved in producing a syntactically well-formed utterance, discourse analysts have recognised that a major part of our competence in speaking a language is the ability to fit what we say into sequences of dialogue. Whether Wells and Montgomery's model takes adequate account of the sequential relationship between utterances, and of the significance of that relationship for the ways in which utterances are formed, I shall question later. But it is clear that the links between utterances do receive some explicit attention in the model.

However, a major concern of the model is to attempt to describe the 'options' which are available to a speaker, any of which may be employed in a given turn at talking. Thus, as I understand it, what a speaker 'means' when he says something is taken to be a product of the decision to employ a certain set of those options (and, possibly, not to employ other available options?), though what 'meaning' refers to in this context is not quite clear – the closest explanation of that being, that 'Combinations of options from each of these systems [of 'commodity' and 'discourse role'] define the basic communicative acts of Demand . . . Question . . . Statement . . . Answer' (p. 219). Thus, a speaker's 'meaning' looks, roughly, to be the action he performs through the selection of an utterance the features of which can be described according to the range of options it employs. The model employs a coding grid the categories of which describe features, some of which any utterance will possess. All utterances are taken to involve the assignment of a role to the speaker (e.g. whether he initiates something, or is responding to a prior speaker), the exchange of some commodity (e.g. goods or services, or information), and whether or not the 'content' (which seems to be treated as synonymous with referent) of a prior turn is incorporated in the utterance. Then, reading the grid from left to right, one successively uncovers more detailed aspects of a speaker's selection from the available options represented by the grid.

Since the generality of the model lies in the fact that any two utterances may be compared to see which, if any, features (categories) they share, it already, almost necessarily, fulfils the first and last requirements for such a model (see the contribution by McTear in this volume). However, whether it satisfies the middle two conditions, concerning the model's ability to depict a *developmental* process of language acquisition, will depend on its ability to describe the systematics of talk at any particular stage in development, or adequately to characterise the 'competence' which children gradually acquire. Early on, it is suggested that the model itself already represents possible stages in the acquisition process:

> The notion of progressively more delicate sub-categorisation can also be taken as a powerful hypothesis about the sequence of development. Our initial exploration of this hypothesis, drawing

> upon consecutive recordings of the same children, suggests that development over time does indeed take the form of the gradual addition of further functions which quite largely correspond to the sub-categorisation that one would make in carrying out a more delicate description of adult discourse. (pp. 219-20)

Accordingly, only the categories towards the left-hand side of the model should be applicable to the utterances of very young children; their development of skills in talking (conversing) would then be traced by the successive acquisition of the 'more delicate' categories to the right of the model. That strikes me as unlikely, if only because some of the earliest, one-word utterances are easily categorisable as options towards, or at, the extreme right-hand side of the model. Thus one finds very young children Requesting Acknowledgement, Complying with and Rejecting parents' requests – all of which are options to the right of the model, representing the repertoire of options, or skills, claimed to be more characteristic of adult speakers. This is not to say that there may not be differences in the way children often design utterances in order to accomplish certain actions, compared with how adults manage the same actions. For example, a feature of initial turns in request sequences in adult conversation is that pre-request forms are frequently used. Instead of making a direct request in initial position, someone wishing to make a request may first ask the intended recipient a question concerning the object of the request – a question which is routinely treated by the recipient as projecting a next move in the sequence, i.e. the request. An 'answer' to a question recognised as leading up to a request – i.e. a pre-request – may be designed not to address the literal question, but with a view to the anticipated request, and thus formed, for instance, as a 'granting' (and perhaps, by virtue of the fact that the request has not yet been made, as an 'offer').[2] By contrast, children apparently use pre-request forms much less frequently, and more often use some 'direct' request format.[3] But it should be emphasised that quite young children may sometimes use pre-request forms, just as adults use direct request forms in initial position: so the difference is probably not due to any lack of competence on the part of the children.[4] What I want to draw from this is, firstly, that an apparent difference between the ways children, and adults, manage the same interactional tasks such as requesting might be established through careful analysis of the design of the initial (sequence) forms, and the sequential implicativeness of those forms. The relevant features of their design will *not* be located through more detailed coding ('sub-categorisation') of those utterances, since both direct and pre-request forms can presumably be coded in a very similar fashion (according to the model, both might be treated, and hence coded, as Initiating, designed to have recipient Give on Request, and may be built to get the recipient to Comply, i.e. to have the recipient grant the request). The second point is that, even then, the differences which emerge may not be so much a matter of children's lack of competence, or the unavailability to them of particular forms for managing activities, as the result of certain interactional difficulties which children may face. So I doubt that one could identify stages in conversational/linguistic development simply by sub-categorising either the 'basic speech functions' (activities) or the 'options' constituting those functions, in the way proposed: the sub-categories are likely to be equally applicable to young children's utterances and to talk in general (i.e. including adult talk). It is in this respect that I think the model obscures not only much of the richness of the data collected, but also some aspects of the systematic character of conversation. In setting out a system of options available to speakers, the model also makes some attempt to specify the 'constraints' which might operate on the type of action which should properly be done by a next speaker in response to a prior turn. However, what this seems to miss is the significance of the specific management or design of a turn in order to accomplish a given activity type. Given that an activity can be managed through a variety of possible alternative formats or designs, I shall argue that we need to ask what considerations are involved in the selection of particular designs, or what interactional work a given format achieves. The importance of these questions is stressed by the fact that *initial* turns in sequences may be subject to other interactional considerations, which are not really constraints, but which may be systematic with respect to their implicativeness for subsequent talk. We can begin to see something of the importance of how turns are designed so as to accomplish certain activities, by considering a fragment from some data discussed in Wells and Montgomery's paper, a transcript of a video-tape: in this fragment, a teacher, T, is holding a book open and pointing with a pencil at successive items in the text for the child, R, to read out.[5]

(1) (BLDP: School Extract C)
R: I / am / tall / said / the / –
(2.0)

((T looks from text to R. Shapes lips to indicate sound))

R: Tower
→ T: Chimney
R: Chimbley
T: ↓ Its a big factory chimney isn't it.

In this fragment, T corrects R's misreading of the text ('Tower') by citing the correct item, 'Chimney': but there are other familiar ways in which a recipient may initiate the correction of a first speaker. For example, T might have pointed back to the word which was misread, perhaps also asking R to try reading each syllable in order to make up the word. Another method might have been to repeat the item which is taken to be incorrect (in this case, to repeat 'Tower'), as in these examples:[6]

(2) (TW: Ca, E, 57)
D: He wants some oil
→ M: Oi:l
D: Petrol
(2.0)
M: Has he no petrol
D: No cos he's =
M: = His car won' go very far will it

(3) (GJ: FN)
((3 children playing tag: St. has been tagged, and is now 'it'))
St: One, two, three, (.) four, five, six (.) eleven eight nine ten
→ Su: Eleven? eight, nine, ten?
St: Eleven, eight, nine, ten
→ N: Eleven?
St: Seven, eight, nine, ten
Su: That's better

In each of these extracts, recipient(s) treat some item in prior speaker's utterance as possibly incorrect, by repeating that item: in (2), that is 'Oi:l' and, in (3), Su repeats that part of St's utterance in which the error occurred, stressing the incorrect item[7] – and when St fails to correct the error in his subsequent turn, N repeats just that item,

'Eleven?', again with stress. St then corrects, to 'Seven', as does D in (2), from 'oil' to 'petrol'.

Yet another way of initiating a correction of prior speaker is illustrated in another fragment from the Bristol data.

(4) (BLDP: Extract A)
M: Whats the time / by the clock
R: Uh
M: Whats the time
(3.0)
M: (Now) what numbers that
R: Number two
→ M: No its not
M: What is it
M: Its a one and a nought

In (4), M initiates a correction sequence by drawing explicit attention to an error – i.e. that the number is not 'two', as R proposed. However, M locates the error but without also supplying the correct version. Even when R does not respond (as 'No its not', 'What is it', and 'Its a one and a nought' are transcribed as separate turns, I take it that there are spaces between them in which R might have begun a self-correction), M continues attempting to elicit a correction from R and does not herself supply the correct item until several further attempts (see data, Extract A, p. 211). Notice that even her prompt, in her last turn in (4), withholds naming the correct item (i.e ten).

Another way in which recipients may seek to have first speakers correct a suspected error – if, indeed, it turns out that an error has been made – is to design their turns as possible hearing or understanding checks (with, for example, 'Pardon', 'What', or a partial repeat + 'what'):[8] these forms, together with their sequential significance in terms of how they are subsequently treated by first speaker, are discussed by Langford in another paper in this volume. But I want to focus back on the three formats just outlined through which T might have initiated the correct sequence in (1): by *pointing back* to the word which was misread (non-verbal); by *repeating* the incorrect item (i.e. 'Tower', probably with upward question intonation); or by explicitly *rejecting* R's proffered version, in a negative format (e.g. 'No, not tower'). It will be noticed that, in each case, recipients design their turns so as to *withhold* the correction in the turn immediately subsequent to that in which an error is being located. They may all manage to draw first speaker's attention to the occurrence of an error, but they are designed to allow first speaker the opportunity to *self-correct*: recipients do not themselves immediately make the correction – even the negative 'rejection' format can leave the first speaker to come up with the correct item. These formats, together with 'hearing' and 'understanding' checks, etc., may all be treated by the speaker whose turn they follow as invitations to self-correct.

In that respect they contrast with the format which T in fact uses in (1).

R: I / am / tall / said / the / –
(2.0)
((T looks from text to R. Shapes lips to indicate sound))
R: Tower
→ T: Chimney

Here T's initial turn post the located error is designed as an outright correction: it does not allow R the opportunity to self-correct, as might alternative formats which could have been selected.

Thus, two general alternatives available to a speaker who recognises or suspects an error in prior speaker's utterance are: either to withhold a correction, albeit by possibly inviting self-correction (though not necessarily; recipient may let the error pass); or to do a correction, by supplying the item which should have been there. But, as Schegloff, Jefferson and Sacks (1977) show, these are not equivalent alternatives. In short, self-corrections are preferred activities, and other-corrections (i.e. corrections by recipients) are dispreferred activities. 'Preference' here does not refer to the psychological proclivities of individual speakers, but to organised and systematic features of turns in which these activities are managed. For example, self-corrections may be done at an earliest opportunity, interruptively – a speaker may interrupt himself in mid-turn or even mid-word to correct something earlier in the same turn, as in:

(5) (PT, 7)
→ E: .hhh B't anyway we played golf et San or Bud played
et San Ma:rcus so I went down with 'im yihknow . . .

(6) (US, 5)
M: °Yah. Th't's w't I jus' checked ou(hh)t ma:n, .hh No
→ she's bitching about sh– he gave me d'clock.

By contrast, corrections of other speakers tend to be withheld, not only by not being done interruptively in the turn in which an 'error' is located, but also by not being done at an earliest opportunity on the completion of that turn – so pauses systematically occur in such environments. Recipients further withhold corrections by designing their initial turn post the 'error' as an invitation to self-correct, as described above. Therefore, recipients are passing over at least three opportunities to do a correction – immediately post the item to be corrected, immediately on completion of the turn in which the 'error' occurred, and in their initial turn post that in which the first speaker made an 'error': thus they withhold or delay the dispreferred action, an other-correction. They design their initial turns (and some subsequent ones, as in (3) and (4)) to enable first speakers to self-correct, and thereby to provide opportunities for the preferred action, self-correction.

Moreover, even when recipients do correct first speaker, such other-corrections are built to display their dispreferred status. A case from child-adult conversation is this:

(7) (TW: 430-1) ((R and L are children))
R: Ma:↓=
L: = He's sayin mamee in't 'ee↑
M: Uhuh
(5.0)
R: Dadada::↑
R: ( )
L: He's saying mummy↑
(1.2)
→ M: He was (.) I think he's sayin dada now

M's correction, 'He was (.) I think he's sayin dada now', is first of all delayed (by the 1.2 second pause); it is then done with an agreement component in the first position in the turn, 'He was', which finds something in L's prior turn with which to agree. The correction, 'dada', is treated as possibly an interpretable matter (rather than a strict case of truth/falsity) by being made into something M *thinks* he's saying. Finally, the correction is not done with overt negations of

L's position – M avoids such forms as 'No he's not, he's saying . . .'

The sequential features associated with withholding other-corrections (e.g. pauses, initial turns inviting self-correction), and features of the design of turns in which other-corrections are done (the correction may be delayed in the turn; it may occur with, or be preceded by, agreement and other mitigating components; and the avoidance of negative forms), are what are referred to by the dis-preferred status of other-corrections. This is no more than an outline of the preference organisation for correction sequences such as those occurring in (1) and (4) from the Bristol data (for further points see Schegloff, Jefferson and Sacks, 1977, and also Pomerantz, 1977; Wootton, 1978a, discusses how the preferred character of grantings of requests is exhibited in child-adult talk). Yet already, I think, there are a number of implications for the kind of model which Wells and Montgomery propose.

The usefulness of the model for analysing any given corpus is derived from the applicability of the categories of options to all kinds of talk: hence any two utterances may be compared in terms of those 'options' they share, and those which are distinctive to each. But, to begin with, the options in the model may quite ignore the interactional work achieved in the design of the turn. For example, we saw that in the turns in which recipients initiate correction sequences, in (2) and (3),

D: He wants some oil
→ M: Oi:l

St: One, two, three, (.) four, five, six (.)
eleven eight nine ten
→ Su: Eleven? eight, nine, ten?

are designed as *repetitions* of part of prior speakers' turns, inviting self-correction. Thus recipients manage the twin interactional tasks of drawing attention to a possible error, whilst avoiding doing an outright correction and thereby leaving it to prior speakers to self-correct. Looking at the correction in (1),

R: Tower
→ T: Chimney

we can see that, although T straightaway corrects R, she does so avoiding the use of an overt correction format, negating or rejecting prior speaker's version. For instance, in extract (4), M designs her turn as a rejection of R's version:

M: (Now) what numbers that
R: Number two
→ M: No its not

A similar format in (1) might have been, 'No its not tower, its chimney'. However, T avoids such a format and instead simply supplies the correct item without that being explicitly marked as a correction. This is perhaps emphasised by what follows that fragment.

R: Chimbley
T: ↑Its a big factory chimney isnt it

R's acknowledgment of the correction is an attempted repeat of the correct item, an attempt which does not quite succeed. T then manages to correct R's lexical inaccuracy, or perhaps dialect form ('Chimbley'), again avoiding an explicit correction or rejection form, by embedding the correct pronunciation in something like an extension of the topic, continuing to talk (and getting R to talk) about the object in the picture.

Now, according to the model, a distinction might be made between Implicit and Explicit rejections (see Wells and Montgomery, p. 222 above), though this does not, of course, account for how rejections can get to do the work of, and be treated as, corrections. Moreover, coding utterances in this way does no justice to sequential properties of such turns (especially the delay of outright corrections), and aspects of their design (e.g. delay of the correction component in the turn, pauses, agreement and 'I think' prefaces), through which overt corrections may be managed in a variety of interactionally 'delicate' ways. The model might presumably be further refined to show how some implicit corrections are invitations to self-correct, by coding cases of the latter as, perhaps, Text-Contingent (category) plus Reiterate (option). In once again overlooking features of how a turn may be designed to invite self-correction (its delay; pauses; emphasis used to locate the error in the prior turn, etc.), a major difficulty with such a solution is apparent: a full or partial repeat of a prior speaker's turn may be used to do – and may be treated as doing – a variety of interactional work besides inviting self-correction. For example, a few lines later, in the 'Rosie' (second school) extract, the teacher repeats a comment of Rosie's:

(8) (BLDP: Extract C)
R: I don't like that one
T: You don't like it
R: ((shakes head))
T: Why not
R: I only like little ones

In common with other (partial or full) repeats, this could be coded in the same way as those repeats which invite self-correction (i.e. as Text-Contingent Reiterations) – though clearly T's repeat in (8) does not appear to invite R to correct anything in her comment and nor does R treat it as such. Instead, the repeat here, in this sequential environment, seems to be bound up with seeking some elaboration from R (which it eventually gets). So a critical question is what sequential aspects, and what features of their design, make certain partial/full repeats recognisable as invitations to self-correct, whilst others are (or are treated as) requests for elaboration, requests for clarification, etc. – and it's just this question which is central to Langford's chapter in Part Two. Only detailed investigation of the sequential position and design of turns can yield an answer to that question: coding it according to the categories/options in the model rather obscures how turns are managed to do what they do. The alternative proposed here – and what seems fundamental to conversational analysis, represented by the papers in the previous section of this book – is to treat utterances (or perhaps parts of utterances) as sequential objects: look for what a turn does in a sequence of turns, and find a general description for that work as, for instance, 'invitation to self-correct'. From a collection of such structurally similar objects, one can then begin to find some of the systematic, regularly occurring features associated with, and through which the turn is designed to be, that kind of sequential object.

Recall that we are considering different ways in which recipients may initiate correction sequences, by supplying the correct item, as in (1) and (7), or using types which withhold the correction, for example in (2)-(4). Another general implication for the model is that types of turns in which recipients initiate correction sequences are *non-equivalent* – while the model, as it stands, lists them as apparently equivalent, equally selectable alternative forms. There is nothing to suggest that the combination of options which might be used to code differently preferred correction formats could be both differently available according to what has gone before (as I mentioned above) and differently implicative for what may follow. Yet now we can see that some allow first speaker the opportunity to self-correct, whilst others do not, but correct other speaker instead: the former are *preferred*, whilst the latter, other-correction forms, are *dispreferred*. The differential status of the types as preferred and dispreferred activities may be reflected in their differential distribution, their placement in sequential positions (other-corrections may be less likely to occur in first position in correction sequences) and the kinds of components in the turns (particularly with respect to the components which may co-occur with outright corrections). Of course, this is only intended to illustrate a general point about the model, that certain options may be ordered relative to one another (e.g. some preferred, some dispreferred is one such ordering), and certain options may systematically co-occur, so that utterances are not formed out of random bunches of 'options' or components.

Now, whilst Wells and Montgomery discuss at some length the importance of sequential constraints in very broad terms, it is unclear specifically how the options in their network may be sequentially organised, or how sequential patterns or structures come to be generated in talk. I want to turn now to discuss some of the interesting sequential patterns associated with corrections in the Bristol data, patterns with which the model does not help us much.

The different formats used to initiate correction sequences are fitted with, and make their turns into, differential sequential objects. I do not have much to say about that first sense, of being fitted with different sequential objects, though that can be illustrated briefly in the case of T's correction in (1):

R: I / am / tall / said / the / –
(2.0) ((T looks from text to R. Shapes lips to indicate sound))
R: Tower
T: Chimney

After a two-second pause in which R fails to read the word in the text, T makes an attempt to have R complete, by non-verbally showing her the sounds in the word. So T does the correction, 'Chimney', post R's failure to read the text and also her failure to match the prompted sounds to the text. Thus, T's selection of a correction instead of a form inviting self-correction, e.g. by repeating 'Tower', might be fitted to R's two failures, by treating R's attempted reading as a guess based on the picture, and not just a 'slip of the tongue' in reading the text. In using an invitation to self-correct, recipient may treat an error as an unintended slip, whilst the outright correction form treats the error as something the child doesn't and couldn't know or is not able to read. So the selection of a given form through which to initiate the correction can display recipient's understanding of what kind of error prior speaker has made: the type of 'repair' selected characterises or accounts for the repairable item. Once again, the model does not capture the ways in which the selection of a particular type of turn subsequent to a first object displays recipient's differential treatment of what that object is.

However, the differential formats for initiating corrections are different sequential objects in another sense: they have different implications for what is done in at least the next turn in the sequence. Where recipient does a correction, by supplying the correct item, in first position post the error, a sequentially relevant next action by the speaker who made the error is an acknowledgement.

(1) R: Tower
T: Chimney
→ R: Chimbley

(9) H: On Her Majesty's::: Service er:::
S: On Her Majesty's Secret Service [That's right
→ H: [Secret Service yeah.

R and H respectively acknowledge the corrections by repeating the corrected items. Thus, acknowledgement in (9) is a partial repeat of that part of S's turn in which the correction is done; it is also followed by another acknowledgement or confirmation token, 'yeah'. A basis for the acknowledgements in such positions can be that, as was discussed for (1), the corrections are done without explicit negative or rejection components, and so are not marked as being corrections. That applies also in (9), where the addition of 'Secret' to the title of the book is embedded in a repeat of H's version (instead, S might simply have said 'Secret Service' to correct H). Given that the corrections are unmarked, an issue might be whether they have been received/understood; and thus this is confirmed in the next turn by an acknowledgement.

Recipients may draw attention to a possible error, though without making a correction, by inviting first speaker to check what he has just said and, if necessary, make a self-correction. Thus, invitations to self-correct may get a correction in the next turn.

(2) D: He wants some oil
M: Oi:l
→ D: Petrol

Alternatively, first speaker may confirm the repeated item; but notice that, while the child in the next sequence confirms the number of yoghurts as eight, he also treats the repeat as having attended to a possible error.

(10) (TW: Ca, E, 059)
D: He's gonna buy eight yoghurt
M: Eight
→ D: Yes (0.5) Is that a lot

So the two general types of initial turns in correction sequences implicate different objects – or relevant next actions – in the subsequent turns: corrections in initial position provide for the relevance of *acknowledgements* by prior speakers; while (forms of) invitation to self-correct occasion *confirmations* or *corrections.*[9] However, the constraint on those subsequent turns is not that which operates for adjacency pairs: following the production of the first part of an adjacency pair, recipient should then do a second part from that pair. But the turns subsequent to 'corrections', 'invitations to correct', etc. seem to be less closely constrained, perhaps because the initial turns allow for some specifiable set of options in next position.[10] At any rate, identifiable sequential structures are associated with the forms used to initiate the sequence – by virtue of their implicating the relevance of (one of a set of) subsequent actions on the part of first speakers. The 'prospective/retrospective' links in Wells and Montgomery's model do not help to locate such identifiable structures of actions in sequences, because happening to refer back to something in prior speaker's utterance, or retaining a topical link, is treated in the model as equivalent to, say, producing the second part of an adjacency pair, or acknowledging a correction – i.e. all would be coded as 'retrospective'. However, they ought not to be taken as equivalent, because a topic of a prior turn may be incorporated in a subsequent one, without the subsequent turn being implicated in, or constrained by, the prior (as, for instance, is the action performed post the first part of an adjacency pair).

Some actions, then, may be taken to occasion the relevance of a next; a specifiable (set of) subsequent action(s) is an expectable occurrence. Trying to identify how certain actions may be organised into sequential structures might be of considerable interest in the Bristol data. Many sequences in the data are seemingly bound up with *instructing* children. Such sequences occur in both the school and the home data, so it is not that we should investigate the talk as though it were setting specific, but we should begin to ask whether there are systematic features of the sequences in which adults instruct children, wherever.

I want to make some observations about aspects of the data which seem to be associated with how what is going on might be treated by co-participants as 'instructing'. Firstly, we saw that, in (1), T does an outright correction. Though not marked as a rejection of R's version, it supplies the correct version. It is a case of 'other-correction', the dispreferred activity, and we saw that a basis for that is T's treatment of 'Tower' as a guess – the kind of remedial T selects displays her understanding of R's 'problem'. What T is not doing, therefore, is permitting the child's version to stand: it is not treated as a matter of R making up a story, and thereby being in control of what is or is not correct. This contrasts with what then happens in fragment (10):

D: He's gonna buy eight yoghurt
M: Eight
D: Yes (0.5) ↑Is that a lot↑
→ M: What else is he gonna buy

Here M passes over the opportunity to do a correction (provided by D's question '↑Is that a lot↑') and instead asks a question back to D which enables him to continue the story/game. In (1), however, T retains control over what is to stand as correct in that position.

A related observation is that those turns in which recipients initiate correction sequences in the Bristol data – e.g. (1) and (4) –

(1) R: Tower
→ T: Chimney

(4) M: (Now) what numbers that ((Pointing to position of hands on the clock))
R: Number two
→ M: No its not
M: What is it

do not display recipients' uncertainty or doubt as to whether an error has, in fact, been made – though some forms might have been selected which hedge on speaker's certainty.[11] Again, what is (going to) stand as correct is not treated by T and M as a negotiable matter, or one over which the child has the same access to a possibly correct version as they do.

Both the correction in (1) and the rejection in (4) occur post first attempts by R; and, in (4), R has two prior opportunities to answer.

M: Whats the time / by the clock
→ R: Uh
M: Whats the time
→ (3.0)
M: (Now) what numbers that ((Pointing to position of hands on the clock))

R's hesitancy, and particularly her silence after M's question 'Whats the time', are treated by M, not as signs that R is withholding an answer – that she knows the answer but refuses to give it – but as indicating R's inability to answer. That characterisation of/account for R's non-answer is displayed in the way M proceeds to break the task of 'telling the time' down into component parts for R: M thereby shows R a way of approaching the initial question so as (possibly) to arrive at an answer. The particular way M reformulates the question – where other reformulations/aids are conceivable – treats R's problem as due to her inability to read off the clock, and not due, for instance, to her not knowing where to find the clock, or to her not having heard/understood the question. So the reformulation she uses seems integral to the character of the sequence as instructing the child, rather than being some kind of clarification sequence. Reformulations of questions post children's silences are very common in the Bristol data. Two other cases from the School Extract B, reproduced in Wells and Montgomery's paper, are these:

(11) (BLDP: Extract B)
T: Whats / what are those
(3.0)
→ T: What d'you think he uses them for

(12) (BLDP: Extract B)
T: He uses those / to go down –
(5.0)
→ T: Is it a hill or a mountain

Notice that such reformulations are compatible with the speaker (i.e. questioner) already possessing the answer. It is specifically because these reformulations are built to show the child another route to a correct answer (and do not merely 'clarify' what was asked) that they display the speaker's prior knowledge of the answer. It is on that basis that we – and recipients of such questions/reformulations – can begin to distinguish questions to which the speaker does know the answer, from those to which he does not (the latter being 'genuine' requests for information).

Thus, it might be that recipients (children) face a particular interactional problem in such sequences, and in this respect their silences post question, as in (4), (11) and (12), are interesting. For some questions, not having an answer may be treated by recipient as simply a matter of not happening to know, in a reply such as 'I don't know' – which can, furthermore, take the line: if I don't know, neither of us does. In such cases then, a non-answer ('I don't know') may not be delayed or withheld. However, silences, such as those occurring in (4), can display recipients' understanding that it is expected that they should know the answers, not merely that they might know the answers. Hence, recipients (in (4), R) treat their own problem as being, not that they just happen not to know the answer, but that they ought to know (are being expected to know) and don't. This looks like a problem which might be associated with being in the position of the recipient of instruction.

These initial observations very much tie in with an apparent structure for 'instruction' sequences. Routinely, sequences in which one party asks co-participant questions as part of instructing recipient are not completed by the production of an answer; instead, the questioner generally confirms that the answer is correct.

(13) (BLDP: Extract B)

	T:	Is it a hill or a mountain
	R:	A hill
→	T:	A hill / yes
	T:	And whats on the hill
	R:	Ice
→	T:	Yes / ice

In each case in (13), T confirms R's answer by repeating the answer, together with an affirmative (in other cases, affirmatives such as 'Yes, that's right' are also used). Thus, the actions in such sequences are organised into this structure:

A: Question
B: Answer
A: Confirmation

The importance of this sequential structure is that it differentiates instruction sequences from information sequences. Were A's initial question to be treated as simply a request for information, A would not then confirm B's answer, for by confirming an answer, A makes it into one which he already knew, and over which he retains control to decide its correctness.

However, in cases where an answer to the initial question is not forthcoming, that 'basic' sequential structure seems to be modified in at least two ways. Firstly, the sequence may be expanded by A's production of a reformulation (or series of reformulations):

(14) (BLDP: Extract B)

T:	What's / what are those	(Question)
	(3.0)	(Non-response)
T:	What d'you think he uses them for	(Reformulation)
	(4.0)	
R:	Go down	(Answer)
	(2.0)	
T:	Go down –	
		((R rubs both

		eyes with backs of hands))
T:	Yes / You're right / Go on	(Confirmation)

The expansion here is complicated a little by T's treatment of R's answer 'Go down' as only part of an answer, through her prompting R for more. But broadly – and this can be found in other data presented in the section – the 'basic' structure is expanded by first speaker's reformulation of the question, post recipient's non-response to the initial question; from then on, the sequence is organised as before, with B's production of an answer, followed by A's confirmation.

In other cases, though, the structure is more clearly altered, and not just expanded. These are cases in which, post recipient's non-response to the initial question – or post an incorrect answer – the questioner provides the answer in the subsequent turn.

(15) (BLDP: Extract A)
M: What is it
→ M: Its a one and a nought
R: Nought
R: One and a nought

(16) (BLDP: Extract A)
M: Whats one and a nought
R: Um / that
→ M: A ten
R: Ten

In (15), R does not answer the initial question 'What is it'; so M subsequently provides an answer, 'It's a one and a nought', which R repeats. In (16), R hesitantly attempts to answer, unsuccessfully; again, M provides an answer which is repeated by R. The structure for these sequences is, then:

A: Question
B: Non-response/incorrect answer
A: Answer
B: Acknowledgement (or Display)

The 'basic' structure I outlined has thus been modified in two ways:

it is the questioner, and not the recipient, who provides the answer: that has the consequence that recipient, B, completes the sequence (not A as before) with something like a display. The last part is, therefore, a different sequential object from before: even though questioners' confirmations may have superficial similarities with recipients' displays (e.g. both may involve repeats of the correct answer), recipients clearly do not confirm A's answer in these latter sequence types – an indication of this is the fact that displays generally do not include affirmative components. What the repeats in the latter sequences may do is to display or acknowledge that A's prior turn has been understood as an answer to the initial question – much like recipient's acknowledgement of an other-correction, as in (1).

R:	Tower	
T:	Chimney	(Correction)
R:	Chimbley	(Acknowledgement)

It is these kinds of sequential structures which can be identified in the Bristol data – and, of course, elsewhere in child-adult discourse – which might be well worth investigating further, given that they seem to be closely associated with the character of much of the talk as involving 'adults instructing children'. Naturally, many other kinds of sequences, not all of which involve instruction, may be found in adult-child talk. I have merely discussed these sequential structures as an example of an orderly and systematic quality in the data – and thereby an aspect of the competence children and adults have in talking, sensibly and coherently, with one another – which I think the model developed by Wells and Montgomery largely misses. Some of the points made in this latter discussion about structures of actions serve to emphasise part of my earlier argument – that coding aspects of utterances cannot capture much of the interactional and sequential work which a turn may be designed to achieve. For instance, just coding utterances as 'repeats' or 'reformulations' would not describe what interactional work they achieve in given sequential environments, or systematic aspects of their design for that work. It is this understanding of turns, and components within turns, as sequential objects, the features of which are managed with a view to their sequential placement, which the model seems to miss – but which is fundamental to our ability as speakers to fit what we say into orderly discourse.

Notes

1. I should emphasise this particularly, because when I wrote this response I had seen only an early draft of Wells' paper, outlining a preliminary version of the model being developed in Bristol. The version which appears in this volume, co-authored with Montgomery, is considerably revised: and in some respects it is clear that their model does attempt to capture some of the systematic features of conversation which I discuss here. I have therefore made some modifications to my original draft, to take account of, and do a little justice to, ways in which the model may try to handle such features as constraints operating on options available to next speakers, the design of turns, etc. However, the revisions which Wells and Montgomery have made do not seem to me to alter the main lines of my argument or my contention that such a model cannot adequately or satisfactorily capture such features. But what I have to say should be regarded not as a detailed assessment/critique of the prior paper, but as an attempt to show how their data might be more satisfactorily analysed. That should not obscure the interests we share in investigating the sequential management and orderliness of naturally occurring conversation.

2. See Atkinson and Drew (1979, Ch. 5) for a discussion of pre-sequences, including pre-requests.

3. Two of the most common forms children use to initiate requests are 'I want' forms, as in

(TW: Ha/M/16)
C: Mummy I'm wantin my be::ll offa the Christma:s tree:

and 'Can I' types

(TW: Ga/M/104)
C: Mummy why can't a .hh mummy in the afternoon please .hh please can I 'ave Shona's (ball)

In calling these 'direct' request forms, it should be remembered that such forms may nevertheless be designed to obtain a granting of the request, and hence may be sensitive to something like the 'imposition' the request makes on the recipient. For instance, they may include 'politeness' forms, such as the 'please(s)' in the above extract; and they may seek to reduce the scale of what is requested. For an analysis of some systematic properties of such request forms used by children to adults, see Wootton (1978b).

4. A case is the following:

(TW: Ca/E/493)
C: Da:ddy
(1.5)
F: °What
C: Wh–
C: When are 'or gonna sho:p for mummy again
(2.0)
F: .hhh Why d'you want t'come
C: Yes
F: An will ye show me where all the things are
C: Yes

The child's inquiry is treated by F as projecting a request on the part of C to go shopping with him, an understanding displayed in his not actually answering the question 'When . . .?', but going on to ask why she wanted to know (i.e. what next action hangs on the outcome of the answer). And C confirms that she was asking because she wanted to go. So C initiates the request sequence, not with a 'direct' request, but with a question which leads up to, or projects, the request. Such questions may be designed to elicit whether, if a request were forthcoming, it would be granted.

5. For extracts taken from the Bristol Language Development Project data (BLDP), I have for the most part retained their transcription symbols – despite some misgivings about them. For instance, some of the symbols appear to capture, not what is heard on the tape, but the analyst's interpretation of what was intended by the sounds. The effect of this might easily be to collect together things which on the tape are quite dissimilar sounding, on the grounds that a similar intention underlay them. But, surely, a case should be made out for how dissimilar objects, sound patterns, etc. should be doing the same thing, and not presuppose that in the very data to be analysed. (I also mistrust the timings, since none under 2 seconds appear, and all have been timed to the nearest second.)

6. All other data extracts are transcribed according to the conventions current in conversation analysis: see Sacks, Schegloff and Jefferson (1974: Appendix). I am grateful to David Langford, who transcribed many of the extracts to which I refer in this paper; and especially to Tony Wootton, from whose data the extracts are taken. Extract (3) is from Jefferson (1972).

7. It is noticeable that, where only part of a word is taken to be incorrect, the speaker may repeat the word, stressing just that part to be corrected:

(GTS: 11/2/54)

K: 'E likes that waiter over there,
(.)
→ A: Wait-er?
K: Waitress, (.) sorry

Throughout the paper I refer to 'errors'. I am uneasy about this because things other than errors may be corrected, as here.

(Syracuse)

C: .hhh I was um: (0.3) I war' u– (.) I spoke t' the gir–
I spoke to Caryn. (0.2) .hh andum . . .

Though 'girl' is not strictly incorrect, C corrects it with a naming, Karen. Schegloff *et al.* (1977) describe some of the many things, other than errors, which may be repaired through corrections. I continue to use 'errors' here, partly as a shorthand – and partly because the initial turns by adults in the correction sequences discussed in this paper do treat something the child has said as an 'error', as something which is wrong (rather than, 'not quite right').

8. 'What' and 'Pardon' may thus invite self-correction, though embed that in a hearing check. In contrast to invitations to self-correct done with repeats of the incorrect item, the 'hearing check' forms a hedge on whether an error was made, or which item was incorrect. Nevertheless, hearing checks are routinely treated by recipients as finding an error in what was just said, though it may be ambiguous as to whether the What/Pardon was intended to notice an error – as here:

(TW: Ca/E/055)

C: Is Derek a nice boy
→ M: Pardon
→ C: Is Derek a bad boy
M: Who

C: Derek
M: No:

9. Where self-corrections are done in these slots, post invitations to self-correct, they are often accompanied by apologies, as in the extract in note 7.

A: Wait-er?
→ K: Waitress, (.) sorry

The ways in which specific forms of invitations to self-correct (e.g. 'What/Pardon', partial repeats, elliptical repeats and full repeats) are systematically treated by first speaker, in their production of various subsequent objects – especially corrections and confirmations – are discussed by Langford in his chapter in Part Two of this volume.

10. Pomerantz has worked on orderings between actions, in which a subsequent action is implicated in an initial action, though that implicativeness is not due to a constraint deriving from an adjacency pair. She calls these 'action chains'. A rule for adjacency pairs is that, following the production of a first pair part, recipient should then take a turn, and produce a second part from the pair type of which the first is a member. By contrast,

> With 'action chains', what is being proposed is that an $Action_2$, or a 'second pair part' is not a *should* but a *may* for recipient i.e. an option among several specifiable options. In part, it is in the doing of the second that a prior becomes treated (formulated) as one or another first action which is linked with that given second. Although some number of appropriate $Actions_2$ may be available subsequent to a given prior, initial evidence suggests that those alternative options are themselves preferentially ordered relative to each other. (Pomerantz, 1977)

11. It was mentioned above (note 8), that 'hearing checks', such as 'What' or 'Pardon', can invite recipient to check what he just said for a possible error, whilst managing that in a form which displays only a difficulty hearing. Of course, they are unspecific as to which item might be the source of the error. Such forms (and possibly others) are compatible with speaker being unsure that an error was, in fact, made, or where it might have been made – and thus are less committed in this direction than a repeat of the item taken to be incorrect. This seems to be the case, for instance, in the following extract, in which the mother does a partial repeat with a 'what' inserted for the uncertain item, 'canet'. Despite a repeat of the word by the child, M continues to query that item, with a repeat of it. But notice that she does not propose her version until some considerable time later and, even then, she does not pursue/insist on her version, post C's disconfirmation.

(TW: Ga/E/212)
M: It's supposed to be a a Space .hh
D: Cane:t
→ M: A space what darling
D: Space Canet
→ M: Cane:t
D: Ye:s a Space Canet
M: ah:: [:
D: [After my movie [my .hh m[ovies
M: [oh (.) [( )
D: My movie =

M: = Oh I see [I haven'
D: [Not my movie
M: I haven't [really listen'
D: [no this one
M: Ah ha
D: n. this one
M: I know what you mean but I .h haven't listen' to it really
D: The the one ↑Whacky Races↑
M: Whacky yer Whacky Races that's [right
D: [After Whacky
Races the Space Canet is that right they're [Space Canet
→ M: [n Space
→ Cad:ets (.) is that it
D: No
M: No
D: Space Cane:t
→ M: .well you could be right (you)

References

Atkinson, J.M. and Drew, P. (1979). *Order in Court: The Organisation of Verbal Interaction in Judicial Settings.* London: Macmillan

Jefferson, G. (1972). 'Side Sequences'. In D. Sudnow (ed.), *Studies in Social Interaction*

Pomerantz, A. (1977). 'Agreeing and Disagreeing with Assessments: Some Features of Preferred/Dispreferred Turn Shapes'. Unpublished MS, University of California, Los Angeles

Sacks, H., Schegloff, E. and Jefferson, G. (1974). 'A Simplest Systematics for the Organization of Turn-Taking for Conversation'. *Language*, 50, pp. 696–735

Schegloff, E., Jefferson, G. and Sacks, H. (1977). 'The Preference for Self-Correction in the Organization of Repair in Conversation', *Language*, 53, pp. 361–82

Sudnow, D. (ed.) (1972). *Studies in Social Interaction.* New York: Free Press

Wootton, A.J. (1978a). 'The Management of Grantings and Rejections by Parents in Request Sequences'. *Semiotica* (forthcoming)

— (1978b). 'The Organisation of Initial Request Turns by Children'. Unpublished MS, University of York

14 INTERPRETING CHILD DISCOURSE

Sue Foster

Approaching Child Language

The general view amongst students of child language in the 1960s and early 1970s was that early utterances were little more than inadequate adult sentences, and consequently communicatively inefficient. There had, however, been earlier attempts to view such utterances as communicative units involving the utterance and the non-verbal context. Such an approach saw early language as much richer, and more communicatively efficient, than the restricted, utterance-based, approach allows.

Stern and Stern, for instance, in work spanning from 1907 to 1928, having failed to classify satisfactorily children's one-word utterances as parts of speech, declared that the young child's verbal units did not belong to any consistent word class because they were not words but sentences (see Greenfield and Smith, 1976, p. 18). De Laguna (1927) viewed single-word utterances as actually complete, though undifferentiated, sentences and emphasised that these utterances could function as sentences because they were used in particular contexts and the missing linguistic elements could be seen as being supplied by the situation. So an utterance 'gone', said by a child as his mother left the room, could be interpreted as 'mummy has gone'. She also recognised the importance of non-verbal gesture, which could serve to add to and explain the verbal utterance. Thus she recognised, for instance, that a child could utter a word for an object while looking and pointing to it and thus indicate the particular object referred to. Guillaume (1927) also stressed the communicative approach to early language and noted that verbal and non-verbal elements could be combined together – a single verbal element often being capable of combination with a variety of non-verbal elements.

These early communicative approaches to child language, together with Bloom's work on the context of utterance (1970), the semantic approaches of those like Fillmore (1968) and the work of Piaget, have aided the formation of an approach to language development which involves detailed observation of both the non-verbal and verbal elements of communication. Piaget's view, that symbolic representation in general, including language, grows out of the sensori-motor schema of cognitive development, encouraged non-verbal action schemata to be seen as communicative, and moreover as being the precursors of verbal abilities. In Piaget's view, children can be regarded as evolving, from non-communicative action patterns, communicative units which express, by non-verbal means, relationships between elements in the real world. These same non-linguistic relationships will later be realised through verbal language. So, for instance, as Lock (1978a) has documented, from an action of raising the arms – which is unavoidable when being picked up – a child develops the ability to raise his arms in anticipation at the approach of an adult in order to initiate the adult's action of picking him up. Later, when language emerges, the child can produce the same result by verbal means.

There is now a sizeable body of literature (for example, the edited collections of articles by Schaffer (1977) and by Lock (1978b)) which reflects the development of this kind of approach – that is, an approach which recognises that an understanding of early child communication must involve examination of more than vocal utterances: it must view the non-verbal elements of communication as being as intrinsic as the verbal, and must account for the early stages before verbal language is well established. A concern with all the elements of communication provides a much fuller description and a much more useful one. If we are to make any real attempt at elucidating the course of communication development in the young child, we, as analysts, must make prudent use of all the data available.

Analysing Discourse Skills – Conversational Strategies and Topic Handling

In studying very young children from the age of a month and a half up to two years, a detailed examination of the kind of discourse skills children develop has led me to consider the relationship between the vocal (including the verbal) and the non-vocal elements of early child discourse. Originally, I had intended to analyse early interactions in terms of two theoretically distinct 'strands' of conversation, these being, firstly, the strategies[1] involved in handling a conversation and, secondly, the topic and how it is handled. In other words, I had intended, first of all, to look at behaviour clusters[2] that could be categorised as joint attention strategies (attention-getting and attention-directing by the child), conversation maintenance strategies (turn-taking and floor-holding)[3] and ending strategies. I then proposed to see how these functioned, by examining their relationship with the topic of conversation. I had hoped that form and topic could be handled separately and that an examination of the correspondence between form and content would then be possible.

Problems arose at all stages. First, it had seemed plausible to separate out bundles of behavioural features in communication and to categorise them as discourse strategies. So, for instance, a child who leaned towards his[4] mother, vocalised or verbalised while looking at her and putting out a hand to touch, poke or grab her would be regarded as attempting to attract her attention. However, not all cases were as clear in terms of the child's presumed intention. What about the child (and this was particularly the case with the youngest children of under six months old) who mught simply cough or look at his mother and succeed in attracting her attention? Clearly, not only are there problems of whether a very young child can intend to attract attention and how this can be deduced, but there are also problems of defining the objective function of behavioural features. The question is, should an attention strategy be categorised as such, based upon criteria in the child's behaviour (i.e. essentially what the observer deems to be behaviour constituting attracting attention), the mother's response to that behaviour, or the inferred intention of the child? In view of the wide variety of child behaviours which can result in the mother's attending to him, it seemed sensible to define attention strategies as behaviour which involves the child acting in such a way as to result in attention being shared with the mother so far as the observer can determine. Moreover, attention getting is usually followed by the directing of attention to an object which is then shared in attention by mother and child (see Carter, 1978, on attention directing, and Bruner, 1977, on joint attention). The child's behaviour should, therefore, usually result in mother and child sharing attention to something which was not shared prior to the behaviour in question. I say 'usually' because, on occasion, an object of joint attention fails to be established, not because the child's attention-getting strategy failed (though this does happen very occasionally), but because the child, having gained the mother's attention, for some reason does not try to direct it.

Quite obviously, there is a problem in defining joint attention initiation in terms of its result: it means that the only plausible way of defining this particular behaviour is in terms of its position in relation to the topic and that is what the study had originally aimed to avoid. Moreover, in addition to the fact that there is a wide variety of behaviours which result in joint attention, it is also true that most behaviours exhibited in these strategies also occur in ordinary turns within a topic. So, for instance, if we are dealing with a child older than about nine and a half months, who has developed the ability to monitor the mother visually during interaction, the distinction between an attention strategy and a monitored turn-take (Schaffer *et al.*, 1977) is based solely on its position in the flow of the topic.

Turning now to the definition of topic and topic change, a topic is defined simply as the object of joint attention, whether it is a material object in the real world or an abstract idea. This object can change either to a completely new topic or to a sub-topic within a single general topic. Here again there are problems. For instance, if a mother and child are playing together with toys and the child changes the object of joint attention from one toy to another, should this be seen as a complete change of topic or a shift to a sub-topic? It might be suggested that, if the child changes the attention from a car at one end of the room to a train at the other, this is a change of topic; but how far apart, or how different, do two objects have to be to constitute a complete shift of topic rather than a change to a different sub-topic? Perhaps in the light of these problems it is unrealistic to make this distinction between topic and sub-topic. However, I would defend this distinction on the basis of numerous examples, such as that examined in the section on Transcript 2, where the child moves from a concern with obtaining some more apple to a consideration of how the apple he is handed has come to appear as though someone has bitten it. Quite obviously, the particular concern has changed, though the overall topic remains the apple (see Keenan and Schieffelin, 1976, on topic).

While keeping these problems in mind, it seems that, when looking at early conversation, the most sensible way to determine what is going on is by examining the whole behaviour of the child (both vocal and non-vocal). It is necessary to make use of all the available clues and come to decisions about the status of particular items by building up as complete a picture as possible of the child and the interaction. His capabilities, personality, preferences, idiosyncracies of conversational behaviour, as well as the features of the particular interaction under analysis, must be taken into account. The value of the mother's reactions and responses to the child should be exploited, together with the interpretive or hermeneutical[5] judgements that the observer can make. Any observer will inevitably bring to the analysis her/his own knowledge of being a participant in discourse, and this knowledge cannot be ignored. The use made of it in analysis should, of course, be judicial, but to be aware of observer effect on analysis is a far more honest approach than trying to pretend it does not exist.

Two Examples Discussed

In the remainder of this chapter, I shall discuss two short examples of mother-child interactions involving a child (Ross) of two-and-a-half years old. My aim is to show, by means of a descriptive commentary, how an understanding of what is going on can be built up by looking at the verbal and non-verbal data available from mother and child. (However, here I shall only refer to the mother's behaviour in so far as it helps explicate the child's.) In the final section, I will mention some of the other kinds of data which have a bearing on interpreting these interactions.

The transcriptions are taken from a much larger body of video-taped recordings.[6] Each line of transcription (see Figure 14.1) represents both mother and child behaviours as they occur. Items which occur at the same point in time are placed directly above one another. The beginning of the first word of the description of a particular behaviour (whether vocal or non-vocal) is to be regarded as the starting-point of that behaviour. No attempt has been made to account for real time: this transcription aims simply to show what happened and what was the temporal relationship between mother and child behaviours.

The vocal line (V) is here represented in almost standard orthography. The original transcription represented the child's speech in phonemic script (phonetic symbols being used for sounds not present in standard adult English), but most of the idiosyncracies of production have been removed as my immediate concern here is not with the child's phonology. Those peculiarities which are represented are intended to give a flavour, no more, of this child's stage of speech development. The line of gaze (G) shows, quite simply, where each participant was looking (as far as could be ascertained from the tape); and, finally, the line of movement (M) shows the major gestures and movements each participant makes during the conversation. The movements transcribed were of two kinds: firstly, those that were obviously communicative such as reaches, grasps, points, giving and taking and so on (only such movements are referred to as gestures)

Figure 14.1: Transcription System

MOTHER	V	. . . . thats not a flower . . . . .
	G	own food ——— C ——— plate on C's right ———————
	M	- shakes head - - - - - - - -
CHILD	V	. . . . yes dat's flower . . . .
	G	plate to right ——————— M ———————
	M	- - - - - - - - - - - - point to plate on right —— hand down - - - - - - - - - - -

and, secondly, those movements which help to explicate the transcript for the reader/analyst. This second category covers manipulations of objects not involving interaction with the mother, eating motions, wriggling in a chair or whatever. If neither of these types of movement occurred or the movement was not clear on the tape for some reason, a broken line is used. It is perhaps worth making a point about the recording of gesture in the transcription. It should be observed that, in transcribing, conventional terms such as reach, point, etc. were avoided except where the child appeared to be using the gesture deliberately with intent to communicate in some way. For the youngest children in the study, where this was obviously not appropriate, because of the difficulty of ascribing particular intentions to a child of this age, descriptions such as 'hand out, palm down, fingers extended' would be used instead of 'reach'. As a human observer, one cannot help but be aware of the similarity between this description and what constitutes reaching, but it is necessary to be as cautious as possible when describing child behaviour.

Transcript 1

Both transcripts discussed here are of a boy, Ross, aged two-and-a-half years old, in conversation with his mother at a lunchtime. Ross is seated facing the camera with his back to French windows giving a view onto a garden. His mother sits on Ross's left at right angles to him. High on the wall on his right and on his left are decorative plates, one on each side. The plates have pictures of animals surrounded by abstract patterns on them. Figure 14.2 shows the configuration of mother, child and plates.

Prior to the sequence shown in Transcript 1, Ross has been twisting round in his chair trying to see out into the garden behind him. In doing so, he has caught sight of the plate hanging on the wall to his right. Ross opens the topic of the plate with a picture/pattern on it by

Transcript 1 Ross, aged two and a half years, is sitting in a high chair at lunch with his mother.

```
Line 1

       V ............................that's not a flower ..........................
MOTHER G own food ——— C ——— plate on ——————————— C ———— food —— plate on —— C —— food
                            C's rt.                            C's rt.
       M ---------------------------- shakes head ---------------------------------

       V .......... yes dat's  flower..............................................
CHILD  G plate to right ———————————— M ——————————————— plate to ————————————
                                                       rt.
       M ---------- point to ——— hand down ----------------------------------------
                    plate on rt.

Line 2

       V ................it's a plate........with a pattern on  but  it's not like a flower.................
MOTHER G ————————— C ————— plate on C's ——————————————————— C? ———— food ———
                           rt.
       M ------------------------------------------------ shakes head ———— stops ------------

       V ...plate.......................................................................
CHILD  G —— M ——————————————— plate on ————— M ——————————————————— M's food
                              his left
       M -------------------------------------- 'points'apple at      ---------------------
                                                lft. plate & then to mouth

Line 3

       V ........................................................ ooh dear ....................
MOTHER G ———————————————— C ——— plate on C's ——————— down to food ———————————————
                                right
       M - (eats food)------------------------------------------ dribbles tomato---------------

       V .......... it's a flower pattern..............flower..................... dis another plate there
CHILD  G ——————————————— M ——————— plate on his rt. ———————————— plate on —— M ————
                                                                left
       M ------------------------------------------------------------ 'points' apple at left plate
```

Line 4

MOTHER
V.................. mm..
G glances bet. C and plate ———————————— C ——————————————
M ----------------- points plates and away ---

CHILD
V ....dook..............................buvers........buvers ....
G ———————————————— rt. plate ——————————— M ———— left plate ————
M hand back--------------------------- rt. hand out to rt. plate lft. hand out to lft. plate ——————————hands back----------

Line 5

MOTHER
V......what did you say what was that word..............what did you say.....................................
G——
M---

CHILD
V ....ehe:..............
G———————————— M ——————————————————— plate on left———camera——away ————
M-------------------------------------- manipulates apple in mouth ——————————————————

Line 6

MOTHER
V.....that's too much apple in your mouth at once.....................
G ————————————————————————————
M---- shakes head ————stops--------------------------------------

CHILD
V..
G——— M ——————————————————————
M————————————————————————————

Transcript 2 Ross, aged two and a half years, is sitting in a high chair at lunch with his mother.

Line 1

MOTHER
V .... do you want another drink ....
G ———— C ———— apple ———— C ————
M peeling apple ———— stops. eats apple ------------

CHILD
V .... Rossy eh eh Rossy have a apple ....
G plate ———— M ———— M's food ————
M ———— takes plate off cup ———— hand out grasps in air then back. ------------

Line 2

MOTHER
V ...... mm well I'm having some too .... haven't you finished
G ————————
M -------- nods head ------------ shakes head --------

CHILD
V .... me .... Ross .... have a apple ....
G ———— M —— M's food ———— M ————
M ------------ plate down ——— hand forms point ——— points to apples ————

Line 3

MOTHER
V ... yet .... oh dear ....
G ———— apple ———— C —— apple ————
M ------------ gets another apple and prepares it ————

CHILD
V .... more apple .... ho dear ... oh dear .... oh dear ....
G ———— folls M's hand/apple ————
M —— hand down to plate ------------ shakes head ------------ shakes head ------

Line 4

MOTHER
V ....this is your last piece........positively the last........you can have this piece of apple but
G ——————————————————————————————
M ——————————————————————————————

CHILD
V ...want more apple oh dear.................................... more more ....
G ———————— camera ———————— M's hand/apple ———————— M ———————— apple in M's hand
M --

Line 5

MOTHER
V no more ....
G ——————————————————————— C ———————— own food ———————— C
M ——————————————————————— puts apple on C's plate -------------------- eats apple

CHILD
V ....no more (voc:.........)ba:...........pooff ....mmmmm ....(scream)..........
G ——————————————————————— folls. piece ————————————————
M ------------------------------------ hand out ——— hand back ------------------ picks up apple ——————
to apple covers mouth and away

Line 6

MOTHER
V ....(laugh) I haven't bitten it (laugh) ....
G ———————————————— down ——— C ————————————————————————
M ---Shakes head

CHILD
V ...hey..........bitten it .... daddy bitten it ....
G ———————— M/piece in hand ———————— M ————————————————————————
M ———————— extends piece to M ———————— apple back as wipes ———— extends apple again and back ------
nose on back of same hand + smiles

Figure 14.2: Diagram Showing Configuration of Room

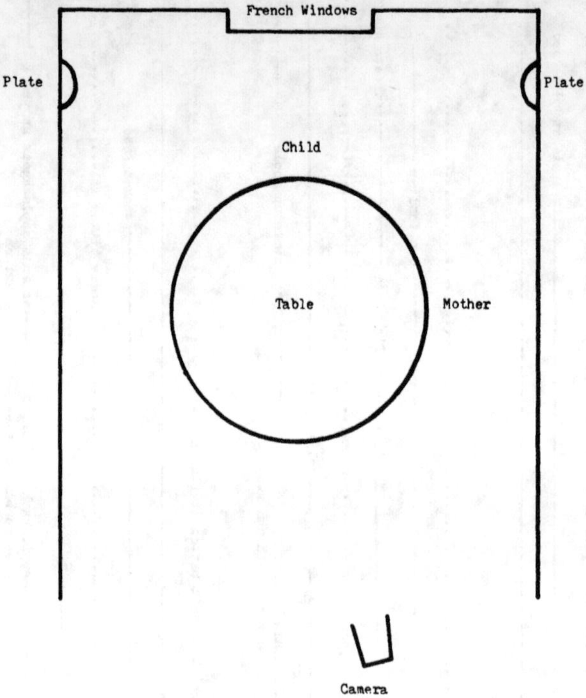

saying 'yes dat's flower', by looking and pointing at the plate which forms the object of his attention and then checking to see that his mother is responding appropriately (that she shares his attention). In view of the fact that this episode occurs within a much longer conversational sequence, Ross already has his mother's attention and is not, therefore, attracting but checking it as he moves to a new topic. This is not a sub-topic shift because it is so different from the 'birds in the garden' topic which had previously held their attention. The 'plate' topic could only be seen as a sub-topic if the superordinate topic were regarded as 'things in the environment'. This would, however, cover almost every conversation at this age and is not, therefore, a useful way of categorising it.

Having opened the topic, Ross then remains relatively passive while his mother takes her first turn of this topic: 'that's not a flower'. There is a pause during which Ross gazes towards the plate and his mother concerns herself with her lunch, though glancing up at Ross and the plate. Ross takes his verbal turn 'plate' and monitors his mother visually as he does so. The 'effect' is to 'cause' his mother to look at him and she comments on the plate. Notice that, during this fairly long turn, Ross notices the other plate (on his left) and reaches out to it in the same way as he had done to the one on his right. He checks attention again too. This is not the only possible interpretation of what is going on: it could be that Ross is momentarily distracted from what his mother is saying and then returns his attention to her, signalled by his resuming looking at her. Again, it could be that, at this instant, he has noticed the similarity between the two plates and is looking at his mother to see whether she has noticed the similarity too. How is it possible to come to any conclusions as to which interpretation is correct? Obviously, we can never be certain, but there are various points that can be made here. Apparently, Ross has not been totally absorbed in the other plate because he seems to have heard something of what his mother has said as evidenced by the way he incorporates the word 'pattern' into his next turn. He may not have heard exactly what she said (or if he did, did not understand her) because his next utterance stands in contradiction to what his mother said. She said, 'it's a plate with a pattern on but it's not like a flower', to which he replied, 'it's a flower pattern'. When Ross looks again at the plate on his right and remarks that the one on the left represents 'another plate', we see the importance of the gaze and gesture data. Not only would the referent of 'this' in 'this another plate there' be obscure if we were unable to see his eye movements and gesture, but we would not be able to build up the picture of a child noticing a connection in vision and in gesture: he makes the same outstretched arm gesture towards each plate which might aid his awareness of the similarity or be a result of it. Having made the connection, he seems to realise the similarity and attempts to share his realisation with his mother in the frequent glances at her during his turns, culminating in the declaration 'brothers', combined with the stretching out of his arms towards the plate. (His mother fails to interpret this utterance, and one wonders whether Ross ever tried this new knowledge out on his mother or other adults in later interactions. Unfortunately, my tapes do not include it if he did.)

What is perhaps most striking in this short sequence is the smooth and synchronised nature of the exchanges. The child co-ordinates gesture, gaze and verbal skill into a neatly executed sequence of turns, checking and monitoring his mother's attention frequently and placing his turns at appropriate points in the interaction, so that a kind of interactional rhythm is evident (c.f. Condon, 1977).

Figure 14.3: Schematic Representation of Transcript 1

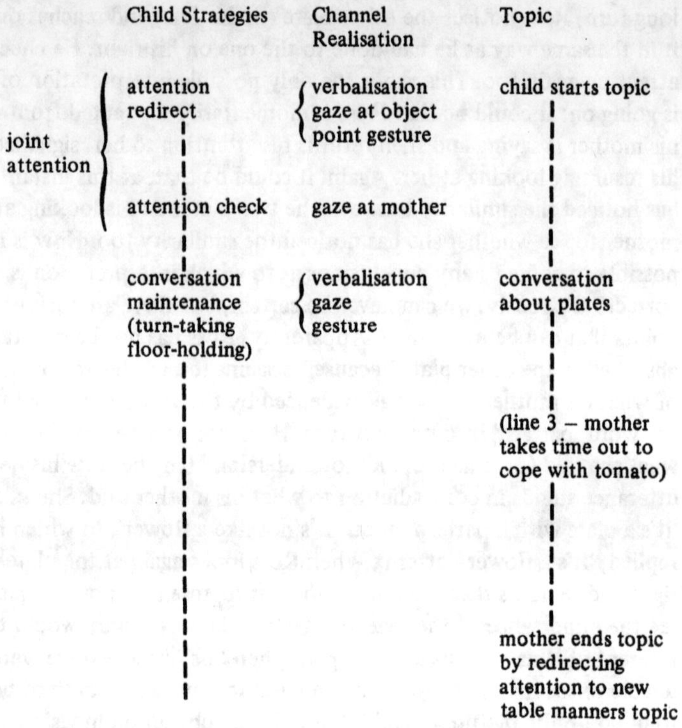

This short extract can be represented in schematic terms, as shown in Figure 14.3.

Transcript 2

Transcript 2 is of interaction occurring a few minutes after the first. Mother and child are still in the same positions, and the meal continues. During the interaction which occurs between the two transcripts, Ross and his mother have talked about the apple he is eating, Ross has claimed to have got out of bed in the middle of the night and run around, which has been discussed, and, immediately before Transcript 2, he has been told to stop playing with his plate (putting it on top of his mug). His mother says, 'will you put your plate down ple— have you finished yet?' The full transcript covers the interaction from this point.

As with the previous example, the child's skill in handling conversation and topic is evident. We see a child who can imitate not only verbally but non-verbally, as when, in line 3, he says 'oh dear' and shakes his head. Note that this is not exactly what his mother had done: she had shaken her head when she said, 'haven't you finished yet?' (line 2). I would suggest that this child can, not only control gesture and language as separate communicative behaviours, but has also a concept of appropriateness when combining them. He produces something which is actually a comical reflection of his mother's behaviour.

Notice, as before, the use of gesture, gaze and verbalisation. An interesting turn is that in line 1 where Ross is reintroducing the apple topic by demanding some more. He certainly checks his mother's attention as he takes his plate off his cup, as he has been asked to do, but, as he reintroduces the topic of 'the apple and having some more', he fails to check her attention. He does not look at her again until after she has taken her turn ('mm, well I'm having some too'). What he does is to gaze intently at the apple he wants, making a grasping gesture towards it, saying 'Rossy have a apple'. (The 'eh eh' represents a fretful cry vocalisation.) The over-all impression is that he is somewhat agitated. The intonation and speed of delivery support this interpretation, and it is noticeable that the sophisticated monitoring behaviour apparent elsewhere is replaced by intent gazing on the apple he wants. In the light of this and similar data elsewhere in the study, it seems plausible to suggest (though far more work needs to be done to substantiate this claim) that states of high emotion can be correlated with a decline in efficiency of communicative behaviour. In addition, it is possible that the more sophisticated the skill, the more likely it is to be replaced by less efficient behaviour. The child seems to revert to earlier communicative forms, and there are several instances in my study of the skill of efficient visual monitoring being abandoned when the child is frustrated: the object desired seems to become more important than the means of getting it. A similar lack of precise monitoring seems to be in evidence when a child is angry or upset.

A further feature of interest in this particular turn is the language he actually uses to realise his demand, and its interpretation by his mother. What Ross says is 'Rossy have a apple'. In terms of adult grammar, he actually states that he has an apple, though the intonation and non-vocal concomitants of gesture and gaze clearly show that he intends a demand. Note, too, that because of the form of words he does use, his mother, though it is fair to assume that she does understand a demand, can and does exploit the ambiguity and respond to the statement made (the locution) rather than to the act performed (the illocution) (c.f. Searle, 1969).

Figure 14.4: Schematic Representation of Transcript 2

	Child strategies	Channel Realisation	Topic
joint attention	attention check	gaze	child introduces 'more apple' topic
	attention redirect	verbalisation gaze gesture	
	conversation maintenance (turn-taking floor-holding)	verbalisation gaze gesture	conversation about getting 'more apple'
	redirect to sub-topic	vocalisation	sub-topic shift to 'bitten apple' topic
	(attention check)	verbalisation gaze gesture	
	conversation maintenance (turn-taking floor-holding)	verbalisation gaze gesture	conversation about 'bitten apple'

Another feature of analytical interest in this extract and which is again possibly the result of heightened emotion, is that Ross violates the smooth sequence of turn-taking so evident in the previous extract. He interrupts his mother in line 2 and again in line 4. At the beginning of line 3, too, the beginning of his turn overlaps the end of his mother's (see Schaffer *et al.*, 1977, on overlapping turns). That Ross can, to some extent, control his frustration is shown in line 2 when, following his mother's 'inappropriate' response to his demand, he uses an explicit pointing gesture at the thing he wants rather than the inexplicit grasping motion he had used previously.

Towards the end of this extract, Ross changes the topic to what can be viewed as a sub-topic of the apple topic. This he achieves by first screaming and then by a 'floor-hold' which involves the integration of visual monitoring, gesture and verbalisation. This is the turn which begins after his mother has put the apple on his plate at the end of line 5. The turn is claimed as he screams. The floor-hold involves him saying 'hey, bitten it', looking at his mother and the piece of apple in his hand and extending it to her. It is not clear, when he says 'bitten it', claiming that his mother has bitten it, whether at this point he is 'joking'. It becomes clear, however, in his next turn, when a broad grin appears on his face and he claims 'daddy bitten it'. As elsewhere, it is the non-verbal elements of the communication which provide us with clues to interpreting data.

This extract can be schematically represented, as shown in Figure 14.4.

Conclusion

In this chapter, an attempt has been made to show that it is not sufficient to analyse discourse only in terms of the words spoken. If real headway is to be made in understanding mother–child interaction, use must be made of the many small details of non-verbal communication. Attention must be paid to the integration of verbal and non-verbal behaviours. It is not enough to be aware simply that use is made of the various channels of communication (vocal, gaze and movement); fruitful analysis must involve examination of how these channels are combined and how, embedded in the interaction, they express the communicative intent of the speaker.

In this chapter, I have attempted only a description of two very small extracts from a much larger sample. The conclusions I have drawn, however, are backed up by extensive analysis of the whole sample, employing a multi-category scoring system. This kind of micro-analysis is not, however, the whole story. As well as looking at the kind of data illustrated in this chapter, we should be aware of the variety or other types of data which can be used to build up an even fuller interpretation of adult–child interaction. In the two short extracts discussed in this chapter, for instance, we could extend the analysis to cover such features as the kinds of expectations mothers[7] have of their children's behaviour at mealtimes. We could look at what the sequence of imitation in Transcript 2 and the use of the word 'pattern' in Transcript 1 (briefly discussed above) tell us about the child's capacities of speech production and reception. We could consider what the child's ability to suggest that an absent father has bitten the apple reveals about the child's developing powers of imagination and his more general capacity for internal representation. We could look at what that grin accompanying that suggestion tells us about the child's knowledge of the function of mischief: we might call it his knowledge of the rules for breaking the rules.

In drawing all these types of information together, there is a real need to approach child language, and child development generally, from a perspective which integrates approaches from all the human science disciplines. Moves in this direction are being made, and there are valuable contributions towards integrating and unifying approaches (Halliday, 1973; Bernstein, 1971; and Rommetveit, 1974), but there is still much to be done. The central problem involved here is in attempting to elucidate exactly what the relationship is between an individual, his language and society (family, peer group, school and so on). Studying young children who are developing their personality, their cognitive and motor capacities, their language and their understanding of society provides us with the kind of material appropriate to making this attempt.

Notes

1. The use of the word 'strategy' is not intended to imply that the child is necessarily behaving in a *consciously* strategic fashion. The term, as it is used here, simply covers behaviour sequences which have the effect of accomplishing the structuring of discourse.

2. 'Behaviour': where not specified otherwise, 'behaviour' refers to both the verbal and non-verbal.

3. 'Turn-taking' and 'floor-holding'. The term 'turn' is applied to a normally unbroken stretch of communicative behaviour which is a participant's contribution to a conversation. The normal pattern of interaction is that the participants alternate their turns, first one speaking, then the other. This alternation of communicative behaviours forms the basis for maintaining a conversation. When a speaker takes a turn, he can simply claim his place in the flow of conversation, by saying 'hm' or 'yes', for example. Alternatively, he can, having claimed his turn, exploit the right he has to continue with his contribution before allowing his interlocutor to take *his* turn. If a speaker chooses to extend his turn in this way, then such extension is termed the floor-hold.

'Monitoring' a turn (either a simple turn take or a turn involving a floor-hold) means that the speaker checks his hearer's face during the turn. This checking is employed to ascertain whether the hearer is responding appropriately.

4. When referring to the participants, for reasons of convenience only, the child is always designated by the male pronoun.

5. 'Hermeneutical': this term has been applied to the analysis of communication by Shotter (1978). It describes a kind of analysis which, instead of attempting to search for objective knowledge by experimental testing of theories, seeks to interpret the meaning of people's actions. It looks for the reasons for people's actions. As Shotter says, 'It takes as given that we all have as human beings a certain special "insider's" view of human behaviour, and concerns itself

with the task of transforming the vague and perhaps mistaken understandings of human phenomena we already possess from that insider's point of view into more precise and effective ones' (p. 51).

6. The data from which the extracts are taken comprise a total of 19½ hours of video-recordings obtained from five children. At the initial filming, the children were aged 1½ months, 5½ months, 9½ months, 16 months and 2 years. The same children were filmed again six months later. All filming was undertaken in the home. Care was taken to allow both mother and child time to become accustomed to the equipment, a period of about five days being spent with each dyad (a few hours each day), and in most cases actual recordings were not made until the second or third day. Disturbance of the daily routine was kept to a minimum and the only constraints put upon the data collected were that they should include at least one mealtime, several play sessions and, where possible, a bath-time. The equipment used comprised a Sony-matic portable video-recorder, portable hand-held Sony camera, Sony AC power adaptor and Sony V-60H tape.

7. All the data used in the study are of middle-class mothers. The kinds of expectations which these mothers have of mealtimes may not be those of working-class mothers. A full interpretation of adult-child interaction needs to be sensitive to possible differences of this kind.

Acknowledgements

This work is supported by a (UK) SSRC Studentship. I am grateful to the Department of Psychology, University of Lancaster, for technical assistance, and to Andy Lock and Mike Breen for much help and encouragement.

References

Bach, E. and Harms, R.T. (eds.) (1968). *Universals in Linguistic Theory*. New York: Holt

Bellugi, U. and Brown, R.W. (eds.) (1964). *The Acquisition of Language* (Monographs of the Society for Research in Child Development, 29). Chicago: University of Chicago Press

Bernstein, B. (1971). *Class, Codes and Control 1: Theoretical Studies Towards a Sociology of Language*. London: Routledge

Bloom, L.M. (1970). *Language Development: Form and Function in Emerging Grammars*. Cambridge, Mass.: MIT Press

Braine, M.D.S. (1963). 'The Ontogeny of English Phrase Structure: The First Phase'. *Language*, 39, pp. 1-13

Brown, R.W. and Fraser, C. (1964). 'The Acquisition of Syntax'. In U. Bellugi and R.W. Brown (eds.), *The Acquisition of Language*

Bruner, J.S. (1977). 'Early Social Interaction and Language Acquisition'. In H.R. Schaffer (ed.), *Studies in Mother-Infant Interaction*

Carter, A.L. (1978). 'From Sensori-Motor Vocalisations to Words: A Case Study of the Evolution of Attention Directing Communication in the Second Year'. In A. Lock (ed.), *Action, Gesture and Symbol: The Emergence of Language*

Chomsky, N. (1957). *Syntactic Structures*. The Hague: Mouton

— (1965). *Aspects of the Theory of Syntax*. Cambridge, Mass.: MIT Press

Condon, W.S. (1977). 'A Primary Phase in the Organization of Infant Responding Behaviour'. In H.R. Schaffer (ed.), *Studies in Mother-Infant Interaction*

Fillmore, C.J. (1968). 'The Case for Case'. In E. Bach and R.T. Harms (eds.), *Universals in Linguistic Theory*

Greenfield, P.M. and Smith, J.H. (1976). *The Structure of Communication in Early Language Development*. New York: Academic Press

Guillaume, P. (1927). 'Les Débuts de la Phrase dans la Langage de l'Enfant'. *Journal de Psychologie*, 24, pp. 1–25

Halliday, M.A.K. (1973). *Explorations in the Functions of Language*. London: Edward Arnold

Keenan, E.O. and Schieffelin, B.B. (1976). 'Topic as a Discourse Notion: A Study of Topic in the Conversations of Children and Adults'. In C. Li (ed.), *Subject and Topic*

de Laguna, G.A. (1927). *Speech: Its Function and Development*. New Haven, Conn.: Yale University Press

Li, C. (ed.) (1976). *Subject and Topic*. New York: Academic Press

Lock, A. (1978a). 'On Being Picked Up'. In A. Lock (ed.), *Action, Gesture and Symbol: The Emergence of Language*

— (ed.) (1978b). *Action, Gesture and Symbol: The Emergence of Language*. New York: Academic Press

McNeill, D. (1966). 'Developmental Psycholinguistics'. In F. Smith and G.A. Miller (eds.), *The Genesis of Language*

Miller, W. and Ervin, S. (1964). 'The Development of Grammar in Child Language'. In U. Bellugi and R.W. Brown (eds.), *The Acquisition of Language*

Rommetveit, R. (1974). *On Message Structure: A Framework for the Study of Language and Communication*. New York: Wiley

Schaffer, H.R. (ed.) (1977). *Studies in Mother-Infant Interaction*. New York: Academic Press

—. Collis, G.N. and Parsons, G. (1977). 'Vocal Interchange and Visual Regard in Verbal and Preverbal Children'. In H.R. Schaffer (ed.), *Studies in Mother-Infant Interaction*

Searle, J. (1969). *Speech Acts: An Essay in the Philosophy of Language*. Cambridge: Cambridge University Press

Shotter, J. (1978). 'The Cultural Context of Communication Studies: Theoretical and Methodological Issues'. In A. Lock (ed.), *Action, Gesture and Symbol: The Emergence of Language*

Smith, F. and Miller, G.A. (eds.) (1966). *The Genesis of Language*. Cambridge, Mass.: MIT Press

Stern, C. and Stern, W. (1907). *Die Kindersprache* (4th revised edn, 1928). Leipzig: Barth (cited in Greenfield and Smith (1977))

Part IV

TALK AND SOCIAL RELATIONS IN THE CLASSROOM

15 ANALYSING CLASSROOM TALK

A.D. Edwards

'Loose Linguistic Sociology'

In his inaugural definition of a 'sociological linguistics', J.R. Firth defined its task as the description of the speech appropriate to the relevant social roles in 'contexts of situation which are typical, recurrent and repeatedly observable' (Firth, 1957). In so far as classrooms constitute such typical contexts, they have seemed to be a suitable case for sociolinguistic treatment. Some of the resulting studies have been concerned with the general task of showing 'how language is organised to serve social ends', and with developing methods of discourse analysis applicable to any situation where social relationships are 'sufficiently well-defined for us to expect clear evidence of this in the text'.[1] More applied research has examined (for example) the difficulties confronting children unprepared for, or unwilling to display, the communicative skills appropriate to formal learning, and has treated 'repeatedly observable' features of classroom talk as evidence of teaching strategies or the permeability of knowledge boundaries.

My own interests lie on the 'practical' side of this obviously over-simplified division of labour. More particularly, I am concerned in this chapter with how analysis of classroom talk can reveal the structure and structuring of teacher-pupil relationships.[2] As a sociologist rather than a sociolinguist, I take comfort from the claim that priority in a 'sociological linguistics' is quite properly given to sociological concerns, and especially to the ways in which social structure is realised in language.[3] But I am also aware of the danger of what Firth called 'a loose linguistic sociology without formal accuracy', a narrowly utilitarian manipulation of linguistic data in the service of whatever the social scientist takes to be his real concerns. It is tempting to treat speech simply as a medium through which to get at other things, and it is a temptation which classroom research has certainly not escaped. Most of it betrays an 'entirely unprincipled use of isolated surface features' as direct indicators of sociological categories, and Stubbs is right to argue that such manipulations are inefficient as well as unprincipled (Stubbs, 1976, 1977). Far more account has to be taken of how the talk is organised *as discourse* if the researcher is to move convincingly from recording what is said to making statements about teaching strategies or the strength of knowledge boundaries.

In the mainstream of classroom research, that of systematic observation, speech has largely been treated as a transparent stream of data to be filtered through the appropriate observational categories. Knowing what to look for, the researcher extracts the essentials from the surrounding 'noise'. Even when these 'events' are coded as they occur, that coding can be done in the confidence that similarly trained observers would confirm the record. Confidence in the validity of that record, however, displays a remarkable blindness to the difficulties of matching form and function, a largely unexplicated reliance on contextual knowledge in identifying what is 'really' going on, an almost entirely denotational and representational conception of talk, and a consequent neglect of allusive and provisional attributions of meaning. The apparently 'hard' data provided by systematic classroom observation 'objectify' the researcher's presuppositions. They are the product of a highly unsystematic identification of speech with social action.[4]

What kinds of evidence, then, would be made available by a more linguistically sensitive and systematic analysis? With priority still being given to sociological concerns, how is the structure of teacher-pupil relationships to be read in the forms of classroom talk? The three 'working assumptions of a thorough-going linguistic sociolinguistic approach' are described as follows by Dell Hymes. A social relationship entails the selection and/or devising of communicative means which are considered appropriate and perhaps specific to it; they will be organised in ways which may not be disclosed apart from that relationship, and the communicative means available in the relationship will condition both its nature and its outcome (Hymes, 1977). From this perspective, forms of social relationship are seen as being signalled, and as being reproduced or modified or challenged, in the act of speaking and in ways which are embedded in the particular context or type of context. Now, such an analysis might still focus on specific surface features, like modes of address, as sufficient evidence of the relevant semantics of power and solidarity. Teachers have many situationally conventional resources for maintaining or relaxing social distance, for mitigating the authoritative 'tone' of their encounters with pupils by means of various politeness formulas and 'indirect' commands, and for announcing shifts from one stage of the lesson to another without making their control too obtrusive.[5] The following example shows both the 'softened' imperative and the indirect imperative framed as a statement or a question, while 'right' and 'now' are typically economical switch signals available to someone in control of the interaction.

> Right, would you be quiet please and all look this way (pause). Can we do that again – uh, could you be quiet please (pause). There's still two people who've got their coats on (pause). Now, you should all – you've all got a booklet for homework so . . .

Such routine devices can be significant markers of hierarchical relationships without being constituents of a consistent style. Indeed, I have argued elsewhere that accounts of the special 'languages' (or registers) associated with school subjects have tended to exaggerate the depth and frequency of their distinctive syntactic characteristics and to underrate the interactional significance of intermittently esoteric vocabulary in the marking of knowledge boundaries and disciplinary identities (Edwards, 1976, 1978a). But it is unlikely that more basic features of syntactic choice can be similarly treated as direct evidence of the particular situation being constructed and maintained. Attempts to base a diagnosis of teaching styles or disciplinary strategies on detailed analysis of, for example, tense forms, indefinite articles or choice of pronouns often conceal their dependence on the researcher's knowledge of the context in identifying the interactional significance of those structural details.[6] Except in highly ritualised situations, there is likely to be 'almost no correlation between the linguistic distinctiveness of the relevant variables and the social information they carry', no way of specifying in advance the nature and delicacy of those variables, and no necessary consistency in their social meaning through successive phases of the interaction (Gumperz and Hymes, 1972). When Hymes warns social scientists that only linguistic analysis as painstakingly detailed as that demanded in literary criticism can reveal 'the depth and adequacy of the elliptical art that is talk', he is using a misleading analogy for the very reason he recognises – that in familiar and conventional relationships, the talk may be very elliptical indeed. Most formal cues to meaning will then be 'efficient i.e. slight in scale', and even close scrutiny of the text may not reveal them (Hymes, 1977). It could be argued, of course, that the formal transmission of school knowledge requires a shift away from any pervasive expectation of shared frames of reference and, therefore, a heavy reliance on the verbal channel as the primary carrier of meaning.[7] Nevertheless, too 'painstakingly' close analysis of structural details may lead the researcher to downgrade the importance of what teacher and pupils are taking for granted about the topic and about each other, and of those tacit references on which the coherence of their discourse may largely depend.

Bernstein has confronted some of these difficulties in his accounts of how the form of social relationships 'acts selectively' on what is said, and of how the 'social structure of relevant meanings' determines their linguistic realisations. Because his work represents an ambitious attempt to develop a 'tight' linguistic sociology *with* 'formal accuracy', I want now to consider whether it offers a 'principled' source of data in the study of classroom interaction.

Semantic Options and Linguistic Realisations

Asserting a causal connection between 'the structure of social relationships and the structure of communication', Bernstein seeks to show how forms of social relationship 'generate distinctive texts'. As he comments laconically, this is a matter 'of considerable sociological and sociolinguistic interest'. The central link in his explanatory chain is the 'meaning potential' of the contexts being studied. What the participants 'can mean' is significant sociologically as a reflection and an expression of social structure; it is significant linguistically in so far as it accounts for related features of linguistic choice.[8] The relevant sociological analysis is not concerned with actual constellations of person, place and topic, but with abstract dimensions on which contexts can be located. If the meaning potential of some typical context is, in Halliday's words, 'rather closely specifiable', it is not because the particular meanings being exchanged are predictable, but because those meanings can be characterised as predominantly closed, ready-coded, impersonal and verbally inexplicit.

In many classrooms, the 'social structures of relevant meanings' could be described in these terms. Unlike Bernstein, I do not assume that the classroom is normally 'predicated upon elaborated codes and their system of social relationships'.[9] Making deliberate reference to his own analysis of open and closed roles, I would typify meanings in the 'regulative context' as being realised largely through imperatives and through positional appeals in a restricted code, and describe pupils as having to 'step into' a predetermined set of 'instructional' meanings and 'leave it relatively undisturbed'. It is surely an unusual classroom in which pupils find frequent opportunities for 'disturbing or changing' a body of received knowledge, and so of 'achieving meaning' on their own terms. But it is not my purpose to exchange typifications. I want instead to ask how we would know where to locate classroom talk. What would be the linguistic evidence for asserting, or denying, that what pupils can mean is normally contained within the boundaries of what the teacher considers to be relevant, appropriate and correct? Even if Bernstein's theory of educational transmission is strong enough to specify 'the structures of semantic options', are their 'grammatical and lexical realisations . . . also capable of specification'?[10]

The question is complex because the main dimensions of sociolinguistic codes – now-coding or ready-coded meanings, positional or personal control, the elaboration or restriction of verbal forms – do not necessarily fit together.[11] Teachers often expound traditional versions of 'the facts' in verbally elaborated ways which admit little or no questioning, while groups of pupils who know one another well may engage in a collaborative construction of meaning through talk which is still 'highly elliptical' because bases for their agreement are residues from past interaction which need only be referred to implicitly. The complex relationships between semantic options and their linguistic realisations can be illustrated from the conventional model of 'transmission-teaching'. Where the teacher-as-expert is transmitting skills or information of which he is initially the sole custodian, he must assume a gulf between his knowledge and his pupils' ignorance which has to be crossed with words. These conditions 'should' then generate speech 'with an explicit logical structure oriented either to accurate or precise statements of meaning, or to developing special or novel meanings' (Cook-Gumperz, 1973). More specific predictions might then be made – for example, that the cohesion of such speech would be achieved largely in the text itself (by frequent repetitions, precise labelling of objects and events, explicit references to what has been said and is to be said next) rather than relying on the listener's tacit knowledge of the context. But the 'either/or' in the statement on which these expectations were based indicates the difficulty of 'reading off' the semantic options from textual features like these. Meanings may be verbally explicit because they are 'news' to their receivers, or because the speakers are jointly engaged in constructing some shared but novel understanding. In classrooms, teachers are often passing down information which is ready-coded for themselves to learners who have little choice but to accept it as fact, and the very fullness of the exposition excludes alternatives by presenting the explicit and authorised version. Any pupil contributions to that exposition are likely to be brief and allusive. They are a framework on which the teacher can hang the necessary details.

T: So God made this universe . . . and now there are these two forces Yin and Yang to control his universe. Two forces – how can we understand that? Anybody help us? How can we get to that? What does the word force mean?
P: Two messengers who tell you what to do.
T: Two messengers, that's one way we can think of it, yes, good. That's some sort of idea, yeah.
P: Sir, powers.
T: Two powers – that's even better isn't it, I think. So God sent out these two powers and the Chinese call them Yin and Yang. But it's not easy for Yin and Yang – it's not easy for this earth to be controlled by Yin and Yang because they're opposites. What's opposites? Somebody else have a go.
P: Sir, enemies.
T: OK, they don't necessarily have to be fighting all the time, but opposites are –
P: Sir, different from each other.
T: Different from each other, and when he says enemies he's got the right idea . . . (continued exposition by the teacher).

In this example, the pupils' contributions seem to be made for instant elaboration. They fit more or less neatly into the slots in the developing exposition. Knowing what he wants to hear, the teacher either waits for the relevant surface appearances or else expands (and, if necessary, translates) what is said into something he can use. The completed version can be seen as the product of his management. For the pupils, it has to be taken rather than made.

It must be emphasised again that what Bernstein is offering is a theory of semantic choice, in which it is recognised that meanings may be verbally explicit and closed. The later studies carried out in his Sociological Research Unit show an increasing awareness of the complex and situationally variable relations between structure and function, and of the consequent problems of coding talk in terms of the semantic options available to, and taken up by, the speakers. Although the intention is still to identify the ground rules from which speakers may generate quite different speech performances in different contexts, and to show the semantic compatibility of these diverse realisations, the focus is quite clearly on the kinds of meaning being transmitted, however this transmission is achieved. It is from this perspective that the assumption that classrooms are 'predicated upon elaborated codes' has to be questioned. Depending on the context, elaborated codes may or may not generate verbally elaborated speech. What they do express, essentially, is a reflexive relationship to the social order, in which the bases of action and belief are made explicit, alternative forms of meaning are explored, and there is some sense of the permeability of the social and cultural 'world'.[12] Even as generalisations at a very high level of abstraction, this hardly describes the conditions created by transmission-teaching. In the 'regulative context', teachers seem to assume that pupils will 'know what they mean' once the grooving-in process is completed, and their disciplinary talk tends to be highly abbreviated and indirect. In the 'instructional context', they seem to assume that pupils will not 'know' something until it has been 'taught'. But, even in this context, once-elaborated meanings accumulate to provide an increasingly extensive backcloth of knowledge which is presumed to be shared and which has been authoritatively defined. In a direct application of Bernstein's theory to the teaching of Nuffield science, Cooper (1976) is surely justified in coding utterances entirely by their situational function and not by their form. He categorises as positional-control any instances of teacher disapprobation which 'rely on status or power for their effect', however verbally elaborated they may be. He also categorises as particularistic any verbally explicit instructional meanings which are tied to the immediate task in which the pupils are involved, and which do not make available general principles from which they might solve problems for themselves rather than passively receive the solutions offered to them.

In that study, then, there is no reliance on how things are said, even when displayed in the organisation of extended texts, as 'hard' evidence of the structure of social relationships and of semantic options. There *is* extensive reference to the researcher's knowledge of the relevant context to support the interpretations being offered. The problem therefore recurs which Bernstein's early, confident listing of code-indicators seemed prematurely to have overcome – namely, that of grounding the researcher's account in something more solid than an implicit invitation to trust his sense of what was 'really' going on. For example, the initial attempts by Barnes and Todd (1977) to discover quantitative indices of 'exploratory' and 'collaborative' classroom talk (e.g. hesitations, intonational markers of tentativeness, frequent use of modal auxiliaries like 'might' to express uncertainty) were soon replaced by qualitative analyses of how meanings were marked as being open to question, modification or challenge. This functional approach identified collaborative talk in (for example) the frequency of questions, the infrequency of overtly evaluative responses and a sharing of responsibility for summarising the gist of the talk so far. But, as the researchers recognise, their account is vulnerable to the criticism of being linguistically unprincipled and unsystematic. It moves 'intuitively' from what is said to an interpretation of what is 'going on', making no attempt to cover the talk in an exhaustive and hierarchically ordered set of categories. Similarly, my own recent research with John Furlong was concerned with showing how instructional meanings are shaped and controlled in the course of classroom interaction, and with how the teacher's authority is routinely expressed and reproduced. Our analysis was 'checked' with the teachers we observed, and it is 'supported' by transcript material from which (it might be claimed) readers can draw their own conclusions. The extracts we present 'both exemplify and are the basis of the particular interpretation being offered', and so provide the image rather than the reality of a 'proof' (Edwards and Furlong, 1978). The problem therefore remains of providing a more systematic and less prematurely coded warrant for an account of classroom interaction.

Sinclair and Coulthard (1975) claim to have done this by locating everything that was said in a hierarchy of categories (acts, moves, exchanges, transactions), and so identifying 'in the text' how turns were distributed, topics introduced and changed, and coherence achieved through whole sequences of utterances. Their attention is firmly fixed on speech as social action, and on a functional interpretation of 'utterances of a particular grammatical form' which is grounded quite explicitly on the sequential position of those utterances and on knowledge of 'the social purposes and expectations of the participants'.[13] The method of analysis is admitted to depend on discourse with a relatively overt and predictable structure of 'roles, objectives and conventions', in which the interactional significance of what is said should rarely be in doubt. In classrooms, that structure is provided by the authority of the teacher. 'One participant has acknowledged responsibility for the direction of the discourse, for deciding who shall speak when, and for introducing and ending topics.' The acknowledgement of that responsibility, by the teacher and by the pupils, was evident in the transcripts they studied in, for example, the teacher's virtual monopoly of the acts labelled as 'Starters', 'Markers', 'Elicitations', 'Checks', 'Directives', 'Informatives', 'Prompts', 'Nominations' and 'Evaluations', and in the virtual restriction of pupils to the acts of 'Bidding', 'Acknowledging', 'Replying' and 'Reacting'. The analysis is both systematic and comprehensive, and it provides useful documentation of the severity of the functional constraints on what pupils could 'do with words'. In the context of my own argument, it suggests some of the communicative consequences of a highly asymmetrical distribution of semantic options. Yet, as Hammersley argues elsewhere in this book, it also betrays an excessively static and consensual notion of 'normally competent' classroom interaction. That orientation to the norms of 'appropriate' usage is quite deliberate. Sinclair and Coulthard are interested in investigating talk in status-marked settings, and they are explicitly uninterested in 'ordinary, desultory conversation', which they describe as being the 'least overtly rule-governed' form of discourse and so as lying beyond their analytical methods. Now, conversational analysts might admit that the rules governing turn-taking and topic-switching are less 'obvious' in contexts where no participant enjoys predetermined special rights and where the others are under no obligation to wait for his 'rulings'. They would also argue, however, that the relevant rules are no less systematic, and that they both are sensitive to differences in, for example, power, prestige or expertise between speakers and provide communicative resources for displaying that sensitivity. In short, their methods can cope with talk between 'equals' and with the inequality displayed in classroom talk. In the final section of this paper, I want to consider how these methods can provide a more 'principled' source of data than the approaches I have outlined so far.

Classroom Knowledge and Classroom Discourse

In 'ordinary, desultory' conversation, turn-taking is managed turn by turn as the interaction proceeds. In formal debates, all turns may be pre-allocated. Between these extremes lie various mixes of local management and pre-allocation. The differences between them are rarely a matter of practices specific to a particular situation, but rather of the tying of certain activities (such as questions or the initiation of opening and closing sequences) to one or more of the participants, and the frequency of such features as interruptions and 'invited stories'. Social facts like the relative power of the speakers are only introduced into the analysis 'where warrant can be offered for the relevance of such characterisations of the data from the data themselves' (Sacks *et al.*, 1974). That warrant has been offered in ethnomethodological studies of, for example, group therapy sessions, courtroom cross-examinations, television interviews and police interrogations.[14] More directly relevant to this chapter is the investigation of talk between adults and children, in which the adult's 'ownership' of the interaction may be evident in her evasion of questions, insistence on the listener's attention and unilateral termination of the conversation. The child may experience difficulty in getting turns, and have those turns subjected to 'open scrutiny, blunt correction and inattention' (Speier, 1976; see also West and Zimmerman, 1977). Elsewhere in this book, Wootton shows how children cannot rely on such 'normal discourse constraints' as the obligation on someone asked a question to offer immediately something recognisable as an answer or a preparation for an answer, and how their frequent difficulty in getting a hearing leads them to 'overbuild' their utterances. When they go to school, their difficulties may be intensified but not necessarily changed. More research (of the kind described by Willes in Part One) is certainly needed into how children learn to cope with the communicative demands of classrooms, but the problem is *not* to show how 'the five-year-old who speaks when he wants to' becomes 'the ten-year-old who waits to be nominated' (Sinclair and Coulthard, 1975, p. 113). The five-year-old will already have experienced various forms of nomination and, even where he can speak when he wants to, another's response is necessary if the speaking is to constitute a 'turn'. As Drew suggests in an earlier chapter, there are systematic features common to sequences in which adults instruct children, whatever the context of that instruction, and the participants' orientation to the activity of instruction will be displayed in the organisation of their talk.

With that cautionary comment on the danger of making the analysis too situationally specific, I want to examine the organisation of turn-taking in 'typical' classroom talk. In ordinary conversation, it is usually only at the moment of decision that it becomes apparent who will enter and who will control the upcoming turn. Along the continuum of turn-taking systems, classroom talk is much closer to the formality of debate. Briefly summarised, 'the speech exchange system is largely preallocated', the small locally-managed component is 'largely the domain of the teacher', and 'only teachers can direct speakership in any creative way' (McHoul, 1978).[15] Contained in this summary is a systematic basis for what has long been 'known' about classroom talk, and an explanation for why it so often displays the characteristics of a play script. Overlapping turns are infrequent, whether these constitute breaches of the one-speaker-at-a-time rule, attempts to estimate where a turn transition might occur, slightly mistimed entries, or examples of co-ordinated talk. Such overlaps are normally avoided because there are so few possibilities of the talk being opened up to a self-selecting first starter, with the attendant 'risks' of competing bids for the next turn and of intrusions into a turn not yet completed by someone eager to gain the floor. Where the current speaker is a pupil, the next speaker will normally be either the teacher or someone whom the teacher selects, or someone whose bid the teacher accepts. Unequal rights are, therefore, pervasively evident in the teacher's almost exclusive access to current-speaker-selects-next-speaker techniques. This is so even when the form of a teacher's question seems to open the floor to competitive bids ('Does anyone know?'), and when starting to speak (or raising a hand) in the absence of competition from other pupils may seem to constitute self-selection. In each case, the upcoming turn has to be ratified by the teacher.

T: Could anybody tell me what – sssh! – tell me and the rest of us what you can see in that particular piece of stone that you've got? Put your hands up please and tell me. Yes?
P: Sir, it's a shell.
T: There's a shell in yours, OK. Anybody see anything else? Yes?
P: Another shell.
T: Another shell.

The duration of turns is also decided by the teacher. As the one who knows, his own contributions can be prolonged at his discretion, whilst his responses to (and interpolations into) those contributions he has invited from pupils define their limits by indicating when an adequate (for the moment) answer has been achieved and when the pursuit of adequacy has to be continued. Pauses are therefore likely to be longer and more frequent than in ordinary conversation, because there is less need for the current speaker, whether teacher or pupil, to protect a turn from possible interruption by leaving no gap which might be 'misheard' as a turn-transition point. Nevertheless, the teacher's responsibility for maintaining topical coherence and for achieving a 'common' understanding of that topic may lead him not only to protect a current pupil turn by repelling intruders, but also to 'close out' a turn if what is being said seems inappropriate to the business at hand and opens the floor to others.

This control over the information being transmitted is evident in the sequences of question-and-answer so characteristic of classrooms. The frequency with which teachers comment on the relevance, correctness and explicitness of the reply has led many classroom observers to describe these as triadic sequences of question-answer evaluation.

Within the analytical framework being outlined here, it is more appropriate to refer to embedded adjacency pairs, in which a teacher's question is often followed by a pupil's question (a request for clarification or further information) which is heard as a necessary preliminary to the 'real' answer, and a pupil's answer is often followed by the teacher repeating the question or asking a supplementary question which serves to narrow down the area of search. Since this process of managing a sufficient answer by means of clues, cues, repetitions and so on may need to be prolonged, the conditional relevance of what is said on what has been said before may be displayed over long stretches of talk (Mehan, 1978). The following examples gives only the edited highlights of such a sequence:

T: But what is it that makes a housing shortage in parts of Britain?
P: The bricks?
T: No.
P: The land?
T: No. (The pupil then tests out a series of answers relating to the *making* of houses.)
T: Look, forget about the houses and think about who's going to live in them.
P: The people who build them.
T: The people who build them are going to live in them? In *this* country?
P: Oh, in *this* country – oh, we get people to build them.
T: But why is it that in some places there are not enough houses for the number of people in that place?
P: There are not a lot of workers.
T: No.
P: They've got vandalism?
T: No, don't think of it – you're thinking of it from the wrong end, the houses.
P: Which end do you want us to think from?
T: I want you to think of it from the other end, which is the number of people.
P: Yes, cos there's a lot of people – too many people after one house.
T: *Right*, in some areas there's simply too many people . . .

In this kind of 'invited story', it is the person doing the eliciting who retains control over the interests of the information which he wishes to obtain (and which he may claim to know already), and the respondent is denied the normal 'story teller's' rights to tell the story in his own words, to sequence it in his own way, and to avoid revealing any discrediting areas of ignorance. The teacher is therefore able to interrupt, to interpolate additional information and, if necessary, to contradict what is being said. There are some obvious organisational similarities with cross-examinations and with police interrogations. More diffusely, it is worth looking closely (as Drew does in this book) at how corrections are managed and how the conversational 'preference' for 'self-corrections' is modified in situations involving an accredited expert. It is important, however, not to make the shaping of 'correct' answers appear too predictable and too remorselessly efficient. Indeed, the frequent vagueness of the teacher's initial outline of the area of search, the ambiguities in subsequent clues and the frequent improvisation and negotiation of criteria for a sufficient answer make it necessary to look closely at each sequence of this kind (French and MacLure, 1979). Yet underlying the *ad hoc* nature of particular exchanges is a general 'orientation on the part of teacher and selected student to have that student produce sufficient answers, where the decidability of that sufficiency is a matter for teachers and teachers only' (McHoul, 1978).

Such an orientation has important implications for the teacher's task as listener. When turn-taking is managed locally and interactionally, each speaker's contributions are closely contingent on the contributions of others, and a wish to speak involves 'a corollary obligation to listen' (Sacks *et al.*, 1974). In classrooms, the teacher's listening has a special character. He is likely to listen to the 'talk thus far' in relation to what only he knows of the talk in prospect. His tendency is, therefore, to listen for what is relevant to instructional purposes. More generally, he has a pervasive responsibility for monitoring what is said and for repairing breakdowns of all kinds. In other words, occasions when the achievement of orderly discourse becomes a topic in its own right are dominated by the teacher. It is almost always he who says, in so many words, what has happened, is happening and will happen, and who regularly sums up what has been achieved so far. In a study of such formulations in the context of radio interviews, Heritage and Watson (1979) distinguish between the frequent and decisive formulations of the 'bringers of news' and the relatively infrequent and tentative formulations of those who receive news. When it is the news-bringer who 'gives the gist' of what has been said, the receiver is unlikely to be invited to do more than signal that the summary has been understood; but when it is the receiver who provides the summary, often by explicit invitation and as a *check* on attention and understanding, then a confirmation or contradiction by the informant is likely to be immediately adjacent. In terms of this analysis, the teacher is a persistent bringer of news, the transmission of which is rarely seen as a smoothly self-explicating process. Pupils' attention to what is being said, and their competence in comprehending it, cannot be taken for granted. Occasions will be unusually frequent when the business at hand is to announce what has been achieved so far, exhibit meanings which should now be 'shared', or else display some failure to understand which has now to be remedied. These activites are normally tied to the role of the teacher:

T: Right, do you notice what we've done? We started off saying we're going to look at ideas around the world, how people explained the world long ago. But what else have we done, and this is very important, what else have we done?
P: Saw how men looked at women.
T: We saw how men looked at women – you're nearly there. What exactly do you mean? Can you say? Tell us a bit more, go on.
P: How he doesn't like her, and how he thinks she's weak.
T: Yeah (tentatively). So we've also looked then – anybody else before I say it . . .

In ordinary conversation, formulations are often contested and rejected as accurate characterisations of the talk so far. But in classrooms, as in other contexts where the participants are oriented to the production of an agreed outcome and where the responsibility for its achievement is very unequal, there is an 'authorised' source of definitive statements. In the particular context of transmission-teaching, it is the teacher's 'right' to provide the final version of what has 'really' been learned.[16]

It is in the pre-allocation of turns, and of certain kinds of turn, that the fact of the teacher's authority is displayed and confirmed. The features I have outlined are not specific to classrooms. Indeed, this analytical approach reveals basic similarities between superficially different settings – for example, between many situations involving the not-yet-competent or where a 'clear-cut task is central, information exchange or knowledge testing is primary, and there is high role differentiation'.[17] It also makes it possible to compare situations in terms of the nature and scope of pre-allocation. The frequency of 'invited stories' or the distribution of formulations will make evident 'in the text' the predetermined clarity of the task and the rigidity of role differentiation. Such analysis can, therefore, fill the empirical void in Bernstein's theory of educational transmission by showing how the strength of the classification and framing of school knowledge is 'realised' in the organisation of classroom talk. In relatively 'open' classrooms, the greater range of semantic options available to pupils may be evident in more overlapping talk, more pupil-selected next speakers, more self-selected next speakers, more interruptions by pupils, fewer pauses, fewer invited stories and fewer but more tentative and more widely distributed formulations. In short, more of the speech exchange system will be locally managed, and pupils too will be able to 'direct speakership in a creative way'.

In so far as such an analysis seeks to account for why the talk was organised as it was, it is open to criticism from ethnomethodologists for misusing their methods for the purposes of 'doing explanations' (which are none of their business) and for positing some 'reality' external to the talk which is seen as constraining how things are said. But many sociolinguists would entirely agree that forms of social relationship are signalled, and are reproduced or modified or challenged, *in the act of speaking*. To study classroom discourse is to study simultaneously the framing of classroom knowledge and what seems to be obvious to the participants about the options open to them. What is actually said is supported by a great deal of implicit communication 'in the form of unexpressed propositions, some specific to the immediate events and some providing persistent points of reference' (Labov and Fanshel, 1977). In 'typical' classrooms, the point of persistent reference is the authority of the teacher as expert, which provides a more or less continuous interpretive context. A basic presupposition of teacher knowledge and pupil ignorance is a main resource from which both teacher and pupils accomplish mutually comprehensible talk. Where the teacher's authority has been partly relinquished or eroded, then the resulting interplay of alternative frames of reference and relevance will be evident in the discourse.

Notes

1. Classroom research as basic research in sociolinguistics is a main theme in Dell Hymes's introduction to Cazden, Hymes and John (1972). Sinclair and Coulthard (1975) present an analysis of classroom discourse as part of a larger investigation of talk in status-marked settings.

2. My argument relates, largely implicitly, to a recently published empirical study by Edwards and Furlong (1978). The transcript examples are taken from that book but the argument itself is a continuation rather than a repetition of that work. Indeed, the method of analysing classroom talk outlined in the last section of this present paper is not one we used ourselves. An earlier version of the paper was extensively criticised by Douglas Barnes, Peter French, Dianne Phillips and Rod Watson. I am grateful to all of them for helping me to clarify some of my confusions.

3. The claim is the more persuasive for being made by a linguist – see Halliday (1973, p. 80).

4. These criticisms are elaborated in Edwards and Furlong (1978, pp. 38–45) and in Furlong and Edwards (1977). See also Walker and Adelman (1975, 1976).

5. The use of conventional 'buffer phrases' to restore social distance is well described in Waller (1965, pp. 279–86). The indirectness of teachers' deviance imputations is examined in Hargreaves, Hestor and Mellor (1975).

6. The implicit references here are to Mishler (1972) and Torode (1976). My objection is not to the substance of these accounts, but to the warrant offered for them. Both base the 'firmness' of the analysis on what was made evident in the talk without explicating the contextual knowledge which made it possible to fill out the meaning of the words.

7. The extent to which an orientation to the verbal channel is strategic for educational success is examined by Donaldson (1978), and in Edwards (1978b).

8. See Bernstein (1977, pp. 11 and 30). The congruence of Bernstein's approach with that of Michael Halliday is apparent in Halliday's contribution to Volume Two of *Class, Codes and Control*, and in Halliday (1975).

9. Bernstein's assumption is made explicit in *Class, Codes and Control*, vol. 1 (p. 212), and open and closed role systems are defined in the same work (pp. 178–9). But very different assumptions about classroom relationships underlie Bernstein's writing on the curriculum, where strong classification and framing is seen as implying impermeable sets of meanings and positional forms of control.

10. A positive answer to this question is given by Turner (1973). Turner admits, however, that the theory is only strong so far in relation to the regulative context.

11. The argument that the code-dimensions 'sort separately' is in Hymes (1977). A similar point is made by Edwards (1976, p. 94).

12. Both the functional emphasis and the analytic sensitivity to the immediate context are apparent in one of the last publications by Bernstein's Unit – Adlam (1977).

13. See also Coulthard (1977).

14. Examples include Turner (1972), Atkinson and Drew (1979), Heritage and Watson (1979) and several currently unpublished papers by Rod Watson on murder confessions elicited by police interrogation. My own application of contrastive analysis to classroom talk has been greatly influenced (possibly against their will) by Paul Drew and Rod Watson. I am grateful to both of them for letting me see work not yet in print.

15. McHoul (1978) is the only attempt known to me to provide a 'simplest systematics' for classroom discourse.

16. See Heritage and Watson (1979). For a sociolinguistic approach to metacommunication see Stubbs (1976).

17. This is a reference to similarities between teaching situations and those involving an educational tester (or child-language researcher) with a young child. See Ervin-Tripp and Mitchell-Kernan (eds.) (1977, pp. 4-5).

References

Adelman, C. (ed.) (1977). *Uttering Muttering: Reporting and Using Talk for Social and Educational Research*. Mimeo. Bulmershe College, Reading

Adlam, D. (1977). *Code in Context*. London: Routledge

Atkinson, J.M. and Drew, P. (1979). *Order in Court: The Organisation of Verbal Interaction in Judicial Settings*. London: Macmillan

Barnes, D. and Todd, F. (1977). *Communication and Learning in Small Groups*. London: Routledge

Bernstein, B. (ed.) (1971) (1973) (1977). *Class, Codes and Control*, vols. I, II and III. London: Routledge

Cazden, C., Hymes, D. and John, V. (eds.) (1972). *Functions of Language in the Classroom*. New York: Teachers' College Press

Chanan, G. and Delamont, S. (eds.) (1975). *Frontiers of Classroom Research*. Slough: NFER

Cook-Gumperz, J. (1973). *Social Control and Socialisation*. London: Routledge

Cooper, B. (1976). 'Bernstein's Codes: A Classroom Study'. Sussex University Education Area Occasional Paper no. 6

Coulthard, M. (1977). *An Introduction to Discourse Analysis*. London: Longman

Dickenson, A. and Lee, P. (eds.) (1978). *History Teaching and Historical Knowledge*. London: Heinemann

Donaldson, M. (1978). *Children's Minds*. London: Fontana

Edwards, A. (1976). *Language in Culture and Class*. London: Heinemann

— (1978a). 'The Language of History and the Communication of Historical Knowledge'. In A. Dickenson and P. Lee (eds.), *History Teaching and Historical Knowledge*

— (1978b). 'Social Class and the Acquisition of Meaning'. Paper presented to the Sociolinguistics Programme of the World Congress of Sociology, Uppsala, Sweden

— and Furlong, V. (1978). *The Language of Teaching*. London: Heinemann Educational

Ervin-Tripp, S. and Mitchell-Kernan, C. (eds.) (1977). *Child Discourse*. New York: Academic Press

Firth, J.R. (1957). 'The Techniques of Semantics'. In *Papers in Linguistics 1934-51*. London: Oxford University Press

French, P. and MacLure, M. (1979). 'Getting the Right Answer and Getting the Answer Right'. *Research in Education*, November 1979

Furlong, V. and Edwards, A. (1977). 'Language in Classroom Interaction: Theory and Data'. *Educational Research*, 19, pp. 122-8

Gumperz, J. and Hymes, D. (eds) (1972). *Directions in Sociolinguistics*. New York: Holt

Halliday, M.A.K. (1973). *Explorations in the Functions of Language*. London: Arnold

— (1975). *Learning How to Mean*. London: Arnold

Hargreaves, D., Hestor, S. and Mellor, F. (1975). *Deviance in the Classroom*. London: Routledge

Heritage, J. and Watson, R. (1979). 'Formulations as Conversational Objects'. In G. Psathas (ed.), *Recent Studies in Ethnomethodology and Conversation Analysis*

Hymes, D. (1977). *Foundations in Sociolinguistics*. London: Tavistock
Labov, W. and Fanshel, D. (1977). *Therapeutic Discourse*. New York: Academic Press
McHoul, A. (1978). 'The Organization of Turns at Formal Talk in the Classroom'. *Language in Society*, 7, pp. 183-213
Mehan, H. (1978). 'Structuring School Structure'. *Harvard Educational Review*, 48, pp. 32-64
Mishler, E. (1972). 'Implications of Teacher Strategies for Language and Cognition'. In Cazden *et al.* (eds.), *Functions of Language in the Classroom*
Psathas, G. (ed.) (1979). *Everyday Language: Studies in Ethnomethodology*. New York: Irvington Press
Sacks, H., Schegloff, E. and Jefferson, G. (1974). 'A Simplest Systematics for the Organization of Turn-Taking for Conversation'. *Language*, 50, pp. 696-735
Sinclair, J.McH. and Coulthard, R.M. (1975). *Towards an Analysis of Discourse*. London: Oxford University Press
Speier, M. (1976). 'The Child as Conversationalist: Some Culture-Contact Features of Conversational Interactions between Adults and Children'. In P.E. Woods and M. Hammersley (eds.), *The Process of Schooling*
Stubbs, M. (1976). 'Keeping in Touch: Some Functions of Teacher Talk'. In M. Stubbs and S. Delamont (eds.), *Explorations in Classroom Observation*
— (1977). 'Linguistic Data in Educational Research'. In C. Adelman (ed.), *Uttering Muttering*
— and Delamont, S. (eds.) (1976). *Explorations in Classroom Observation*. London: Wiley
Sudnow, D. (ed.) (1972). *Studies in Social Interaction*. New York: Free Press
Torode, B. (1976). 'Teachers' Talk and Classroom Discipline'. In M. Stubbs and S. Delamont (eds.), *Explorations in Classroom Observation*
Turner, G. (1973). 'Social Class and Children's Language of Control'. In B. Bernstein (ed.), *Class, Codes and Control*, vol. II
Turner, R. (1972). 'Therapy Talk'. In D. Sudnow (ed.), *Studies in Social Interaction*
Walker, R. and Adelman, C. (1975). 'Interaction Analysis in Informal Classrooms'. *British Journal of Educational Psychology*, 45, pp. 73-6
— and Adelman, C. (1976). 'Strawberries'. In M. Stubbs and S. Delamont (eds.), *Explorations in Classroom Observation*
Waller, W. (1965). *The Sociology of Teaching*. London: Wiley
West, C. and Zimmerman, D. (1977). 'Women's Place in Everyday Talk: Reflections on Parent-Child Interaction'. *Social Problems*, 24, pp. 521-9
Woods, P.E. and Hammersley, M. (eds.) (1976). *The Process of Schooling*. London: Routledge

LIST OF CONTRIBUTORS

David Brazil. Department of English Language and Literature, University of Birmingham
Deirdre Burton. Department of English Language and Literature, University of Birmingham
E.C. Cuff. Didsbury School of Education, Manchester Polytechnic
Paul Drew. Department of Sociology, University of York
A.D. Edwards. School of Education, University of Newcastle-upon-Tyne
Sue Foster. Department of Linguistics and Psychology, University of Lancaster
Peter French. Department of Language and Literature, College of Ripon and York St. John
Martyn Hammersley. Faculty of Educational Studies, Open University
David Hustler. Didsbury School of Education, Manchester Polytechnic
David Langford. Department of Language and Literature, College of Ripon and York St. John
Margaret MacLure. School of Education, University of Bristol
Michael F. McTear. School of Communication Studies, Ulster Polytechnic, Northern Ireland
Martin Montgomery. School of Education, University of Bristol
Michael Stubbs. Department of English Studies, University of Nottingham
Gordon Wells. School of Education, University of Bristol
Mary Willes. Department of Humanities, West Midlands College of Higher Education
A.J. Wootton. Department of Sociology, University of York

INDEX

For Product Safety Concerns and Information please contact our EU representative GPSR@taylorandfrancis.com
Taylor & Francis Verlag GmbH, Kaufingerstraße 24, 80331 München, Germany

www.ingramcontent.com/pod-product-compliance
Lightning Source LLC
LaVergne TN
LVHW010619300926
849162LV00001B/6
* 9 7 8 1 0 4 1 3 1 7 2 6 5 *